CREATURES OF POLITICS

CREATURES OF POLITICS

Media, Message, and the
American Presidency

Michael Lempert & Michael Silverstein

INDIANA UNIVERSITY PRESS

Bloomington and Indianapolis

This book is a publication of

INDIANA UNIVERSITY PRESS
601 North Morton Street
Bloomington, Indiana 47404-3797 USA

iupress.indiana.edu

Telephone orders   800-842-6796
Fax orders   812-855-7931

*Manufactured in the
United States of America*

Library of Congress
Cataloging-in-Publication Data

Lempert, Michael.
  Creatures of politics : media, message,
and the American presidency / Michael
Lempert and Michael Silverstein.
      p. cm.
  Includes bibliographical references and
index.
  ISBN 978-0-253-00745-2 (cloth : alk.
paper) — ISBN 978-0-253-00752-0 (pbk.
: alk. paper) — ISBN 978-0-253-00756-8
(ebk.) 1. Communication in politics—
United States. 2. Presidential candidates—
United States—Language. 3. Rhetoric—
Political aspects—United States. I.
Silverstein, Michael, 1945– II. Title.
  JA85.2.U6L46 2012
  320.97301'4—dc23
                                    2012015064

1 2 3 4 5 17 16 15 14 13 12

TO JAMES MADISON,

"Father of the Constitution,"
who, despite his best intentions,
breathed life into creatures of politics.

This idea that you can merchandise candidates for high office like breakfast cereal . . . is, I think, the ultimate indignity to the democratic process.

—ADLAI STEVENSON,
at the 1956 Democratic National Convention

CONTENTS

PREFACE & ACKNOWLEDGMENTS

In this book we bring together, adapt, and blend material we have been separately developing over the last decade. Mutually discovering that each of us has been following American electoral politics—particularly, American presidential politics—with a similarly attuned linguistic anthropological eye and ear has animated this collaborative effort.

Contemporary linguistic anthropology moves analytically in several concurrently applied ways. Trying to understand how a particular focal communicative event has had certain effects (even effectiveness in some social realm) inevitably leads the analyst to investigate the cultural values illustrated or frustrated by the key signals—verbal, gestural, behavioral, sartorial, and so on—that participants generate, as revealed in the transcribed record of the event. Generally this involves looking at any particular communicative event in a documented or putative trajectory of other events with which it can be associated for one or another reason—for example, an event and other events that report that the first event took place. (This last relationship is central to political news and commentary, of course.) We are concerned with matters of a politician's personal style against a backdrop of what appear to be normative expectations of how particular kinds of events "should" take place, and with the strategies and frames that license or animate the display of the stylistically distinctive.

In all of these chapters focusing on various creatures of politics, our concern is not merely to present a bestiary, mythical or real, as the case may be. Our concern is to explain, as anthropologists, the sense of how the central communicative mechanisms of American politics operate as institutional forms in that corner of the American sociocultural world shaped by processes of electoral politics. Needless to say, this is a field that has long been the analytic province of the rhetorician, the political scientist, the specialist in mass communications, and one where practitioners of the art keep materializing as its commentators, frequently in between gigs in practical service. However, we believe that our perspective on political communication, achieved via the lens of the "how" as distinct from the "what" of politicians' communicative behavior, adds fresh insight into matters long treated differently as a matter of course.

In spring 2004, while the U.S. presidential campaign was in full swing, Michael Lempert was finishing his dissertation in linguistic anthropology on Tibetan Buddhist debate, a visually arresting educational practice, reestablished in the exile monasteries of India, in which monks wrangle about the niceties of philosophical doctrine. Brash monk-challengers hurl invectives and punctuate their points with hand claps that explode in the direction of the seated defendant's face. These over-the-top histrionics fascinated Lempert: one had to contemplate a kind of argumentation that is much more than a sober, if competitive, exercise in linking premises to a conclusion. But it turns out that Tibetans in exile were themselves busy reflecting on this style of argumentation, trying to square it with liberal-democratic ideals of clear, civil, rational communication—ideals that the Dalai Lama and the Tibetan Government in Exile have been eager to adopt. Lempert sensed parallels between these reflexive debates over "debate" and complaints at home about the purportedly impoverished state of communication in and around electoral politics: that "The Issues" were chronically neglected; that the televised primary and presidential debates were mere theater, privileging style over substance.

And then there was the matter of George W. Bush, in whose speech many could hear, from this normative perspective, only deficiency. By 2004 his malapropisms and gaffes had already accumulated into an impressive archive of "Bushisms." But this didn't begin to explain why it was that so many people thought his communicative style was appealing. Lempert found his explanation in a slim volume by Michael Silverstein, *Talking Politics: The Substance of Style from Abe to "W"* (2003a), which extended methods and theories from linguistic anthropology to the domain of political communication. Inspired by Silverstein's work, and by a few effective forays into electoral politics by other linguistic anthropologists, such as Jane Hill and Asif Agha, Lempert began to write essays in a similar spirit, his special interest being the manner in which debates serve as sites for what are in effect presidential character contests.

Michael Silverstein had been researching the semiotics of ritual performance, and in particular political ritual, since the 1970s. In 1998 he began to use this approach to analyze the text and ritual occasion of Abraham Lincoln's 1863 "remarks" at Gettysburg, Franklin Roosevelt's Fireside Chats of the 1930s, and John Kennedy's inaugural of 1961, among other presidential moments. Around the period of the 2000 electoral cycle, the particular communicative style of first candidate then president George W. Bush became a focus of interest in relation to the sociolinguistics of the phenomenon termed "register" in American English. Stylistically contrasting Lincoln and Bush as political communicators became the theme of that little book, *Talking Politics,* commissioned by Marshall Sahlins for his Prickly Paradigm Press series. (It is freely downloadable as a pdf file at the press's website.) By the time the presidential electoral cycles of 2004 and 2008 were upon us, Silverstein had been invited many, many times to address both general and specialist audiences with linguistic anthropological commentary; several of the accompanying chapters emerged as reshaped records of those occasions. He is very grateful both to his sponsoring hosts and to the lively, interlocutory audiences—really, communicational addressees—on those occasions. One piece here, "What Goes Around . . . ," began, thanks to Professor John MacAloon, as an annually delivered lecture in the introductory course in the University of Chicago's Master of Arts Program in the Social Sciences, where Silverstein undertook to explain and illustrate "symbolic interactionism," as it is termed in the field of sociology. The point is that its viable continuator at the present time is the linguistic anthropology of events. The piece is also an homage to our late, much-missed friend Erving Goffman, one of the great masters of symbolic interactionism, whose unerring eye for the interactional grotesque alighted on the very event at the center of chapter 7.

Several of the chapters that follow originated in invited presentations, acknowledgments for which are recorded in their original print form. To those who facilitated and shaped their later print appearance in earlier published form—photographers, cartoonists, journal editors, and anonymous reviewers—we offer many thanks. And to the editors and publishers of the earlier versions, thanks again for their cooperation in our enterprise of rewriting and adapting them as chapters of this book. Each of us has originated three chapters and we have jointly produced the introductory one. Hence, overall authorship is listed alphabetically.

Chapter 2, "Getting it Ju . . . st Right!" reworks material in two essays by Michael Silverstein: "The Poetics of Politics: 'Theirs' and 'Ours'" (2005b) and "The 'Message' in the (Political) Battle" (2011b). We are grateful to Lawrence G. Straus of the University of New Mexico, editor of *Journal of Anthropological Research;* to Elsevier, Ltd. (by contractual residuals); and to political cartoonists Rick McKee, Scott Stantis, and Jack Higgins; to Tribune Media Services (on behalf of cartoonist Dana Summers); to Universal Press Syndicate (on behalf of cartoonist Pat Oliphant); and to the Associated Press, for licenses and permissions to reprint copyrighted material.

Chapters 3 and 4 draw on our individual contributions to a special 2011 theme issue of *Anthropological Quarterly* called "The Unmentionable: Verbal Taboo and the Moral Life of Language" (edited by Luke Fleming and Michael Lempert). Chapter 3 is adapted from Lempert's essay "Avoiding 'The Issues' as Addressivity in U.S. Electoral Politics" (2011a). Chapter 4 draws on Silverstein's "Presidential Ethno-Blooperology: Performance Misfires in the Business of 'Message'-ing" (2011a). We are grateful to Roy Grinker, editor of *Anthropological Quarterly,* and to associate editors Alex Dent and Joel Kuipers, all of George Washington University, for permission to reprint copyrighted material.

Chapter 5, "Unflipping the Flop," is based on Lempert's 2009 article "On 'Flip-Flopping': Branded Stance-Taking in U.S. Electoral Politics." Thanks to John Wiley and Sons for permission to reprint.

Chapter 6, "The Message in Hand," incorporates material from Lempert's article "Barack Obama, Being Sharp: Indexical Order in the Pragmatics of Precision-Grip Gesture" (2011b) and is published here with kind permission by John Benjamins Publishing Company. Our special thanks go to Jessica Krcmarik for artistic renderings of Barack Obama's gestures.

Chapter 7, "What Goes Around . . ." draws on Silverstein's essay "What Goes Around . . .: Some Shtick from 'Tricky Dick' and the Circulation of U.S. Presidential Image" (2011c). We are grateful to the American Anthropological Association and Wiley-Blackwell (by contractual residuals) for license to reprint. We also thank Pars International (on behalf of the *New York Times*) and Dorothea Alke of the CBS Corporation (holding rights to material of the *Philadelphia Evening Bulletin*) for permission to reprint copyrighted material. Figure 7.7, from the White House via Wikimedia, is in the public domain.

We are very grateful to Rebecca Tolen of Indiana University Press, who saw merit in this project and has remained its champion; to the kind (and no longer anonymous) reviewers of our book prospectus, professors Richard Bauman (Indiana University), Don Brenneis (University of California–Santa Cruz), and Adam Hodges (Carnegie Mellon University), whose guidance we have sought to follow. Michael Lempert wishes to offer a special note of thanks to Hannah DeRose-Wilson, whose assistance has been truly invaluable, and to Brooke Burgess and Travis Gonyou for their assistance with parts of chapter 6. He also thanks the Office of the Vice President for Research of the University of Michigan for a published subvention. He also thanks the Office of the Vice President for Research of the University of Michigan for a publication subvention. As authors who are as well scholars of language and its use, we thank copyeditor Jill R. Hughes and project editor Nancy Lightfoot, whose focused connoisseurship has made the text more reader-friendly—and saved us from several potentially embarrassing gaffes!

Finally, we acknowledge the various "creatures" of the realm, whose "deeds done in words" (Campbell and Jamieson 1990, 2008) we—and, apparently, the entire American electorate—find compelling.

CREATURES OF POLITICS

One

"Message" Is the Medium

If the genius of the Clinton campaign was its disciplined
focus on message—"The economy, stupid"—the Clinton
transition stumbled slightly out of the gate.

Although it harnessed masterfully the new prestige of the president-
elect with Clinton's symbolic reaching out to common people during
his walk on Georgia Avenue last week, it has also endured a torrent
of stories about such "off message" matters as homosexuals
in the military and the role of Hillary Clinton.

—*Washington Post, 22 November 1992*

What Is "Message" in American Politics?

In their professional jargon, political insiders call it simply—and to many
outsiders, misleadingly—"message." It is the politician's publicly imaginable 'character' presented to an electorate, with a biography and a moral
profile crafted out of issues rendered of interest in the public sphere. In
this book we examine the ways in which modern electoral politics in the
United States revolves around contests over "message."

For better or worse, "message" in political parlance is easily confused
with the word <u>message</u> in its everyday colloquial sense or even with its
use by many students of communication. In politics "message" is not

the topic, theme, central holding, or proposition of a swatch of political discourse—what someone is "literally communicating," we might say. Though it sounds like the term should mean what political figures literally say about the state of the world and what should be done about matters under discussion and debate, such as offshore drilling, the debt ceiling, unemployment, health-care mandates, and social security solvency—let alone contraception and same-sex marriage—it does not. In fact, Message (from here on we drop the quotation marks and capitalize instead) does not refer to a politician's communication about Issues so much as what the politician seems to communicate about his or her identity and personal values through selectively taking up some Issues and avoiding others, and in its negative form through identifying a competitor with the dangerous Issues to be kept at arm's distance from oneself. A politician's persona becomes visible as a collage-in-motion of communicative Issue events: through becoming identified in this way with Issues, he or she acquires a political persona. So here is the strategically useful ambiguity of the term. Message as a technical term misdirects the unsuspecting by seeming to steer their attention toward the literal content of political talk—after all, shouldn't politicians still address "The Issues! The Issues!" in the civics books' view of political process?—while Message strategists work diligently behind the scenes. What they are fashioning is an electorally viable political persona through all manner of signs that creatively gesture toward this persona without explicitly describing it, though the political press, the media, can generally be relied upon to do so.

"I will hunt down and kill the terrorists wherever they are!" So proclaimed Democratic presidential challenger John Kerry in his first televised bout with President George W. Bush in 2004—the topic, foreign policy. Senator Kerry was inhabiting a recognizable character: "Tough!"—tough on terror, the television viewers of the debate were supposed to infer, which is just what the Bush campaign had already charged that Kerry wasn't and wouldn't be if elected. Earlier in the primaries, Kerry's positive, self-focused Message became one of genuine—as opposed to ersatz—(and what's more, multiply decorated!) service in the Vietnam War, with its obvious projection into who most likely would be the heroic gunboat commander in the so-called War on Terror. Of course, immediately after

Super Tuesday on 2 March 2004, the Republican National Committee (RNC) rolled out a huge, negative Message campaign about Kerry, true to Karl Rove's signature style, hitting Mr. Kerry precisely in one of his supposed Message strengths. Suddenly we saw pictures—later even a movie made for the Sinclair TV conglomerate—of Kerry's anti–Vietnam War testimony before Congress in 1971, and of his participation in rallies with—gasp!—Jane Fonda (still a negative poster girl for the Republican hard-right base). From March 2004 on, the Republicans mobilized further, fail-safe weapons in their attack against Senator Kerry's war hero Message of tough resoluteness. In Message, Senate votes of twenty years earlier and those of yesterday are artfully compressed. Mr. Kerry, it was asserted, had repeatedly voted against developing and procuring key weapons systems in the "Star Wars" Reagan years, yet was now posturing as a warrior. The senator was irresolute on the Iraq invasion, which Dubya had dubbed the current War on Terror; there were even video clips of Kerry saying he voted now one way, now another. He was not only less than stand-tough and pro-military on these matters of the national defense; he was, in Message-ese, a "flip-flopper"!

But worse. In late summer 2004, Senator Kerry was caught in widely disseminated still photographs and on video windsurfing, in clinging spandex no less, on the waters off patrician Nantucket Island. When the footage was set to the tune of Strauss's "Blue Danube" waltz, as the Bush campaign did in an attack ad released on television right before the first presidential debate, the pointed visual metaphor consolidated the critique of Kerry as not merely a flip-flopper, but an *effete* flip-flopper— tacking back and forth in the wind, unable to make up his mind: *not* a strong, decisive leader. No wonder that in that first debate, in that line about hunting down and killing terrorists, Kerry would try to sound like someone who would lead the "war" effort and pull the trigger himself, not like someone who would push a policy pen at the behest of his advisers.

Compare Senator Kerry's performance with a similar tough-on-terror point made in an altogether different style by then Sen. Barack Obama in the first Democratic primary debate of 2007, held in late April in South Carolina (MSNBC 2007b). Co-moderator Brian Williams of NBC News asked Obama what he would do as president if "we learned that two

American cities had been hit simultaneously by terrorists and we further learned beyond the shadow of a doubt it had been the work of al-Qaeda."

"Well . . .," the senator began in response—he often began turns this way—and then started to unfurl a plan, an interminably lengthy plan. When he finally got around to saying concretely what he would do in response to the hypothetical terror attack, he seemed to bury this action deep in the lower strata and clauses of lawyerly syntactic convolution: "The second thing is to make sure that we've got good intelligence, a., to find out that we don't have other threats and attacks potentially out there, and b., to find out, do we have any intelligence on who might have carried it out, *so that we can take potentially some action to dismantle that network*" (emphasis added). The would-be president's "tak[ing] action," qualified by "potentially" and hedged with "some," sounds tentative, noncommittal—in fact, hardly like "taking action" at all after all that! And though the quotation as we give it does not show this, the otherwise tough-sounding final complement clause that follows—"*to dismantle that network*"—compounds Obama's poor rhetorical showing, slowed fore and aft as it were, as if with speed bumps, by filled pauses: . . . *uh* . . . *to dismantle* . . . *uh*. . . . To many observers, and certainly to campaign antagonists within the Hillary Clinton campaign, Senator Obama's response sounded ruminatively wonkish, indecisive rather than response-ready, and, in a word, weak. (In fact, Obama recognized that he had veered off Message in his delivery after Senator Clinton nailed her answer with the promise of swift retaliation. He felt compelled to double back and answer it again in his next chance to hold the floor, and wasted no time showing that he, too, would be tough on terror: "But one thing that I do have to go back on uh—on this issue of terrorism. We *have* genuine enemies out there that have to be hunted down, networks have to be dismantled.")

So compare the two: "*hunt down and kill the terrorists*," executed—literally, we can imagine—by a heroic "*I*," a President Kerry himself, versus "*dismantle* . . . *uh* . . . *that* [terrorist] *network*," executed ultimately by an amorphous Obama administration's "*we*" after waiting for two different kinds of "*good intelligence*," and no doubt with bipartisan congressional approval and even European Union support! Two *very* different political creatures seem to be speaking, even though Senator Kerry and Senator

Obama were talking about doing almost the same thing, no doubt both knowing pretty much how such things work in the executive branch. Two very different kinds of Message were being performed for the viewing public.

Consider even something as particular as the pronunciation of a proper name. What do we implicitly understand about politicians who pronounce "Pakistan" differently? In the first cross-party presidential debate of September 2008, many observers seized upon the contrast between Senator Obama's pronunciation of "Pakistan" and Senator John McCain's. For example, *National Review* author Kathryn Jean Lopez (2008) wrote: "When Obama says Pock-i-stahn I have an uncontrollable urge to read the *New Yorker* and find some Chardonnay. Fortunately I have an old copy of *NR* and a Coor's Light to snap me back to reality. Seriously though—no one in flyover country says Pock-i-stahn. It's annoying." Look at the rich, if stereotyped, series of opposed emblems of identity—in this instance, of United States cultural and political geography and political orientation—Ms. Lopez discerns in the very phonetics of a single word in the candidates' repertoires: out-of-it left-liberal coastal elites, the people in the fringe "blue" states, reading the *New Yorker* while sipping their chardonnay (whether French or Californian) versus down-to-earth right-conservative ordinary folks in in-between "red" places over which nonstop airplanes fly between New York and Los Angeles, takin' in vintage *National Review* while drinkin' their Coors, produced by and named for the radically right-wing brewing family. (To be sure, predominantly coastal—and Democratic—intellectual elites had long had a field day with "W's" almost too stagey-by-half semiliterate pronunciations of "Eye-Rack" [Iraq] and "Eye-Ran" [Iran] and his delicious malapropisms and other articulatory fumblings of jus' plain ol' folkdom from Flyover-land. So here is a tit-for-tat blow in the War on *Terroir*—as one says in the wine trade—struck "for the Gipper," as it were, or at least for Senator McCain's and Governor Sarah Palin's peeps.)

To Obama's defense came writers like *Washington Monthly*'s Steve Benen (2008), who has picked up at least on the vowel sounds ("ah") of the name of the country, if not on the emphasis or stress that falls on the final syllable: "Barack Obama pronounces 'Pakistan' correctly, with a soft 'a,' just like a lot of people who know what they're talking about, including Gen. David Petraeus. Apparently, having completely run out of compelling policy arguments to make, some high-profile conservatives have decided to make this their latest campaign hobbyhorse." For viewers who even subliminally registered this contrast in their pronunciations— as most of the audience would indeed do—the candidates seemed thereby to be aligning either with those cosmopolitans who were educated enough not only to know how Pakistanis pronounce the name of their own country but also to care enough to take note, or with those who take comfort and pride in Americanizing country names and other foreign words. So it is not difficult to understand how such contrasts could be construed by commentators to reveal details about the respective candidates, including, for some, liberal versus conservative lifestyles, down to gendered and classed beverage preferences, all the while both candidates were clearly understood by all to be referring to the very same country. From a seemingly minor but pregnant difference in place-name pronunciation comes a cascade of inferences about who—that is, sociologically, from what social and value segments and sectors of the populace—candidates really are. In the chapters that follow, we examine politicians' communication and its close reading by seekers of Message, showing how political creatures are fashioned in-and-by their own political talk and, more precisely, by the talk about political talk that is its hoped-for and sometimes dreaded immediate consequence. Candidates for office become personae who are believable or imaginable as incumbents—or not—through critical readings of what their signs "give off" in the way of (in)coherent Message, as Erving Goffman (1959) once put it in his classic writings on self-presentation. This turns out to be a complex, multitiered process that is embedded and institutionalized in our politics, and we lay bare some of its central workings.

Message Aesthetics: Plotlines and Laugh/Gasp Lines

Transparent naturalism, it should be clear, is not the Message-relevant aesthetic in American politics (recalling the hilarious I-am-what-I-am premise of the Warren Beatty film *Bulworth* [1998] or the melodramatic moments of Steven Zaillian's *All the King's Men* [2006]). Campaigns portray their candidate's virtues without care for preserving nuance and gritty biographical detail—foibles and all—unless they are part of a coherent appeal the candidate can inhabit. The foibles *will* be exposed, by fair means or foul, through media scrutiny and the wiles of campaign antagonists and their 527(c) advocacy arms. And before a candidate even enters the fray, what we might at first think of as gross negatives from his or her past will be preemptively absorbed into a triumphant coming-of-age story, ideally published as memoir, wherein boozy or druggy high jinks and abusive fatherhood and spousal philandering become character-building episodes on the way to today's redeemed, reformed, and rededicated paragon. In this respect even Lincoln, not to mention Andrew Jackson, was lucky as a candidate for office to have been "born in a log cabin"!

So caricatured are the political creatures depicted by campaigns that we are reminded of what theorists of art and literature term the "grotesque." By "grotesque" we don't mean to suggest the fantastic fusions of human and beast, like the creatures that roil in the margins of illuminated medieval manuscripts, satyrs and griffins and sirens, and in the ambivalent and at times repulsive hybrids like Quasimodo and the Frankenstein monster who haunt the worlds of the novelistic gothic (although political creatures can and do incite ambivalence, even revulsion: do we not feel alienated from the figure of the "flip-flopper"?). We mean, simply, an aesthetic of characterological extravagance and hyperbole, where both positive and negative personal attributes are portrayed and inhabited in sharp relief and sometimes with an almost cartoonish flair. That there is a measure of the grotesque in Message politics is also evident from the way Message has, with some interesting exceptions, long foregrounded and elevated "ordinariness" as a measure of appeal. It is a truism, for example, that political candidates must know how to speak in a populist tenor, which manifests itself in everything from the sourcing and deployment of "low," "folksy," and "plain" speech registers to the adoption of disarmingly "casual," purportedly status-lowering and intimacy-enhancing nicknames (Dick or Rick, not Richard; Bill, not William; Mitt, not Milton). Enlisted men rigorously looked up to and saluted Gen. Dwight D. Eisenhower, but every "I" liked Ike! His twice-defeated opponent in the presidential elections of 1952 and 1956, Gov. Adlai E. Stevenson II (is there even a nickname possible for Adlai?) was mercilessly taken to task for seeming to be an egghead, if a witty one, given to complex and elegantly formulated policy analyses in the way of campaign speeches.

With their spectacularly exaggerated features, grotesque figures are designed to steal attention, which brings us to the intricate relationship of candidacy and incumbency to celebrity. A celebrity becomes the collective fetish of the masses, the celebrity's fans (from the word <u>fanatic</u>), for whom every tidbit about the celebrity's physical, sartorial, characterological, discursive, and other biographical features is worthwhile to their attentive collection and appreciation. Even those who are more remote from the celebrity are aware of many of these matters and have strong reactions to them, whether attraction or repulsion. There is an analogy here with the aesthetic of the political grotesque, as constituencies, like would-be fans whose passions are stoked by journalistic attention, whether of the relatively restrained sort—think *Us Weekly*—or the predatory voyeurism of, say, a *TMZ*, are encouraged to cathect over any and every aspect of a candidate's being and behavior, just as one might do for a star. Enroll in a sweepstakes, anyone, to get to have a restaurant (not White House) meal with President Obama?

Let us recall how expansive celebrity is. Mass-media performing stars of stage, big and little screens, radio, and recording have long been the prototypes of celebrity, around whose persons in private life as well as around whose performances swirl a whole secondary mass-mediatization, much of it strategically constructed and promulgated as an instrument of that celebrity itself (since celebrity translates into market share and thence into financial return). Marilyn Monroe, Elvis Presley, and Michael Jackson in life, and now in death, are forever paragons of celebrity. Ditto, though probably with a shorter and more sociologically pallid half-life, Amy Winehouse, who is perhaps of the order of celebrity of other dead-of-drugs-at-twenty-seven singers, who are more generational icons.

Celebrity comes to more than just performers, of course. Figures in areas as widely different as mass-marketed sports ("Babe" Ruth), criminal enterprise (Al "Scarface" Capone), or any other achievement-based walk of life also frequently attain their own kind of celebrity. As the significance of his theoretical physics reached a mass public through decreasingly technical and precise orders of translation, Albert Einstein became a global celebrity, ratified as such, for example, by a portrait on the 18 February 1929 cover of *Time* magazine (and not just for having been awarded the Nobel Prize in Physics for 1921). In fact, Einstein was the subject of the *Time* cover portrait no fewer than five times, culminating in his selection as "Person of the Century" for the 31 December 1999 issue.[1] But, more widely, his style of life in America, his movements, his activities, and his views on matters of politics, no less than of science and technology, were widely sought and widely reported on in the media—even gossiped about. For generations he became the very model of the seemingly unworldly scientist, unconcerned—at least in popular imagination—with anything beyond his mathematical physics (and The Bomb). From this his image still underlies and is immanent as the prototype of a grotesque captioned variously as "the nutty professor," "the (mad) genius," "the brain," and so forth. "Hey, Einstein!" is used sarcastically as a cutting address for someone who has done something stupid or unworldly.

In the way of contributing to Message, celebrity becomes a great asset in the realm of political life in several respects. First, and perhaps most obviously, how can celebrity be made to rub off onto a politician through the art of personal association? As both candidates and incumbents, U. S. presidents have sought for a very long time to have such celebrity personalities and their attention-getting auras nearby, just as publicity machines for such celebrities would emphasize how proximity to icons of governmental power reaffirms and enhances their starlike qualities. The mass media are duly engaged to register and to transmit to the masses something of the sometimes titillating quality of this back-and-forth. President Kennedy and Marilyn Monroe certainly constituted a duo in the latter category, a nexus of privilege and power that continues to be almost irresistible in its attention-grabbing, sometimes prurient interest, whatever the truth to the presumptions of a sexual encounter. Recall as well the fierce competition among political candidates to recruit musicians and Hollywood celebs of identifiable cultural iconism for nearly every category of campaign event. By carefully assembling signs of celebrity around a political figure, publicists seek to stimulate in the public sphere even an unconscious appreciation of the Message-worthiness of the politician.

As the cases of career-changing actors-turned-political figures remind us, politicians can also be recruited from the very ranks of established celebrities. Think of "the Governator" of California, Arnold Schwarzenegger; or his predecessor Gov. Ronald Reagan; or any number of less prominent figures, like *Law & Order*'s Sen. Fred Thompson or the World Wrestling Federation's Gov. Jesse ("The Body") Ventura. Or celebrity may emerge from being carefully stimulated and fashioned anew for a politician as an important aspect of the biographical grotesque through the intersection of many of the same techniques and organizational affordances as apply to Hollywood personalities, talk-show hosts, or rock stars. Note how publicists tried refashioning former Minnesota governor Timothy Pawlenty into a celebrity grotesque called "T-Paw," which the press eagerly took up, eager to find some interest in the then otherwise dull early stages of the Republican Party primaries, filled with essentially colorless men (and two firecracker women, one a candidate, the other a phantom candidate). "T-Paw" indeed, on the model of J-Lo, K-Fed (now Fed-Ex), Ice-T, and so forth; just as in an earlier Democratic succession of Message making we had, on the model of FDR, first JFK, then LBJ. Democratic presidents Carter and Clinton eschewed the use of initials, opting instead for a folksy and relaxed Southern strategy, as it were, as "Jimmy" and "Bill"—or, more colorfully and emblematically, "Bubba." And of course who can forget the celebrity-worthy, and heavily marketed, "Dubya"/"W," promoted by RNC forces as the Texan rebaptism of the scion of a patrician Connecticut family?

Competing campaigns of opposed political candidates monitor each other's attempts of this sort, sometimes being able to use those very salient aspects of an emergent celebrity quality to craft a counter-Message. In the Democratic presidential primaries of 2007 and 2008, once Senator Obama was identified as a "rock star" by virtue of huge, screaming crowds at almost every campaign venue, including his statesmanlike speeches in Europe, the campaign of Senator Clinton contrasted this with the subdued seriousness of its own political occasions, wishing to render Senator Obama a mere celebrity lightweight, a political entertainer of the young, in essence. In the lead-up to the general election, the McCain campaign took up this line of attack with abandon, as in its negative television ad dubbed "Celeb." "He's the biggest celebrity in the world," the voice-over begins—with thunderous chants of o-ba-ma in the background, bursts of lightning-like paparazzi camera flashes, and cuts to shots of Paris Hilton—"but is he ready to lead?" (One wonders if these ads will be recycled in 2012, repurposed as "I-told-you-so's.")

Engaging such would-be celebrity, the chapters that follow offer a glimpse of what is, as it were, a political bestiary. We describe the cultural figurations of presidential persona and such stuff as they are made of: signs on the body, of the body, issuing from the body, by which we can recognize the species and varieties of political figures; signs in time and space framing the persons in the communicative events through which politics is realized; signs in the mass media—words, pictures, and so forth—describing and evaluating the people and events of political life. All of these are the means that make creatures of politics. All of these are part of his or her Message. We examine the humor and pathos through which candidates for office become captioned political creatures with recurrently usable epithets: "straight talkers" and "mavericks," "flip-floppers" and "Washington insiders." These projects of morally inflected self- and other-making—these "character contests" as Goffman (1967) might say—are critical to electoral success as they become the shorthand ways by which celebrity or infamy can be communicated.

The field of competition, the political *agōn* or contest as we term it, is notoriously mercurial in its time-boundedness and time-sensitivity. It shifts, sometimes dramatically and right under one's feet, forcing campaigns to find new footing for their Message. Though most of these shifts cannot be predicted, there is an institutionalized calendrics to any developing political race that helps structure the passage of campaign time. There is, for instance, the phase of the exploratory committee, formed to test the candidate's viability through techniques of information gathering (e.g., strategic polling) and participation in events (some created precisely for the campaign) designed to create buzz—and, most essentially, monetary support—among the party faithful and various interest groups. Not only the participants at such events must become aware of the potential nominee, but also a wider public, among whom are potential future audiences for like events. So there must be some way that news gets widely communicated of a candidate's accomplished "explorations" and likely availability for future ones. Absent preexisting paparazzi-worthy celebrity, this requires stimulating media coverage, commentary, and contention—just what media flacks were created for!

At some point there is a formal announcement of one's bid for office—say, the presidency, on which we focus in this book—which generally is wrapped in the colors of a political party, red, blue, or even, nowadays, green (though in the United States there has been only a sputtering sustainability, for an election cycle or two, of more than two parties at any given period). A candidacy must appear to offer attractive pluses to a multitiered party organization as much as receiving from the party the benefits of its brand-like sponsorship. In many ways, operations like presidential campaigns in effect invade, colonize, and control a political party from the time it is clear that it will be the candidacy in a particular electoral cycle. (This also explains why so many of the third-party movements in the last hundred years have been, in effect, organizations of a single election cycle carried on the back of some particular self-authorizing celebrity candidate who has been unsuccessful with one of the two major parties, disappearing after the votes have been counted.) An "announced" candidate's lot is thus to enter the fray among sometimes many such people seeking its imprimatur.

At every level of electoral political structure, some form of party slating must resolve who among all the announced worthies will get to represent the party against nominees of other parties. At the presidential level, until a few decades ago this took place at generally raucous, even sleazy national-level party conventions, conclaves at which state-level delegations of local party faithful engaged in, well, politics: horse-trading over issues; promises of jobs for cronies; influence for this or that commercial bloc or other interest groups; champagne-and-caviar receptions sponsored by those with money to burn and interests to push on delegates, in smoke-filled rooms big and small. Out of all this, over a week or so emerged coalitions for and against particular candidates and their electoral virtues (and liabilities), thus gradually narrowing the field of viable survivors and, sometimes quickly, sometimes painfully slowly, leading to balloting on the floor of the convention for the eventual party candidates for president and vice president.

At every period of mass media, what fun these have been to follow in the press, whose reportorial investigations of cliques and factions, of deals and double-crosses, and of gossip, gossip, gossip have been riveting high points of the cyclic political process. (Perhaps the drama of papal elections as followed by the press until that moment of white smoke gives the young some sense of an earlier mass public's excitement by peeking into the high seriousness of a conclave's factional intrigue.) By the middle of the 1950s, television began to transform the you-are-there immersive reality of parties' national political conventions and, by the 1960 presidential campaign, the vivid actualization of the whole electoral process, including the innovation of nationally televised debates between the two ultimate party candidates for president, Senator Kennedy and Vice President Nixon. The "gavel-to-gavel" network coverage of the political conventions, with their cloyingly faux patriotic hoopla, and of all the little side dramas of politics as sausage making, though giving the vast television audience a not always flattering glimpse of the process, may well have contributed to the major parties' resolution to put more emphasis on primary electoral contests on a state-by-state basis. Such emphasis would make it possible, at least in theory, for an announced candidate to be popularly chosen by winning the controlling majority of state-level delegates to the national conventions before the actual convention voting even took place, thus taking away the very suspense that animated interest in the media plotline of the traditional party convention.

To be sure, party primaries had long existed in most states, but they were not taken all that seriously when national convention time rolled around. Today, however, in the age of desperate buy-my-Message populism, they constitute one of the most gripping of continuing stories for continuing coverage, with a plotline a little bit like the game of musical chairs (or any generic *Survivor*-like show—perhaps here to be thought of as "The Biggest Winner!"). Primaries plot a sometimes grueling procession through the various regions and states, organized by a calendrics of no reasonable sort save party tradition and current candidate strategizing. Such pyramidically organized time-tiers of primaries (with progressively decreasing numbers of candidates running) presumably test voter popularity that can be mobilized—brought to the ballot box—on behalf of a candidate, winning committed delegates as a more or less direct function of state-level popularity. The geographically meandering slog through primaries in the modern period inevitably keeps narrowing the nomadic field of possible national-level candidates. Those who "also ran," though poorly, pack up their own tents so as to be welcomed into the fold of more successful candidates, whose campaign caravans they are asked to join and whose aspirations they are asked to endorse for the next stage. Musical chairs—*Jeopardy*—even NBA tournament: the whole interest has shifted from the conventions, which have become, as spectacle, dull and drama-less affairs. They are now no longer broadcast except as party-sponsored candidate Message opportunities necessitating FCC equal-time measures. The action for months and months is in—ahem!—(the) primary process, as affectively gripping for the media audience as learning who will be next thrown off the island or voted out of the group residence in a present-day reality show, with which the Message-driven plotlines of political primaries might well be compared—especially the weekly who's-up/who's-down cliff-hanger that the early 2012 Republican series of primaries had become.

This is how we get to a national general election for the presidency every four years, in a cyclic process that really no longer ever ceases, if even pausing for crew changes. It is important to observe that during the whole time within a cycle, critical dates, places, and events attract special attention and have become captioned touchstones or distance markers of the presidency: the Iowa caucuses, New Hampshire, Super Tuesday, the national party conventions—not to mention the marathons of televised debates of increasingly diverse format that are now de rigueur both for the presidential candidates and the vice presidential. In fact, in the 2008 election the latter single encounter between Sarah Palin and Joe Biden was arguably of more interest to viewers than the former three between the presidential contenders, because of then Governor Palin's disastrous interviews with CBS's Katie Couric and ABC's Charlie Gibson. (In the debate, people wondered whether Palin would again display a seemingly astonishing ignorance and ill-preparedness, and whether the brash, gaffe-prone Biden, infamous for having boasted of a high IQ, would incur the risk of picking on her.)

We dwell on the temporality of candidacy in order to call attention to the role of media in which, as we said, a candidate's own Message arises and flourishes to success, withstanding the toxic negative Messages of others, or withers to failure. All the episodes of a candidacy are narrated with the help of professional journalists and political commentators, who do much to serialize the race as a series of culminative decision points, as noted above, parceling it out into temporally bounded episodic intervals between these points through previews and recaps, through tracking ups and downs, and through inviting experts and insiders to remark on the candidates' ever-shifting fortunes.

Thought of in terms of aesthetic style in this way, quite a bit of the media's serialization of politics merits comparison with soap opera. The grotesque figures in campaigns materialize as in soap opera, particularly as in soap opera's technique of heightening and foregrounding a gripping, close-up (and surreal) "ordinary life." In campaign serialization there is even a degree of what Hobson (2003) calls "recurrent catathesis," the periodic spikes in dramatic tension just at the break in a viewing interval that are designed to hook soap-opera audiences, to get them to tune in again to see how their favorite character has fared. Think of all the fretful and dramatic ups and downs of plot for those who supported Hillary Clinton in her failed bid for her party's presidential nomination in 2007–2008: "The Philadelphia Pile On," as one headline recapped attacks on Hillary in a turning-point debate at Drexel University in 2007; the "Comeback Girl" moniker she earned after her dramatic post-choke-up win in the New Hampshire primary, the same state where in early 1992 Bill Clinton had earned his "Comeback Kid" soubriquet after coming from behind and finishing second to then Democratic front-runner in New England, Sen. Paul Tsongas of Massachusetts; the "Clinton-Obama Showdown in Texas" summoning up the drama of a spaghetti Western; and so forth. In addition, insiders and commentators frequently identify major turning points or crises in the plot of candidacy-to-election-to-incumbency as a figure's "defining moments."

These are events that, while not necessarily defined by the strict calendar of the political cycle, are in retrospect inflection points at which a decisive shift suddenly looms in a political figure's fortunes—for good or for ill. For ill, as we take up in a later chapter, who can forget the reaction to Gov. Howard Dean's epic post-loss scream that sounded the knell for whatever viability remained in his 2004 presidential candidacy? Such "defining moments" are, of course, in the eye of the beholder, generally a political analyst or pundit whose spin on an event may not be an ingenuous or neutral report; why a moment calls attention to itself is frequently a function of the Message plotline into which a figure is to be scripted. Notice the widespread manufacture of a defining moment in an otherwise dull patch: Senator Obama, for example, said to have "failed to create a [defining] moment"—that is, to satisfy the soap-operatic plot many commentators had prepared for him—by not ripping into then front-runner Sen. Hillary Clinton when he had the chance in an important Democratic Party primary debate.

The basic point is that Message is not just about inhabiting identities in a field of competition at particular historical points in time. However soap-operatic in playing on the buffeting forces when one ambition meets another, these identities are narrated to publics in such a manner that they seem to follow trajectories of personal development and growth, as in a Bildungsroman, a novel of a protagonist's coming to realize his or her essential character by encounters with life. All sorts of events and social relations test and shape a candidate as the race unfolds. A roller-coaster-like range of events pass in a rather short period, as can be seen by juxtaposing, in roughly chronological fashion—like time-lapse photography—a handful of actual news headlines that trace media representation of the candidate's critical moments and crisis points: John McCain Enters Race; Appears to Be off His Stride; Looks for Support from Christian Conservatives; Attacks Old Target; Loses Some of His Rebel Edge; "Insider" McCain Punches Back; Attempts to Breathe New Life into Campaign; Money's Tight, Turns on the Charm; Shakes up Campaign Again; Delivers First Big Swipe at Rudy Giuliani; Criticizes

Feminists and Liberals in Stump Speech; Says It's OK to Make People Mad; Receives NRA Endorsement; Sends out "Truth Squad" to Counter Whisper Campaign; Forced to Deny Romantic Link with Lobbyist; Rejects the Endorsements of Two Evangelical Ministers; Lambastes Bush Years; Attacks *New York Times* after Op-Ed Column Rejected; Kerry Says McCain Lacks Judgment to Be President; McCain, Kerry Friendship Hits a Rocky Stretch; Last Chance; Fighting Back Once Again; McCain Driving Debate, but Some Fear Swerving; Slings "Socialist" Charges at Obama to Spark Comeback; Hammers Obama as Job-Killing Socialist; McCain Just "Making Stuff Up": Obama; Can't Gain Traction; Gets Angry, Kind of; Temper, Temper; Analysis: McCain Is Running on Angry; John McCain and Joe the Plumber, Together in Ohio; Admits Tensions with Running Mate Sarah Palin; Has Terse Response on Palin Shopping Spree; Looks Lost on "Meet the Press"; Hoping He Has Friends in Pennsylvania; Vows Nothing is Inevitable; The Journey Ends; Looks Ahead; Can McCain Be Obama's Friend in Congress?

Whew! All this in thirty-nine weeks or less of media coverage!

Our favorite characters live in this kind of mass-mediatized paracosm, this separate universe that, like soap opera, bears an uncanny and hypertrophied likeness to our own. From the standpoint of Message building, political figures thus have to emerge on the horizon of a political tableau or diorama populated by many actors, each following a particular plotline, and the figures' Messages cause that tableau to transform—a true tableau vivant—in ways that are understandable according to dramatic coherence, or at least non-inconsistency. There are changes of heart on this or that issue all by itself that are managed in response to circumstances, for it is perfectly understandable that people grow and develop as they face crises, just as do characters in the best Bildungsromane. However, when such change of heart is itself the news, when it seems to be the whole story of strategic self-refashioning, it is suspicious, like the proverbial Kerry "flip-flops" of the 2004 campaign, or those fact-denying ones of Gov. Mitt Romney of the 2008 campaign and beyond, strongly persisting as the major negative Message about Romney's "true (that is, feigned) conservatism" in the 2011–2012 election season (the minor one playing to the Christian Right being the "cult" of Mormonism). But is the change of heart consistent with the cumulative biographical construction of one's Message? Therein lies the difference between media empathy or suspicion, between the public's trust or its distrust of how issues are mediating a figure's Message.

"Logocracy"; or, Why "The Issues" Matter

Central to electoral politics as these dramatic, rough-and-tumble character contests may be, there is a countercurrent. Who, following politics, does not sometimes feel that personalia should be secondary to substantive debate centered on "The Issues"? Is this not a kind of reverence for The Issues, for insisting that politicians should speak clearly and with conviction about issues before the polity, crafting sound arguments that link analytic premises to a conclusion in which a course of action is indicated? Why, in the face of the long-term stability of Message politics in American society, do we still feel moved to appeal to the enduring model of politics as public deliberative debate of The Issues? Why, in fact, in many jeremiads of our day, should there be a strong moral loading to the choice supposedly to be made between Issue and Image, between serious debate and mere theater, between substance and style, implying that the health of democracy may even lie in the balance? Why the abiding suspicion of Machiavellian doings among political figures—that they (gasp!) dissimulate and (oh, no!) engage in verbal subterfuge and (for shame!) say whatever is momentarily expedient to secure support, money, and votes?

We suggest that some of these distinctions and sentiments are traceable to deep-rooted cultural convictions about political process and the role of political communication in it. Such sentiments are inherent outgrowths of our political culture that were institutionalized in the founding moments of the United States; for many they still serve as a kind of standard or measure of how well we are doing politically. These involve the institutionalization of a form of self-governance that Washington Irving, speaking through his fictional foreign observer Mustapha Rub-a-Dub Keli Khan, first satirically dubbed "logocracy," rule by language. About this instrumental role of language and communication in governance, Irving's 1807 *Salmagundi* (a work Irving penned with his brother William and

James Paulding) used his protagonist's astonishment to foreground this new loquaciousness in speech and print, along with the ironic violence and even risk of the restoration of tyranny it permitted—perhaps even engendered. This was, after all, a period of party fractiousness between Democratic-Republicans and Federalists fueled by the "slang-whangers" of the Fourth Estate, the newspaper editorialists who were infamous for dishing out all manner of partisan gossip and abuse. Irving reserved little reverence even for the office of the presidency, then held by Thomas Jefferson, for while there "never was a dignitary better qualified for his station," here was a "man of superlative ventosity, and comparable to nothing but a huge bladder of wind" (155).

All this suspicion directed toward language, resting on familiar dichotomies of language versus action, saying versus doing, harkens back to the storied seventeenth-century anxieties about what John Locke called the "cheat and abuse" of words (see Bauman and Briggs 2003, 36–40), writing as he did in the wake of the English Civil Wars. It reminds us, too, of contemporary complaints about the need for clear, substantive, issue-driven political communication. But the broader point is that Irving's early satire spotlighted the role of language in what was then a new and precarious form of self-governance. In this it recalled the heady spirit of early American federalism, whose architects, the intellectual leaders of the period—Benjamin Rush, James Madison, John Adams, John Jay, and others—had envisioned language playing a critical role in democratic governance.

As with the Enlightenment legacy more generally, language came to be viewed as a crucial cognitive resource and instrument for knowing ourselves and for dealing with the world. Just as in the various fields of natural philosophy—physical and biological science—being revolutionized by a new empirical and experimental sensibility, the words and expressions of language came to be seen as instruments for representing as well what we now term "sociocultural realities." And, like all instruments, the words and expressions of language could and should be improved. For Locke the "cheat and abuse" of words, epitomized by polysemy and fanciful metaphor, could be remedied through reflexive attention to and disciplined use of language. Analogously, for the intellectual leaders of early American federalism, language, if used properly and refined, could be harnessed to improve society. Refined in their meanings, elaborated in how they relate one to another, augmented by new coinages, words could even aid in a particular society's ability to govern itself as a polity. "Governments are instituted among men," meaning humankind, asserts the 1776 United States Declaration of Independence, following Locke's lead in his *Second Treatise,* in order to transform what any social scientist would recognize as a mass society into a polity.

The political science of the time followed, in broad terms, the Baconian and especially Lockean ideas that were so successful in creating a modern scientific sense: that one could come to right and rational action about the world by testing and refining what one knows about it, revealed, of course, in how one talks about the world and otherwise describes or represents it for oneself and for others. Think of the proceduralist account of empirical sciences, where, it is widely thought, one formulates a hypothesis, a representation of the way things ought to be; one applies the representation against the particulars of the world; and, on the basis of how it applies (or not) to the world, judges the capacity of the representation to capture how things work, adjusting the representation accordingly and, starting the cycle over, trying again. There is an internally self-propelling and self-guiding cycle of, if not perfection, at least a promise of *perfectibility* in moving knowledge closer to the reality it models, of creating a more perfect union of conceptualization and practical being-in-the-world.

Down to the early period of American nationhood, Enlightenment theorists of society and polity shaped theoretical ideas about the nature of government as a doubly acting enterprise of this very sort: a mechanism—a machine, as it were—for coming to more rational collective action as a polity, and thus, secondly, a machine of orderly linguistic procedure for creating, refining, and, if necessary, changing the conceptual language with which to formulate and evaluate how to go about doing the first. A great experiment indeed! These ideas first culminated in their application to the American Constitution, which sets out a verbal model for the organization of a federal government and an allocation of at least initially licensed powers to each of its parts. With all of the "shall be"s, "shall consist of"s, and "shall have power to"s, the Constitution gets things going in the hopes that the government will be self-sustaining and self-modifying. These governmental powers for variously elected and appointed incumbents to act in society on behalf of the whole begin and end, of course, in language, in "representative" language. Hence, we can understand Irving's quip about our having not an aristocratic form of government, nor a (directly) democratic one, but a logocratic one—a government in which the formulation and application and reformulation of words is always at issue: a "government of laws," operating on the energy supplied by language as an instrument for rationally acting upon the world of human affairs.

Logos, Aristotle's notion of rational discourse that is humanity's link to cosmic orderliness, surely becomes the very armature of government in such a view as self-governance is seen to be, potentially, a kind of applied science. The state, seen as an emergently natural polity composed of and coordinating its citizens, is indeed like a ship requiring a helmsman (Greek κυβερνής [kyberné:s]), and government serves that (as we now say, cybernetic) function insofar it governs in the *logocratic* mode: that mode of government that rests on the creation, administration, and adjudication of written laws within a representative—or republican—constitutional system.[2]

In parallel fashion, James Madison's account of this new organon of self-governance originates in the legislative formulation of laws as licensed to the Congress by the Constitution; the execution or enforcement of these laws through administering them by the executive branch, headed by the president; and the judgment of whether or not, and how well, the laws as executed are working in people's lives by adjudication in case law of a federal judiciary. It is a tripartite reciprocating engine running on language, in which the never-ending and recursive legislative → executive → judicial → . . . cycle of key terms and expressions repeatedly moving through the system is the only way that words have political meaning. (So much for the "original intent" mystification of constitutional language!)

This is a language-focused pragmatist legacy in the political thought that founded the United States. In it, the very lawyerly proceduralism as practiced by those in political power becomes a route to more precise self-understanding of ourselves as citizens with freedoms, rights, duties, obligations to and claims upon each other, by virtue of government debating and undertaking projects of one or another sort in the name of the polity. "Ahh! Yes!" we may recall: "form[ing] a more perfect Union, establish[ing] Justice, insur[ing] domestic Tranquility, provid[ing] for the common defence [sic], promot[ing] the general Welfare, and secur[ing] the Blessings of Liberty to ourselves and our Posterity." Starting from these lofty and abstract goals of the preamble to the U.S. Constitution, as from any of the other very general authorizations for action by one or another branch of government (or from any of the very generally phrased protections therefrom in the Bill of Rights), everything in logocracy becomes a question of acting or not acting, authorizing or not authorizing, funding or not funding, redefining a situation or letting it be in the various specific and contextualized realms within the purview of those so empowered. And the acting or not, the authorizing or not, and so on inevitably will gore the ox of one interest group while it fattens the heifer of another.

So there is a sometimes very direct, very immediate politico-economic as well as moral consequentiality of language-mediated governmental proceduralism. It should not be hard to imagine, then, why the electorate might expect from our political actors clear, precise, sincere speech that is directed to Issue-centered communication both within government and in the broader public sphere. How will the passage into executed public law of a bill on taxation of widgets from abroad affect the butcher, the baker, the candlestick maker? Tell us why those other gizmos escape such taxation, or at least are taxed at a much lower rate! As we can see, the logocratic culture out of which emerges the founding values of representative republicanism orients both media and their publics to hold politicians accountable to Issues and, when their wits are about them, to be suspicious when anything seems to be in play other than weighing of alternatives in the name and on behalf of the commonweal. Logocracy in its Madisonian ideal holds a normative sway in the electoral imaginary, rendering us all creatures of politics, in the unnerving sense of being so habituated to the surround of what sounds and looks at first sight to be Issue-oriented communication from our political figures that we can easily become oblivious to the fact that Issues are not the Message, but are merely what we might term the "design elements" of that complex professional construction, a political figure's Message. The latter is a social construction of a sort that exists in the public space that encompasses political figures and the concentric social circles around them, a construction of a certain complexity and abstractness, in actuality, around which our electoral politics is shaped.

To get a measure of critical distance on this political environment in which we live, we have to pay special attention to what anthropologists and sociologists call "the breach," moments when participants in a social system—here, particularly, candidates running for office—are thought by others in it to flout conventions and norms, the reactions to which reveal much about what is tacit and taken for granted within that social system. We pay attention to reactions to moments when candidates and incumbents respond poorly to a question, become, as it were, unhinged—scream, shed (real?) tears—get bollixed up, say inane or convoluted things, seem to dodge Issues, flip-flop, go rogue, lose control of their tongue in verbal slips and gaffes, and so forth. At such moments their Message is up for reevaluation, if not at risk. Such moments offer us the chance to see how people in the media and in the public think politicians should talk, act, comport themselves. So rather than focus exclusively on rhetorical eloquence in presidential and other political oratory (*pace* Jamieson 1988), we pay special heed to moments of threatened meltdown of Message. We use the breach as a methodological aperture through which to glimpse what political communication—both as an object of study and a field of study—takes for granted.

Experts in and Practitioners of Political Communication

There is a field generally captioned "political communication" that concerns itself almost exclusively with communication between government (and candidates for incumbencies therein) and a public—for example, the democratic electorate, as mediated by print, broadcast, and web media, thus, "mediatized" communication. Some trace this field of political communication to World War I–era public-relations initiatives and the propaganda studies that emerged in its wake, and note the field's interdisciplinary and somewhat eclectic makeup, which has included psychology, political science, rhetoric, and social-institutional communication studies (see Sanders 2009). Such study of mediatized communication between governmental and public spheres manifests itself in the academy in departments or schools of communication and in comparable sites specializing in government or political science. The focus is generally reflexive, in that the field takes the contemporary organization of explicit or frank politics for granted, mass electoral democracies being the neutral zero point from which things are considered. Research in political communication often involves inquiries into outcomes of communication— that is, communication "effects"—in some particular aspect or phase of the total political process, electoral politics being only one aspect. How does the prime minister influence the vote in the Japanese Diet or the British Parliament through appeals to the public who have elected (and who will [re]elect, or not) their representatives? How does the leader of the opposition rally voters to the polls after a vote of no confidence? What role does television broadcasting play in keeping a dictator's people subjugated to a nondemocratic regime under a communicational state of emergency? What role do Facebook and Twitter play in organizing an effective opposition to this?

These scholarly approaches border on policy science or policy studies in that there are practical applications of their empirical results and generalizations by practitioners who fill various roles in the overall political enterprises of our contemporary world. The field of political communication, so conceived, invites movement of specialists across the divide of what some think of as "theory" and "practice." Indeed, people who have been in political incumbencies, thus experienced in communicating to electorates, move in and out of positions in academia at places like Harvard's Kennedy School, Stanford's Hoover Institution, Johns Hopkins's School of International and Strategic Studies, Princeton's Woodrow Wilson School, and other institutions. And there is a whole world of consultants, advisers, and quasi-governmental go-betweens at all levels of government, from local municipalities to global institutions like the United Nations and the World Trade Organization, who operate halfway between worlds of degreed academic or think-tank reflection, active paid consulting, actual government service, at any time of their careers serving in one or another of these positions. (As we point out below, the merger of political communication and marketing has created a field of "political marketing," which eschews policy for hardscrabble practicalities of success in a public construed as a consumer-like market.) In this world there is a practical intuition about what works and what does not, but there is precious little in the way of theorization of why this may be so, based on what we now know about language and communication in a sociocultural context.

Our task is somewhat different, all the while recognizing that this world of academic and applied political communication exists. We are anthropologists who are interested in exploring political communication by thinking about it as *discursive interaction,* a complex of processes of actual, language-centered communication that take place in sociocultural contexts. To be sure, several activist-intellectuals as well as industry insiders have also studied Message by way of language, explaining, for example, why slogans like "death tax" (not "estate tax"; note the old and popular saying that the only certainties in life are "death and taxes") and "climate change" (not "global warming") work in gaining electoral support (e.g., Luntz 2007); or claiming that partisan politics supposedly turns on purportedly underlying "metaphors" and how issues can be contrastively "framed" through invoking them (G. Lakoff 2004; Feldman 2007). Its embrace of contemporary themes in cognitive science and psychology notwithstanding, this work shares much in spirit with the classical tradition of applied rhetoric, to the extent that it tries to identify effective, persuasive devices for use in political communication. (Some connoisseurs of oratory today tick off devices of classical rhetoric as they listen to political speeches: anadiplosis, chiasmus, asyndeton, and so on, canonized in Greco-Roman times in prescriptive treatises on oratory, like that of the influential first-century Roman rhetorician Quintilian.) Quite a bit of this work tends to focus on a narrow slice of language—namely, easily reportable words and expressions like slogans and shibboleths. (Compare here the "word clouds" one sees in news reports on political debates, in which the relative frequency of word types uttered is translated visually into larger and smaller font size and central and peripheral positionality so that viewers see what words stand out within a billowy, cloudlike diagram. Or, indeed, compare here what is termed, in political science and communication studies, "content analysis," which ironically empties discourse of anything one might term 'content'—that is, sense—and then counts up token instances of a word or expression with no care to what propositional content is actually being communicated!)

Message, however, as we have come to understand it, is multimodal in the sense that it can incorporate all sorts of material, from clothing and staging to gesture and speech. Even for verbal discourse itself, facts of pronunciation, lexis, register, grammar, prosody, textual poetics—any or all of these may become implicated in Message. To create Message and keep a candidate on Message, campaigns try to deploy signs in multiple modalities that should mutually reinforce one another and invite a favorable story about who the candidate is in relation to competitors. Both press and the public have taken note of Governor Romney's "perfect"—apparently heavily moussed—hair and Governor Palin's titanium-frame Kazuo Kawasaki eyewear. And identifyingly newsworthy were Senator Clinton's choking up about perseverance against odds before the 2008 New Hampshire primary, and Rep. Michelle Bachman's "crazy eyes," as some said of her somewhat unflattering photo on the cover of *Newsweek* as she joined the Republican Party group of would-be 2012 presidential candidates. Verbally and in other modalities what is offered are calculated bundles of pungent, eye- or ear-catching phrases and design elements that, once introduced and taken account of, for example, in the media, become emblems to be fought over across the divide of political camps' discursive Ping Pong matches. These are "Message partials," or overtones, that become the usable constituents of campaigns of personal identity and identifiability. (Remember, Message is both positive—what you want for yourself—and negative—how you want to brand your opponent.) For this reason, Message turns out to be the kind of social fact that is best approached expansively, through semiotics—the systematic study of how all phenomena, in implicit as well as explicit events of communication, can be understood as signs of and for things like character, biographical trajectory, and identifiability of a political figure.

A semiotic sensibility toward language in its communicative context is also critical in order to overcome a referentialist orientation to language, itself a legacy of the Enlightenment that informed the Madisonian logocratic imaginary. Without moving beyond the simple fact of words and their frequencies, for example, it becomes impossible to explain how two ways of otherwise saying the same thing (e.g., contrastive pronunciations of *Pakistan,* or the forms of expression *hunt down and kill the terrorists* versus *dismantle that network*) could make a difference in what kind of political figure seems to be speaking in the political public sphere. This aspect of signs in action (semiosis) is crucial to Message, as we develop in this work, showing how what are technically termed "indexical" differences (how signs point to—even create—aspects of their context of occurrence) can be understood to signal attributes of the speaker in systematic ways. To describe and model Message dynamics, we draw on such concepts developed for the study of discourse over the past several decades in linguistic anthropology as well as in related traditions like sociolinguistics and discourse analysis.

While we approach Message as multimodal discursive interaction, this doesn't mean we treat communicative events as if they were neatly circumscribed texts whose meaningful parts and formal organization could be studied apart from sociocultural context. Rather, our approach to Message politics centers on three related perspectives: (1) the semiotic analysis of occasions of communication and how they seem to accomplish the social ends they do or fail to do; (2) the political sociology of institutionalized communicative genres (e.g., candidate debates, post-debate commentary, stump speeches, and journalistic reportage about any of these)—in other words, where communicative events occur in the social space-time centered on institutionalized politics—and (3) the cultural analysis of the values that underlie Message performance (in inhabitable figures like the "maverick" and the "flip-flopper" and the axis of developing biographical authenticity with which political players can be emplotted in them as character types with various strategic purposes and degrees of success).

The qualitative dimensions of communicative events offer answers to questions about: Who and to whom? About whom/what? By what means? For whom? Where in social space-time? So let us consider some of what this entails. If we start with the social anthropological notion that an event of political communication counts as a particular kind of discursively mediated interaction with social cause and effect, how can we interpretatively contextualize it in its, as Max Weber termed it, *institutional matrix*? How can we interpret it against a backdrop of relevant actors' sustained or frustrated or exceeded presumptions about what such communication *does* in the way of an effective outcome?

Where, in a complex sequence of communications leading up to and framing the present one does a communicative event stand, and what is its likely effectiveness in its communicative afterlife, its several possible sequels? In politics, for example, when the going gets tough, the tough distract with spectacle. (One might think here of Mr. Nixon's administration during the onslaught of Watergate, or Mr. Clinton's multiple trips to be photographed with world leaders during the endless impeachment process that took up most of his second term in office.) How do individuals get to enjoy the privileged role of being an agentive source of communication? And who has the access to the event in both direct and mediate or relayed recipient role in respect of the communication? Who is let in to the live proceedings, and who can watch on closed- or open-circuit TV? How many such spectacles are broadcast live all around the world? (Mr. Obama's inaugural ceremony was so broadcast, with perhaps the same level of interest in it as a soap-operatic culmination as one might see in a British royal wedding or funeral.) Observe that government—that is, the political figures in it—frequently makes itself visible through such organized spectacle that, even if restricted in here-and-now physical access, generates secondary, tertiary, and further communication that government figures and bodies come more and more to rely on to get out their Message to the recipient publics on whom they depend for their legitimacy—especially the British royals these days!

Our focus here is on people who can be called "political communicators," particularly those who communicate while aspiring to or are incumbent in roles in government, yet a moment's reflection reveals that all sorts of other potentially relevant vectors of communication exist within the political field. They communicate among each other, as for example a

U.S. president consulting the vice president, a cabinet secretary, or other official by telephone. They sometimes communicate *ex cathedra*—that is, in official and corporate capacity—as for example, a majority decision of the U.S. Supreme Court handed out by the clerk of the court or posted on its website that, though signed, is written "for the majority" as the legally binding decision. Such political communicators are regularly expected to communicate to the public via the self-designated nongovernmental representatives of the public, the political media, for which purpose there are several kinds of communicative events. News bulletins are issued to the press corps from governmental officials and organizational bodies. Incumbent officeholders give both regularly scheduled and extra-cyclic press briefings, sometimes with questions and answers, as in presidential news conferences. The "news" is duly, if usually selectively, relayed to the wider public by being reported in the various media (although complete television and web-streamed coverage has been generally available since the Kennedy administration). Those in power frequently communicate to the world outside government—and thereby, indirectly, to those inside as well—by secret, not-for-attribution "leaks" to the media, perhaps the most famous of which in modern U.S. history was the continuing saga of the Nixon White House's Watergate scandal, the details of which were leaked in 1972 and 1973 by FBI Associate Director W. Mark Felt, aka "Deep Throat."

These exemplify the workings of an organizational matrix that shapes the vectors of political communication. We must think of all this communication in relation to the highly reticulated structure of any government, in which official offices or incumbencies are generally apical positions within multi-person organizational nodes, and, as in any complex, multipurpose firm, all of these nodes are organized in tiered clusters. As was long ago set forth in the U.S. Constitution, these clusters are divided into a tripartite structure following the theory of essential governmental powers: the legislative, the executive, and the judicial. So intra-governmental communication is one essential component of how government works (or does not) and how the people inside government operate within the social organization of functioning bureaucracy. How they operate within this complex functioning bureaucracy frequently becomes "news" that they—or, in the case of bad tidings, someone else—want to have known on the outside of government. Of course, as noted above, extra-governmental interests of various sorts are highly motivated to penetrate the sometimes not-so-secure boundaries of such internal communication and perhaps even to participate in it: go-betweens of various sorts shuttle information via communication between governmental operatives and political interests in business or any large-scale enterprise that would benefit from foreknowledge to shape its strategy in trying to have governmental process turned to its advantage. In our day of lobbying, not only obvious commercial interests but any kind of interest group wants to make direct contact by communicating its hopes/needs/wants/threats to people in government who are working on policy or its implementation. Such interest groups might be universities, "green" nongovernmental organizations, religious denominations, and so on, as well as the Tobacco Institute, the American Dairy Council, or the U.S. Chamber of Commerce, which are to various degrees camouflaged industry agents.

Interestingly, in the arena of still extra-governmental but governmentally oriented political campaigns of candidates within our American electoral system, a whole parallel sort of bureaucracy comes into being, with many of the same internal problems of people working within bureaucratic organizational structure as are obvious in the competitive world of government, along with many of the pressures of communication with financing interests, supporters, media, and so forth. At the level of running a national campaign—as, for example, a presidential campaign—there are complex problems of state- and even county-level political organizations that must be brought into being and kept in communication. In short, there must be a kind of extra-governmental apparatus that parallels in many ways the apparatus of government. In a sense, what soon becomes visible under such circumstances is whether or not the national campaign is sufficiently organized to run like a proper tiered bureaucracy with lines of command and zones of privileged communication in the manner of the government itself. The political media have been concentrating on this theme over many cycles of both primary and national presidential politics, not so subtly suggesting its equivalence to a candidate's deserving office. When campaigns are discovered to be lacking in such functional stability, let alone solid and continuing financing, the media soon discover their flaws and begin reporting this to the public ("Shake-up inside the Doe campaign!" "Doe campaign out of bucks!"), almost always to the detriment of the campaign as the organization that buoys someone's candidacy with a structural platform on which to stand. So-called openness, then, just like multiple communication at cross-purposes, bodes ill for running a governmental bureaucracy, which must maintain a certain degree of internal structure and ultimate non-permeability of its membrane of privileged communication.

Notwithstanding all the complexity of government as a reticulated and tiered organizational form with communication vectors directed every which way, not all of these kinds of communication have received due attention as political communication. This is partly a function of the lag time in assembling and rendering usable archives of relevant communicational artifacts such as written and printed memoranda, directives, and reports, and e-mails among principals. Who can do a social-scientific study of internal bureaucratic communication without day-by-day, even hour-by-hour access to such material? Instead, much of this has to be reconstructed far after the fact by responsible historians, even when, in a kind of frequently misleading and self-serving kiss-and-tell genre of memoir, people who have concluded a period of service in government write about their just-completed service in a strategic bid for self-aggrandizement, absolution, and exoneration. (The culture of celebrity that we have noted and the soap-operatic thematic of our time ensure that such tales can appeal to a certain guaranteed market, especially if government service has been controversial or has been in proximity to controversial celebrity political figures and events. These essentially pre-emptive publications in retrospective Message-ing come cyclically in bursts starting generally in the second year after a change of executive branch administrations.)

In other words, we concentrate here on understanding that communicative events, chains or cycles of such communicative events, structures facilitating such chains or cycles, controlling interests that work to establish and institutionalize such structures (whether positively or negatively), are all part of the way that communication—both in the single event and over a social space-time of many diverse genres of events—is the central, mediating fact of political process.

To trace the dynamics of Message, we look across communicative events and pay special attention to the forms of mediation between political and governmental figures and their presumptive publics. Such institutionalized mediation gets captioned as "the press" and "the media," which we might imagine to form a framing, interpretative ring separating politicians from their publics, what Pres. George W. Bush called "the filter" between him and the public. We must be sensitive to the particular communicative and inscriptional technologies of the time as we study this mediation; they have rhythms of circulation and consumption that interact in interesting ways. The media through which people have circulated Message partials are ever changing, whether through artifacts like handbills, direct-mail letters, or e-mails, or through real-time broadcast media spectacle or secondary excerpts therefrom later in a news cycle— derided, with a wink, as mere "sound bites" by many who nonetheless depend on them. Today in the United States, for example, we rarely get to feel that we live, as in Mr. Lincoln's day, in an era of the dynamite speech on a carefully constructed thematic occasion, which relied on verbatim quotation in newspaper circulation and then many further echoes in popular phraseology for a certain image-building half-life of Message relevance.

What we would call the social sites at which and through which political communication—the real work of electoral politics—takes place are ever changing, too. It has been only fifty years since television joined and displaced radio as the way political figures could actualize in the sensory here-and-now of an electorate. Now there are various new media that allow new modalities of communicative contact and even, sometimes, feedback. A vast organization is required to manage and coordinate all of this beyond live appearances, speeches, and usual news-cycle coverage: from campaign materials (signage, legible clothing blazoned with campaign logo) and texts (relaying "talking points" circulated among campaign operatives and supporters) to websites (needing rapid editing and updating), Twitter (for that youthful insouciance and celebrity feeling), and Facebook (providing an aura of two-way dialogicality).

Interestingly, the advent of television (and now web-streamed) coverage of political spectacles—which has the potential to create a huge number of addressees for a political figure—just does not seem to have sparked a renaissance of the dynamite speech. Certainly among American presidents, for example, until 2004 the last truly stirring address was Mr. Kennedy's only inaugural, in January 1961. We note that at the 2004 Democratic National Convention (DNC), a great new orator, Illinois state senator Barack Obama, materialized as if out of nowhere and delivered the convention's keynote address in a performance that became a central part of his Message and in a sense the spectacular beginning of his presidential campaign. Combining the cadences of the Lincolnesque plain style and the constructional majesty of Mr. Kennedy's lofty and lengthy periods, it was delivered in quasi-sermonesque tones that—framed by Mr. Obama's demographic, which he also thematized in his text—could only remind people of the Rev. Martin Luther King Jr. Several times during the 2008 presidential cycle, Mr. Obama demonstrated these rhetorical gifts anew, and they became a recurrent theme of attempted negative Message-ing by opponents both in the primary campaign and in the general election. During his incumbency, including his own inaugural address on 20 January 2009, these gifts have been very little in evidence, a severe blow to his Message within a sector of his political base, to be sure, both those who are old enough to recall Mr. Kennedy's inaugural triumph and those among the young who have never heard that traditional rhetoric of the American civil-religious presidency.

Majestic and inspiring rhetorical spectacle aside, then, today the techniques of Message that are visible and audible all around us seem to be conceptualized much in the style of contemporary brand-focused marketing. Thus well captioned as "political marketing," here is an approach to political communication designed for an electorate and even wider public who can "buy in" to the Message, with monetary support, votes, enthusiastic "buzz," recognition, and so forth. Professionals in multimodal or cross-modal marketing strategy design the many ways a political figure materializes through all the Message-building components of such a campaign in which the *political persona of the Message*—not necessarily the actual individual politician concerned—is to exist in the communicational interface with the public. Whatever the origins of the term "political campaign" in the metaphorical transfer from determined, goal-directed military action, it has been moving in a direction ever closer to an asymptote in the "ad campaign." We must take note of the complexities of campaign organization (see our remarks above on the quasi-governmental standards to which campaigns are evaluatively held) built around the production and furtherance of a candidate's positive Message and the fending off of any negative Message-ing coming from rivals.

But notwithstanding the various channels through which Message is developed and disseminated, we need to understand the processes that lead a public and an electorate to be able to identify political figures' Messages at the heart of the democratic process, and that depend partly on cultural values, which are too often neglected in studies of political communication. In such study we see that culturally and historically specific dimensions of imaginable identity have been made to count in politicians' coming to visibility, audibility, and survival in the political process. How is communication shaped and imbued with meaning in relation to cultural normativities and commonplaces of various sorts, on which being able to stimulate even implicitly understood plotlines of biographical figuration must depend? Can one imagine "the Governator," former governor Arnold Schwarzenegger of California, in any other way than from his Hollywood role as "the Terminator?" His campaign, after all, stimulated the dissemination of this moniker that was clearly supposed to define who—again, sociologically speaking, what social persona—he was seeking (rather truculently, though perhaps with a sense of justice done) to inhabit in government.

Not everyone aligns with the cultural values of an intended Message, and some may not even register them; such alignments are unevenly distributed through a population as a function of people's social positions in society and of their affiliations with groups that have particular interests. Hence, a central question is, What strategic (or happenstance) role or function does political communication play in relation to the interests that come together in political processes from outside of government? This leads naturally to a critical topic in political communication, that of "addressivity," which, as Mikhail Bakhtin (1986, 95) expansively put it, refers to the way discourse, written or spoken, is felt to have a "quality of being directed to someone." To whom, to which categories and groups of social actors, is political communication, and especially political spectacle, addressed?

Observe in this connection, for instance, the increasing use among political commentators of the concept of a candidate's base, his or her enthusiastic supporters who resonate with the figure's Message as built around Issue slogans and Issue shibboleths and other framing semiotic flotsam and jetsam with which a characteristic demographic or cluster of demographics can identify. Political figures seem to absorb energy—or at least maintain the momentum of their Message—from such a socio-demographic base, expansive or narrow as it may be in relation to the larger public, and woe be to the politician without such a base in the overall system of Message politics.

Observe, too, the complexities of addressivity that lurk behind the notion of "direct" address, like a president's speech "to" Congress or "to" different publics. From a linguistic anthropological perspective, we must consider seemingly direct appeals to political bodies or to the public in their fullness as, in fact, complexly layered communicative events. If we consider something like that modern annual made-for-TV spectacle, the presidential State of the Union Address, we should note that technically it is structured by the Constitution (Article II, Section 3) as a progress report by the chief executive to Congress. There is no stipulation that it be delivered as a speech to the assembled legislature in bicameral meeting (early presidents had a written message read to the Congress by a clerk). Those assembled now prominently include the president's cabinet secretaries, the Supreme Court justices, the Joint Chiefs of Staff of the military, and other notable government figures. It also includes a balcony observers' gallery of the carefully demographically varied yet telegenically blessed "public" sitting along with the First Lady and—since Ronald Reagan's boffo Hollywood-worthy performances—ordinary citizens whose good deeds, hard times, and other soap-opera-worthy tales figure in the speech itself (at which time network television cameras switch to shots of the character come to life before us, now smiling, crying, waving, as the case necessitates). Is it still the president "giv[ing] to the Congress

Information of the State of the Union, and recommend[ing] to their Consideration such Measures as he shall judge necessary and expedient"? In a way, of course, but it must now be understood to be performed in the high-lumen intensity of a ritual enactment that has become one of the pillars of the rhetorical obligations of the presidency in the public sphere. It has become part of the Message strategies of the modern presidency (cf. Tulis 1987) and, as such, attracts all the usual manner of analysis, commentary, and resonance in relation to the president as a political figure (especially pronounced in the second two years of a presidential term of office). In fact, since the president is, of course, affiliated with a particular political party, notwithstanding this address is a stipulated constitutional obligation, networks now offer a token rebuttal time to a senator or representative of the opposite party, confirming their understanding of this as presidential Message.

An inverse kind of communicative complexity can also be seen in how a political figure such as a president can use the explicitly framed occasion of speaking "directly" to the populace in the public sphere as a means for strategically addressing specific others in government. A telling use of this duplex (duplicitous?) communicative framework was FDR's Fireside Chats during the 1930s and early 1940s. Broadcast (in front of a small, enjoined-to-silence audience of administration personnel) on network radio from a studio in the office wing of the White House, the idea was to speak in "non-governmentese" on matters that were vital to the administration's New Deal as though chatting with neighbors in front of the family hearth. The format was put to particularly telling strategic intra-governmental effect in a chat of 9 March 1937, just after FDR's reelection, stemming from the fact that several major anti-Depression measures of the Roosevelt administration passed by Congress had been serially declared unconstitutional by the Supreme Court in cases brought by conservative and business interests desperate to halt the "socialist" New Deal. (Sound familiar to a 2012 readership?) FDR had become frustrated by the intransigence of the "nine old men," who lacked "personal experience and contact with modern facts and circumstances under which average men have to live and work" and who showed "hardening of the judicial arteries," he noted for his radio audience. The administration had asked

Congress the previous month to legislate a counterbalancing increase in the size of the Supreme Court with new appointees to counterbalance those beyond age seventy, a congressional prerogative, to be sure. The battle in Congress was framed by widespread acrimonious attacks against Roosevelt as a dictator who was out to subvert the sacred Constitution.

But something miraculous happened starting at the end of that very month and into April: suddenly, though in some cases by relatively slim majorities, the New Deal legislation was upheld in Court decisions, and one by one, starting at the end of the 1937 term, the older justices announced their retirements. It is widely argued—by legal historians, for example—that Roosevelt's "court packing" caper resulted in a political thrashing for the president, the proposed "Judicial Procedures Reform Bill of 1937" coming to naught in both House and Senate. But the actual addressees of his Fireside Chat—not the explicit ones, the American public—seem to have understood what action was needed on their part, enhancing FDR's Message in the public sphere as someone who would take on the most entrenched interests on behalf of the plain old folks, notwithstanding his patrician pedigree.

And all this is to say nothing of the vast range of addressivity effects that we can discover when we start looking carefully at discourse. Recall, for instance, the almost made-for-parody move by John McCain in the third and final presidential debate of 2008 when he tried to use an anecdote to argue that Senator Obama's proposed tax policy would harm small business and the middle class and thus dampen the entrepreneurial spirit of the American dream with a crypto-socialist plan to "spread the wealth around," as McCain repeatedly put it. McCain recounted Obama's chance meeting with a supposedly successful Ohio plumber, "Joe" (Samuel J.) Wurzelbacher, who worried that Obama's tax policy would adversely affect him. It turned out that Wurzelbacher wasn't technically licensed as a plumber, nor was his first name legally Joe—nor was he as financially successful as McCain suggested—but in the hands of the McCain campaign he was fashioned into the captioned figure "Joe the Plumber." Wurzelbacher's surname was dropped and replaced by first name "Joe" plus the role designator "plumber" following what feels like an archaic binomial formula. "Joe" was no doubt a synecdoche for all the 'ordinary'

Joes, and "plumber" has stereotypic 'middle-class' associations based on cultural taxonomies of the professions, making Wurzelbacher, in effect, a proxy for the laboring lower-middle class. (The hackneyed formula Mc-Cain used made it sound as if Wurzelbacher had been inducted into some ragtag band with all the silly swagger of, say, *Monty Python and the Holy Grail*'s Sir Lancelot the Brave, Sir Robin the Not-Quite-So-Brave-as-Sir-Lancelot, etc. As "Joe the Plumber," Wurzelbacher was now in the class of such figures as "Tevye the Milkman" of *Fiddler on the Roof*, "Sam the Butcher" of *Funny Girl*, and the *Brady Bunch*.) What gave this figure real gravity—real social and political consequences—was the fact that both candidates didn't just refer to "Joe the Plumber" in the third person; they occasionally "directly" addressed him as if he were physically there—and in a sense, he was. Here are a few highlights:

MCCAIN:

> Now, my old buddy [!], Joe, Joe the plumber, is out there. Now, Joe, Senator Obama's plan, if you're a small business and you are able—and your—the guy that sells to you will not have his capital gains tax increase, which Senator Obama wants, if you're out there, my friend, and you've got employees, and you've got kids, if you don't get—adopt the health care plan that Senator Obama mandates, he's going to fine you.

OBAMA:

> And I'm happy to talk to you, Joe, too, if you're out there. Here's your fine—zero.

AGAIN MCCAIN:

> Now, Joe, you're rich, congratulations, and you will then fall into the category where you'll have to pay a fine if you don't provide health insurance that Senator Obama mandates, not the kind that you think is best for your family, your children, your employees, but the kind that he mandates for you.

AND AGAIN OBAMA:

> All I want to do, if you've already got health care, is lower your costs. That includes you, Joe.

In the wake of the debate, Joe—the real Joe, a stand-in for millions of ordinary Joes—made cameos at McCain campaign stops; gave interviews on *CBS Evening News* and *Good Morning America*; published a book, *Joe the Plumber: Fighting for the American Dream* (written with help from Thomas Tabback); inspired pro- and anti-Joe T-shirts, even a bobble-head doll; and, as of the time we write, he has launched his own political run for

Congress. All of this illustrates what can happen when one is hailed in a high-stakes televised debate late in the campaign season and why addressivity is so much more complex, and interesting, than our intuitions about political address to some undifferentiated "public" let on.

The Political Press and Other Players in the Agōn of Message-ing

Of all the vectors of address that have attracted scholarly attention, the most scrutinized has surely been the two-way communicative traffic between government officials and campaigns and their publics—traffic that has been regulated, as it were, by the political press. The so-called Fourth Estate, meaning a free and independent press, has long been recognized as central to the stability of liberal-democratic governance. We have several times noted how essential to the nurturance of Message are the mass media focused on politics. Without web, broadcast, and print relay of political happenings—first as news and second as material for endless response in analysis and commentary—the sayings, doings, comings, and goings of political figures would be one-off unique events with no impact on a set of addressees or an audience privy to the tidings beyond the here-and-now of their occurrence. That something is deemed a significant enough occurrence to be reportable about a political figure already makes it Message-relevant to that figure and to allies and opponents. What kind of treatment it gets in its media afterlife is, of course, precisely the issue and the anxiety, anxiety that is sometimes justified. As candidate for the vice presidency in autumn 2008, Alaska governor Sarah Palin sat for an utterly disastrous two-part television interview with ABC News correspondent Katie Couric. (Given how television footage is reshaped and trimmed in editing, one can only imagine what the omitted footage would have revealed.) So disastrous was it in the immediate reaction of political commentators who were already critical of the candidate's readiness for such high national office—even friendly conservative political commentary was stupefied by what it revealed about the candidate—that it became grist for continuing weekly spoof (frequently using the candidate's own televised responses) on NBC's *Saturday Night Live,* making Tina Fey, playing the governor against Amy Poehler's Couric impersonation, even more of a comic star than before. The McCain-Palin campaign tried using the whole incident to positive Message advantage for Governor Palin to be cast as a beyond-the-Beltway "victim" of the press, who were, of course, presented as biased against non-cosmopolitanites such as composed her most enthusiastic base, for whom she was chosen by McCain in the first place. (Moreover, all of this occurred as a plotline of the Palin family saga unfolded like a televangelical soap opera about rural "trailer trash.") But the snicker-worthy damage had already been done for everyone, except for a certain adoring sector of supporters for whom knowledge of how government works and related factual matters are irrelevant to candidacy or are, in fact, Message-negatives since they connote "insiderhood," a "buy-in" attitude to the justifiable institutionality of government.

The political press corps generally understands how the contributory partials of Message are designed, developed, and fine-tuned by politicians' staffs. (In fact, many political staff members, such as President Obama's David Axelrod, earlier worked as political journalists. In the aftermath of campaigns and administrations, large numbers of such staff members sideline as commentators and analysts of political spin, with a definite whiff of partisan deconstruction of others' Messages.) Much of the very stuff of political reporting requires correspondents to operate essentially as trade professionals of the world of political institutionality, making informed and strategic decisions about precisely what is reportable and what is not, even though the spirit of the celebrity-crazy, soap-opera personalism of our media-saturated times pressures them to traffic in gossip. After-the-fact confessional memoirs by White House correspondents of earlier eras claim that of course the press corps knew about FDR's dalliances with Mrs. Lucy Rutherford (who was with him in Warm Springs, Georgia, when he died) or JFK's quickies with any woman within reach. "You know, the sexist times, the sacred privacy of even a president, the irrelevance to governing, blah blah blah," they have claimed. One can be certain that also in the know was J. Edgar Hoover, who survived for decades as director of the FBI by apparently having dossiers on virtually everyone in Washington (as well as "leftists" and troublemakers like Rev. Martin Luther King Jr.). But media times have indeed changed, and even the tiniest misdemeanor indictment for a senatorial solicitation to homosexual activity in a Minneapolis airport men's room is now racing around all the media markets before the guy's plane lands in Idaho, for goodness' sake!

The point is that as Message dominates politics in the American public media sphere, as celebrity, soap opera, and developing a cult of biography loom ever more centrally in campaigns and visible government, the traditional wall disappears between the politician's "two bodies," on one side a public figure available for reportage, on the other side an individual with rights to privacy of opinion, offstage talk, and solidarity-zone behavior. In the contemporary world of political marketing of Message, this is both an advantage and a real risk, where the unscripted and personal—in the sense of so-called reality TV—can be both mobilized as the political and exposed for its most calculated phoniness. (Who can forget the claptrap about a recent governor of Illinois whose campaign consultants euthanized the small, furry family dog and substituted a golden retriever so that "candid" portraits of the family would have a more normative-looking dog for the Message of vanilla blandness that anchored the campaign after a larger-than-life predecessor in that office? For pictorial aspects of Message, this was approached just like staging a piece of real estate one has put on the market, rendering it one's faux home. [A Springfield reporter must have asked, "Hey, what happened to your dog?"]) The media types with access to both of these realms have thus been relied upon by political figures to respect the etiquette of the times in revealing or concealing erstwhile "private" matters. As president, Harry Truman used to play poker with his press cronies at the Shoreham Hotel on Connecticut Avenue once a week; can one imagine what matters of state might have been casually broached in well-oiled conversation, as well as complaints about the in-laws and the quality of the bourbon? How such information made its way into report and commentary of the times—"a highly placed source noted . . ."; "rumors abound that . . ."; "speaking off the record, a White House official said . . ."—was left to the trusted discretion of such media figures as had privileged access. Even today we pay attention to the verbal formulations and other textual features used by political reporters and analysts—and especially to the punch lines of political cartoons—to keep track of how those who are closest to the Message signal that what they have discovered lies behind both its positive and negative aspects while still responsibly maintaining authorial distance from out-and-out spilling the beans.

The political press thus must play its role in a mutually negotiated institutional form—"politics as usual," let's call it—though the nature of the complex of relationships of media is an ever-shifting one with no fewer than three distinct other players. First, the media corps must secure and maintain relationships with individuals in government, in political campaigns, and in similar places that generate reportables and analyzables. Such friendly sources will, sometimes for their own organization-internal reasons (such as personal advancement, an ideological agenda, etc.) pass along scoop-worthy information, generally not for attribution or quotation, but useful nonetheless as an indicator of the investigative prowess of the media player. Second, the media corps generally participate in news gathering and analysis as employees of or on contract to large media firms at either the "wholesale"—AP, Reuters—or "retail"—*ABC News, Washington Post*—levels. Their positions within such firms depend in no small measure on their access to the personnel of sites that generate newsworthy developments that can be folded appropriately into a wider editorial vision that is congenial to the media brand's overall communicative strategy within highly competitive and tiered media markets. The counterbalanced freelancers flourishing in the blogosphere notwithstanding—a bit like small businesspersons running one- or two-person shops with the same financing (advertisements) as the biggies—most of the media are still very much corporate employees as well as media celebrities, or at least people with recurrent bylines. The third relationship media people have is indeed with the readership/listenership/viewership of the proffered circulating media products, news stories, essays of analysis and opinion, and so on that are increasingly encountered in multiple modes of transmission of text, graphics, clips, interactive features, and so forth.

Consistent with the evolving aesthetic of Message we noted above, there has been an evolution from sober and narrowly wrought verbal news reportage as the reliable platform of coverage of the ultimately dull world of government in the mass media. Congenial to Message, coverage has tended in the direction of "infotainment" across all media types.

Thus, to a certain extent the very personnel of the media corps have been gradually refashioned into personae with their own aura of media celebrity: celebrity among the media corps who are seen/heard/read about in proximity to the aspired-for celebrity of political figures whom they cover, interview, comment on, and analyze. In the grand old days, the *New York Times* would send its "secretary of state," James B. "Scotty" Reston, its most distinguished and respected political columnist, to the Oval Office to interview a sitting president (a relationship so comfortable that many a not-for-attribution revelation from on high would materialize as well in Mr. Reston's opinion columns, by the way). Now we have political candidates for president making the necessary celebrity rounds to NBC star talk-show host Jay Leno's celebrity sofa, to CBS's David Letterman's, and perhaps even to the stage of *Saturday Night Live* (as well as, of course, Comedy Central's *Daily Show* with Jon Stewart!).

Indeed, it is celebrity meeting celebrity, an entertaining spectacle indeed. Each comes to the encounter with his or her own massive media presence not only as a live player but also as a character of great interest to the public in the respective narrated and analyzed world in which they themselves are coverage-worthy—and worthy of attention. (And, recalling here the encounter between Governor Palin and Katie Couric, note how the obvious Message-relevant intent of the McCain presidential campaign was to give the vice presidential candidate some gravitas by sitting down in front of the camera with a reasonably, but not frighteningly, serious correspondent rather than a jokester. What a colossal blunder, although this interview for the history books did come back the second time on *SNL* as farce, to be sure!)

But if the political media must pay careful attention to the gal or guy at the apical top and center of a governmental unit or political campaign, they must be ever more attentive to the complex network of players that develops around the latter, much as lobbyists and similarly determined—and flush!—interested parties spring up like mushrooms after the storm around political figures of government units in power. (Well, it's all "speech," isn't it?—as the U.S. Supreme Court has now ruled in the *Citizens United* case that licenses corporations and the like to "speak" politically through unlimited financing of political expression.) Thus, in respect of getting out a candidate's and a campaign's positive Message, but especially useful in fostering a negative Message among the public for one's opponents, both personal and organizational political surrogates have proved to be essential. These are individuals and organizations beyond the official or traceable chart of personnel and units within the campaign itself, yet who seem to speak and act on cue with a certain partisan authoritativeness. The Republican primaries of 2011–2012 have been an extraordinary demonstration of this system in operation. Beyond the bounds of transparent or traceable seemliness, in which many candidates and their campaign organizations still seem to operate, surrogates are recruited to sling negative Message material in the direction of the other campaign(s).

A particularly florid instance in 2008 was the outburst of the late former House representative and 1984 Democratic vice presidential candidate Geraldine Ferraro, affiliated as an "adviser" to then Senator Clinton's primary campaign. In the early months of 2008, Ferraro asserted several times, apparently to any press people who would listen, that then Senator Obama would not have gotten where he is other than because he is a black man, a remark that was widely disseminated across many media. Senator Obama and his campaign had seized on the positive reaction to his stance of post-racialism in his stunning 2004 convention keynote address to make this a central part of his 2008 election-cycle Message. But here was a respectable senior voice of the Democratic Party literally contradicting the very premise of the Message, which was, in effect, that there were dreams from *both* his Kenyan father *and* his white, Kansas-born mother that, fused, made his biography a microcosm and allegory of America (this despite the happy circumstance of his having married into a genuinely African American family of Chicago's South Side, which would give him political chops in that powerful voting bloc). This was just one of a long series of Clinton campaign surrogacy attempts to indelibly racialize the Obama Message to the advantage of the Clintonistas—one must include here the former president Bill Clinton as well, right after the South Carolina primary. Called out for the never-acceptable voicing of racial sour grapes by a (here, supposedly liberal) white ethnic, seeming to belittle Senator Obama as an unfairly if affirmatively advantaged player,

Ms. Ferraro was called upon to resign from the campaign as an "adviser" aka mouthpiece. (Even Bill Clinton was withdrawn from solo appearances on behalf of his candidate wife for a couple of weeks.)

In the instance, this negative Message surrogacy on the Democratic side of the 2008 primary cycle dovetailed with similar slings coming from the Republican side, already sensing, perhaps, who would be Senator McCain's opponent. For example, at a McCain rally moderated at about this time by Cincinnati radio talk-show host Bill Cunningham, Senator Obama's middle name, Hussein, became a broadcast fetish object for incessant repetition, thus suggestively associating the senator with Islam, particularly with Saddam Hussein, an enemy alien who drove the Bushes and their administrations nuts (and who happened to be the excuse for the American invasion of Iraq in 2003). Following the standard operating procedure, Senator McCain said in a news conference after the event, "I absolutely repudiate such comments. It will never happen again." Exit Mr. Cunningham from proximity to the campaign.

We might compare the use of such surrogates for negative and indeed scurrilous Message attacks to how a chess player must sacrifice many pieces of lesser power and value so that ultimately the king survives to the end of the match. But in the instance of political campaigning, new surrogates seem to spring up at every turn to replace those already expended. The Message-worthiness of getting people to think of Senator Obama as both black and Muslim seems to have persisted well into his presidency, creating a disruptive sideshow that was at times quite frenzied in the classic paranoid style among so-called birthers, who see, retrospectively, a perfect conspiracy concocted by sinister, Al Qaeda–like Muslim forces apparently during the pregnancy of his mother, Dr. Dunham. All during the main presidential campaign, the senator gingerly kept a vast amount of social distance between himself and his geographically mighty close neighbor-in-the-'hood, that paragon of Black Muslim assertiveness, Rev. Louis Farrakhan (whose home is a couple blocks away from the president's in leafy, upscale Kenwood). Yet the two descriptors, invoked time and again for negative Message-ing purposes, took on a media life of their own. This was not helped, either, by the campaign crisis that took shape when recorded sermons by Rev. Jeremiah Wright, the Obama family pastor, came to light in the media. Here was a religious figure whose brand of fire-and-brimstone preaching sounded anti-American—or at least anti-white-bread-American—and an awful lot like what the Reverend Farrakhan had been saying for the longest time.

Such negative surrogacy by freelance celebrities continues because the professionals who run campaigns believe negative Message-ing about the competition is the most effective tactic in benefiting one's own standing with the public. It has the immediacy of creating a distracting flapdoodle that demands resources—time, money, attention—be diverted from the positive Message the other candidate's campaign has been getting out into the public. It attempts to spread sufficient doubt or hesitation with a cloud of what the gossip columnist Walter Winchell termed "insinu-endo." Whole organizations, funded with all the subterfuge of offshore shell corporations, are now plentiful in the "527(c)" advocacy-but-not-endorsement neverland. Who can forget the very prototype, "Swift Boat Veterans for Truth," that was mobilized on behalf of the George W. Bush reelection effort against the increasingly hapless 2004 presidential cam-paign of Democratic challenger John Kerry? (Recall that in clinching his party's nomination, Senator Kerry presented himself as a seasoned war hero of the Vietnam conflict who was ready once more for service—both literally and figuratively—in the so-called War on Terror that the Bush administration declared in the aftermath of the horrific events of 9/11. Kerry's Democratic supporters in the primaries had thought that remind-ing voters of his military service was his strongest shot at a positive, Message-worthy attribute, especially given the persistent negatives about President Bush's evasive—some even claimed AWOL—Vietnam-era mil-itary record. This was a great miscalculation, however, given such archival news footage as the then young Lieutenant Kerry, returned from combat, testifying before Congress *against* the Vietnam War.) Even when they are above-board and transparent in their funding, such as MoveOn.org on the political left, such organizations, which are technically independent of particular candidacies in legal status, serve as particularly valuable ad-junct corporate surrogates usually specializing in negative Messages. (Bil-lionaire Koch brothers–funded organizations have been incredibly busy in the 2012 Republican primaries—for example, smearing contenders with blanket television campaigns in state after state.) Privately delighted but publicly helpless campaign spokespersons, when pressed about such tactics, always note that the campaign just cannot (wink, wink) control them and rein in their zealous negative Message-ing.

Unlike surrogates and endorsers, who presumably are cognizant of what they do, there are many presumably unwitting couriers of Message whom politicians' organizations strategically manage to recruit from within the ranks of professional journalists. As detailed in *Game Change* (Heilemann and Halperin 2010), during the Democratic primary process for the 2008 elections, the Obama presidential campaign decided—as if spoiling for a fight—to telegraph its first punch right before the debate that took place in Philadelphia in fall 2007. Senator Obama sat for an interview with the *New York Times,* and the press dutifully relayed the candidate's threat: "Obama Promises a Forceful Stand against Clinton," read the newspaper's front-page headline. Obama "says he will start confronting Senator Hillary Rodham Clinton more forcefully, declaring that she had not been candid in describing her views on critical issues." The article included a direct quote to this effect from Senator Obama's interview, repeated on the front page: "I don't think people know what her agenda exactly is." The innuendo about a lack of candor or transparency on "critical issues" suggested, of course, a negative Message that the opponent—a prominent incumbent senator already in her second term—was deep in the middle of many entanglements, a "Washington insider," as is commonly said in denunciatory terms, doing—gasp!— politics as usual. Sure enough, debate co-moderator Brian Williams took the bait. He cited the story and even quoted Senator Obama's remark, offering him the opening turn to expand upon and develop it, just as the Obama campaign had hoped.

The space-time of things-that-just-happen-to-happen in determinate spatial or temporal relation one to another, even in spatiotemporal proximity is, of course, made up of people—even politically engaged people—constantly doing and saying things. There is an uncertain and uncontrolled randomness in all this, a backdrop of great and crisscrossing complexity—sometimes seeming like the states of randomness and even entropy of the physicists—against which the emergence of an organized, counter-entropic trend, even groundswell, as they say, of political coherence and direction becomes a discernible wonder. Outcomes look, at least in retrospect, inevitable.

Via the medium of media, political organizations work to compose and orchestrate Message, even if they are really improvising and changing as they go along. Their goal is that at some point a majority sense or intuition—call it "public opinion"—will gel about the "inevitable" positive outcome for their apical public political figure. (Note how during the early 2012 phases of the Republican Party primaries, the Mitt Romney campaign was repeatedly frustrated in its attempts to assert such inevitability for his nomination all the way to Super Tuesday.) The task is to sustain this intuitive feeling until, say, the ballots are counted. Continuous polling of public opinion at every relevant level of the polity is one lens through which all this is revealed to the professionals in political campaigns, which increasingly commission two kinds of polls, both the "public"—for strategically revelatory publication—and the "private"—for strategic decision making (there's strategic art in the first and real social science in the second). And, to believe retrospective accounts of campaign insiders, when then future electoral losers (much more even than electoral winners) get a sense of that inevitability, the wind goes out of them in a kind of terminal deflation that is difficult or impossible to reverse. But until such time as clarity of plot sets in, every element of Message at every moment works to spread a (hoped-for) sense of the inevitable in one or another corner of the political market. Media, then, of which the gatekeepers are the media corps, constitute in this the central stage on which Message unfolds in the reports on and analyses of the doings and sayings of the various players, both the authorized or official and the unauthorized and expendable.

Message as Brand in Late Democracy

The best analogy for Message today may be "brand." No surprise there; campaign dynamics are frequently talked about in terms of the trope of brand within political marketing. It is an analogy that professional Message strategists, increasingly drawn from the fields of advertising and public relations, have taken very seriously for a long time, though with increased intensity since the mid-1990s (see Sanders 2009). Brand generates a sense of trust and reliability among its market share of consumers. An abstract, or conceptual entity, one that cannot itself be touched or kicked in the physical world, brand exists in a differential field of potential economic value of products and services, ever changing as the field of alternatives changes, and hence needing constant rejuvenation through brand-centered (re)design, product-line expansion, and, of course, advertising or marketing. Message, too, in its differential political field has precisely this kind of dynamic and abstract quality, expressed more in the moral and biographical terms of projectable character that its consumers, the electorate and wider public, can identify, so as to identify with, in a political figure.

It may be no coincidence that the notion of Message itself and the expressions "on-message" and "off-message" made their earliest widespread appearance in print journalism in 1992, at the dawn of the Bill Clinton campaign and administration. (Notice how our epigraph, from 1992, encloses the term "off-message" in scare quotes, suggesting its freshness as a coinage to be used in public.) During the Clinton years of presidential politics a dramatic increase began in the political consulting industry, and the second Clinton administration in particular (1997–2001) was renowned for its unprecedented use of strategic polling and psychologistic brand-development techniques, not just for its reelection campaign but also for its guidance in the policies and decisions of governance itself. Much has been made of the importance of professional consultancy, polling, and marketing firms in today's electoral politics, but it is important to recognize how rapidly the expert organizational infrastructures of Message have been changing even since the early 1990s. Though polling, for instance, can be traced to the early nineteenth century in the U.S. context, its regular use for governing is only a few decades old.

Political consultancy underwent professionalization in the late 1960s in the United States (as signaled, for instance, by the founding of a professional group, the American Association of Political Consultants [AAPC; Dulio 2004]), but only in recent decades—again, especially since the 1990s—has its sociocultural visibility spiked among the public. A spate of books by thoughtful, if worried, political commentators in the media and in academia condemn its purportedly corrosive effects on baseline Madisonian republican but democratically electoral governance. Films like 1993's *The War Room* (a documentary of Bill Clinton's 1992 presidential campaign) and the 1997 Dustin Hoffman–Robert DeNiro film *Wag the Dog* depict not only political but also strategic military campaigns as captives of the Message strategies fashioned by consultants to political figures. Memoirs abound of former campaign strategists turned pundits, and the emergence of "celebrity consultants" (Johnson 2007), such as the George W. Bush candidacy's and presidency's Karl Rove or the later Clinton presidency's Richard Morris, has turned some of them into the characters of gossip columns and paparazzi sightings, with their own Message, as it were—in the happiest instance becoming a Message-relevant asset to the boss. And well-known, frequently eponymous consulting firms have become increasingly viewed as assets for campaign fund-raising—a bit like letting people know who is your celebrity interior decorator or couturier—particularly as a way to reassure donors to one's cause that they are investing in the very best shot at one's election and incumbency, and perhaps an ambassadorship for their trouble. Such is the visible value of one's political consulting firm, or firms, that press conferences now trumpet the arrival of a major consultant, and departures rarely escape media attention.

Equally striking has been the application of brand marketing principles and techniques to political campaigns. Though this can be dated to quite earlier in the twentieth century, and especially to the mid-1950s in the United States, brand marketing enjoyed only a rather fitful history until the late 1960s. In recent decades it has come to include branding methods and theories, including "micro-targeting" of specific potential constituencies that has drawn on lifestyle marketing research methods and projective ego-psychological theories of brand personality, thus displacing an earlier concern with straightforwardly demographic variables like sex, age, class, and so forth. Who can forget frightened suburban "soccer moms" or "rednecks with Confederate flags on their pick-up truck" or "limousine liberals"? (Penn and Zalesne 2007; Kavanagh 1995). All of this has often been collectively dubbed "political marketing" (Needham 2006;

Newman and Sheth 1985; Newman 1994; Kavanagh 1995; Mauser 1983),
as we noted above. Brand-focused ideas inform the way professionals
model electoral politics and, more broadly, consultants' arguably "neo-
liberal" sense that voters in the polity's electorate are to be understood
to be consumers exercising their choice from among a set of candidate
alternatives. ("We know you have a choice of candidates, so thank you
for flying with us today, and we look forward to seeing you on another of
our political flights real soon!")

Message is not only being shaped as brand, but, for at least some in
political life, Message *is* brand. Former governor Sarah Palin, for example,
who spent many months in a state of almost presidential candidacy before
declaring that she wouldn't run, and her daughter Bristol, are both celebrities many times over, most recently for cable-network television appearances (the governor's reality show, *Alaska,* on TLC Discovery Channel,
Bristol's *Dancing with the Stars* appearances on ABC). As we write this, the
U.S. Patent and Trademark Office is processing both a 5 November 2010
application for trademark protection of "Sarah Palin®" and a 15 September
2010 application for "Bristol Palin®." The governor's self-branding application claims it is to protect her pecuniary interest in services rendered
providing "information about political elections," "providing a website
featuring information about political issues," and "educational and entertainment services . . . providing motivational speaking services in the
field of politics, culture, business and values." Given the pre-*Dancing* context of the soap-operatic unwed motherhood in which Bristol Palin first
came to prominence during the 2008 election, it is almost breathtaking
to think that her application is meant to protect her pecuniary interest in
"educational and entertainment services, namely, providing motivational
speaking services in the field of life choices." Choose a life? Get a life!
The frank merger here of Message and trademarkable brand is almost too
perfect an innovation for our times.

Critical, then, to candidate branding is mediatization, which has often
been taken to denote the process whereby societal and especially political
institutions become increasingly shaped by and subject to—"mediated
by"—the mass media of print, broadcast, web, and so on.[3] To be sure,
electoral politics involving the electorate and wider public is not the sum

total of institutional politics, as we noted earlier, but it is the most colorful and culturally salient image of the legitimately political in the United
States. If electoral politics has become dependent entirely upon mediatization and, with this development, on the affectively laden vagaries of
brand-like Message, then where, many Enlightenment intellectuals wonder, is there still room for Madisonian rationality and Issue focus? (When
T-Paw dropped out of the race for the presidency after a disappointing
showing in the Republican Party's Ames straw poll in August 2011, he
said he felt he had a strong, "rational" platform but thought "the audience, so to speak, was looking for something different," to which Comedy
Central's Stephen Colbert retorted, in exasperation: "*Yes,* they were not
looking for *rational.* Rationality is the third rail of American politics!"
Many—shall we call them?—Madisonians were reassured by the election
of Barack Obama as president in 2008, since a central part of his Message
seemed to be lawyerly rationality, if overlain by a certain cool blackness.)
With this sense of contemporary politics come now familiar and recurrent anxieties—imagine a kind of visceral "Tea Party" exuberance of 2010
recurring in 2012 and beyond—about the fate of liberal-democratic ideals
and institutions, anxieties inherited largely from the Frankfurt School's
critical social-scientific suspicion of the mass media's power in both re-
producing and ultimately superseding the legitimate hegemony of the
post-Enlightenment state.

One of the most influential stories of mediatization's ill effects on
democratic politics is Jürgen Habermas's account of the rise and fall of
the bourgeois public sphere as the popular font of legitimate mass democratic politics. As Habermas (1989) modeled it, what he termed, in the
Enlightenment tradition, the "bourgeois public sphere" emerged in the
late seventeenth and early eighteenth centuries as a non-exclusionary
space for the formation of the will of the people outside the corridors
of a noble's court or of Parliament. In his ideal-type model it is a space
for rational-critical argument about political matters—issues, policies,
decisions taken and to be taken—that was insulated from both state
control and private pecuniary interest. It is a space for wrangling in as
disinterested a manner as one can about matters of public concern—a
people's parliament, as it were. In keeping with this notion of individual

disinterest as a component of the rhetorical ideals of the eighteenth-century American public sphere, Warner (1990, 1993) has described a "principle of [demographic] negativity," where the "validity of what you say in public bears a negative relation to your person" (1993, 239)—that is, its weight in public discussion is inverse to the marks it bears of one's actual biography as a socially locatable identity with presumptive biases, interests, and so forth. Anonymity, "impersonal reference," and similar rhetorical strategies were designed to neutralize a public speaker's (or writer's) distinctiveness (even if this "impersonalization" through rhetorical strategies of de-personalization ironically served as a badge of distinction [Bourdieu 1984)] to the extent that these practices excluded and minoritized provincial voices [Warner 1993; Fraser 1993; cf. Bauman and Briggs 2003]). Who was that "Publius" who signed all of the contributions to *The Federalist* in 1788? (We now know by statistical study of textual characteristics that it was a triumvirate of Alexander Hamilton, James Madison, and John Jay.) By withholding identity markers in public deliberation, one aspired to address an abstract public and help it to arrive at a disinterested consensus, the latter being the telos of rational-critical dialogue in this liberal-democratic vision (see Habermas 1984).

As Habermas (1989) narrates it, however, this public sphere, this space of rational-critical deliberation where public opinion could be formed as a potential force in the politics of the state, collapsed soon after it arose and later devolved through the corrupting force of the mass media—wide circulators of interesting, perhaps even sensational, communications on a model of market consumption for "interested" corporate profit (see Agha 2011)—into a purely representative public sphere. It was representative as opposed to participatory because publicness became something to be displayed to the many by the capitalized few, in a way, Habermas notes, that was not dissimilar to that of long ago, when the power of apical incumbency in a polity was incarnated, quite literally, in the very person of the monarch or feudal lord regularly, even spectacularly, displayed before the masses as their sovereign incarnate. Habermas (also Lefort and Thompson 1986) called this analogue in the age of mass media a kind of "refeudalization" of the public sphere, where, writes Warner, "public body images are everywhere on display," where "visual media—including print—now display bodies, that is, people identifiable as to biographical characteristics, for a range of purposes: admiration, identification, appropriation, scandal" (1993, 242)—in short, the celebrity sovereign and sovereign wannabe. We seem to have come full circle to the mediatization of the political figure's Message as a circulating abstraction of the "refeudalized" public sphere.

Habermas's narrative of decline is one of many bemoaning the mediatization of politics in the United States and beyond. In communication studies, for instance, there is Tulis's (1987) notion of the "rhetorical presidency," a shift in communicative relations of the office to the public sphere that he traced to the twentieth century, when presidents began to make appeals directly to the people rather than strictly to Congress and others in the government. Besides his campaign methods, which featured all sorts of now standard but then questionable promotional tactics, from songs to badges to the holding of rallies, even Andrew Jackson's heavy use of popular speeches while in office was often fiercely criticized at the time, because it was felt to be an inappropriate expansion of presidential power that risked becoming demagoguery. Evidence of this shift toward a rhetorical presidency can also be seen in transformations like that of the State of the Union event, as we noted above, which evolved from a written report and plan directed at Congress to an oratorical performance designed to persuade, delivered by the president directly to the people via broadcast media over the heads, as it were, of Congress. This new loquaciousness, analysts see, legitimated a president's popular appeals launched into the public sphere so as to bypass the interbranch deliberation chartered by the Constitution. Needless to say, it has been greatly facilitated in the twentieth and twenty-first centuries by the evolving infrastructure of mass mediatization, which increasingly gives such rhetoric the possibility of wide simultaneous reach. For Tulis this poses a challenge to democratic—certainly, to representative republican—governance and has even led to a "decay of political discourse" itself (1987, 178).

We might consider here as well Lim's (2008) pessimistic account of the "anti-intellectual presidency," which also involves shifts in mediatized political rhetoric. Focusing on the history of professional speechwriting in the United States, Lim faults changes that began during the Nixon administration when policy advisers were sequestered from speechwriters. Nixon created the Writing and Research Department, the White House's first formal speechwriting office. Speechwriters used to be "substantive issue men" who had "little patience for matters of style" (81), but the institutionalization of a divide between speechwriters and policy wonks created, or at least reinforced, a sharp division between substance and style. "Indeed," claims Lim, "the division of labor between policymakers and wordsmiths has only exacerbated the differences between the two and made wordsmiths even more furious champions of [mere] style" (88)—that is, of the verbal design elements of Message. To be sure, it was the Nixon presidential campaign of 1968 that first called the public's attention to the "selling"—that is, Message-driven political marketing—of the candidate. These marketing techniques mobilized a new, highly professionalized level of collaborative concern for all the specifics that go into the projective work of each and every appearance of the candidate, of each and every verbal communication. But President Nixon himself worked very hard to project an image of almost stodgy, if calm and lawyerly, seriousness and intellectuality, not its opposite, to which, apparently, the electorate responded as over against the raucous circuses of mayhem that surrounded his hapless, if earnest, Democratic opponents in both 1968 and 1972.

Rather than trying to evaluate these claims of decline and fall as historical arguments, however, we simply wish to call attention to the very "presentist" nostalgias that inform each as it locates a historical locus of change from the mythic era of pre-Message Madisonianism. Thus, whatever else these historical perspectives mean as genealogical explanations for perceived changes in the American presidency's relationship to its publics, they are also interventions in the here and now, critiques of the currently observable state of our mediatized union. In this they seem to echo less aureate "media" critiques—finding a blameworthy messenger for Message—circulating outside the academy, which show up in such mediatized venues as Bill O'Reilly's "No Spin Zone" and, of course, in the various parodies of mainstream political journalism, from *The Colbert Report* and Jon Stewart's *Daily Show* to "Weekend Update" and other skits on *Saturday Night Live.*

The relevant point is that this perceived crisis of mediatization—however that crisis may be conceived—is now found *within* the central mediating industry of Message politics itself. Message strategists seem to acknowledge and have even tried to domesticate the crisis. They have tried to transfigure the crisis of mediatization, real or imagined, into the promise of anti-Message Message, anti-brand brand. Which is one way to view the projective figures of the issue "flip-flopper" and the unfettered "maverick." Together these figures seem to thematize ends of a continuum of candidate authenticity. In this respect such political figurations obviously draw on a host of long-standing cultural ideals and beliefs, including those involving gender and class, but they also seem to give plot and character to the crisis of mediatization, transposing this crisis into an almost therapeutic challenge in *characterological terms* that candidates can then act out in order to "break out."

It is in this respect that we can speak of *late democracy* (cf. the Frankfurt School and Frederic Jameson [1991] on "late capitalism"). By this shorthand we caption this condition of heightened reflexive attention among all the participants centered on the problem of mediatization, specifically, the mediatization that constructs the proscenium connecting—and dividing—politicians from their publics. This is mediatization made painfully aware of itself, that now chases its own tail, if only half seriously, and stimulates what has been termed a "hermeneutics of suspicion" by which people in political publics sift everything with a basic disbelief and even diffidence. Whoever else he is, the maverick is the anti-dramaturgical hero who drops artifice and acts with conviction. His alter, the hollow flip-flopper, needs polls and advisers and scripts to act; he is all Message, all brand, all the time. In such grotesque—one is almost tempted to say burlesque, upping the ante from the mere soap-operatic—form, the sheer extravagance ironically ends up calling more attention to the artifice, the obtrusive proscenium, and the troubled relations between the political figures and "us." Rather than try in vain to scramble to some transhistorical high ground from which to describe and theorize communication in American electoral politics, we locate our inquiry from within these very conditions of heightened reflexivity, a reflexivity trained on and troubled by the mediatization of Message. Our intent is not to jeer at the performers and join the chorus that criticizes the electoral campaigns and other moments on which our studies focus—and the media who follow them—for embracing theatrics, personalism, style, and brand, but to detail in this way the life of our political communicators at work and the peculiar conditions under which they now must labor.

Two

GETTING IT "JU . . . ST RIGHT!"

Many people think about the difference between the 2003–2004 presidential campaign and that of 2007–2008 in terms of the centrality of the Internet, the number of voters of various demographic groups who cast ballots on Election Day, and so forth. One of the important comparisons, however, not to be overlooked if one is focused on how Message politics works in America, is what we can term the "Goldilocks Principle of Message-ing." There is a "ju . . . st right!" use of Message, neither too much—especially of the negative kind—nor too little—especially of one's own positive kind, the communicative weakness or absence of which renders one extremely vulnerable to the other candidates' inevitable barrage of the negative.

So, notwithstanding its apparent effectiveness in shaping the results of the election in 2004 (for President George W. Bush was, in fact, reelected), the powerful Republican Message machine ascribed to the genius of Karl Rove seemed, in retrospect, to call the very enterprise of Message-ing into a kind of official disrepute among the media connoisseurs and much of the public—if, paradoxically, it was still clandestinely admired for its decisive success. Hence, one of the important stances in the 2008 election cycle was to seem to be above, beyond, or in some way independent of Message. And interestingly the two figures who would emerge as the respective candidates of the major parties in 2008 very much embraced an "anti-Message" or "post-Message" Message, at least in their parties' primary campaigns and somewhat beyond. As a demonstration of what we might term reversion to the institutional norm, however, we must note that in the final phases of the 2008 campaigns, Message, and in particular negative Message attempting to define the opponent, was once again in full force. Here we compare these two electoral cycles in more detail in respect of telling moments of "too much," "too little," and "ju . . . st right" Message.

From an ideological point of view, to be sure, our own political institutions are centered on our mass electoral process, which hums away in high gear at the presidential level an incredible two years or more before that recurrent endpoint on the first Tuesday of November every four years. Yet electoral politics at the center of mass democracy is not all of politics by any means. In fact, to judge by participation rates, electoral politics may have definitively become a decreasingly central realm of how the totality of politics operates, in this country as elsewhere. (Even lowering the U.S. voting age has not helped in increasing participation, older people voting at greater rates per population than younger ones—perhaps indicating that the "Chicago Way" of counting votes from cemetery addresses is the only reliable way to increase voter participation!)

Those enfranchised in the United States seem, alas, increasingly to recognize—just read the daily "Letters to the Editor" columns or responses to online articles in the major web news outlets such as AOL/ Huffington Post—that other forms of politics may ultimately be more significant overall in the total political process. They point, for example, to the useful rental of legislative branch representation through campaign contributions and other benefits of corporate "political speech" recently legitimized by the *Citizens United* U.S. Supreme Court decision. To many of the disaffected among actually voting humans, then, politics has just become business carried on by other means, to paraphrase Clausewitz (or are we thinking of Calvin Coolidge?). Politics in such a model is just a business some people engage in, tolerated and legitimated by an otherwise decidedly indifferent public, who mind—and who tend to—their *own* business, knowing that there's an official top business in the state and national capitals that works just like theirs but, alas, not necessarily to their advantage.[1] The 2010 insurrections from the Right of the Republican

Party, however ersatz in their being professionally molded into "The Tea Party" (as most analysts note), and those from the Left of the Democratic Party, "Occupy[ing] Wall Street" and other loci of high finance across downtown America in late 2011 and beyond, are ultimately protests welling up out of the sense of being suckered by the purveyors of participatory politics central to recent-vintage Message. It would seem that the contrast between Message in 2004 and that in 2008 was an early indicator that the political professionals were already sensing a change in how Message must work—if it was to work—in political retailing.

Notwithstanding, electoral politics still continues to be the most interesting part of our political process. It is public spectacle in what we call the public sphere, sometimes indeed to distract from the other (real?) business that seems actually to be at hand among those in so-called public service. How does electoral politics seem to work in contemporary times?

On a regular cyclic basis, the voting—and even the non-voting—public in the United States is mass-mobilized to participation in a drawn-out, if abstract, spectator sport as candidates for elected office compete for web exposure, broadcast time, print and mailbox space, and telephone time with which to secure and sustain differential advantage through the public's ultimate aggregate consequential response: the election. In mass democracies, publics are targeted as addressees of a vast and costly multimodal and multichannel communications environment that is at once designed to saturate and focus people's rational or conscious faculties and to appeal to those unconscious mental processes of affective, gut-level associations bespeaking demographically identifiable, positioned "structures of feeling" (Williams 1977, 128–35).

We caption such communication in the dominant, continuing axis of how electoral politics operates in our kind of political system 'Message politics,' and in light of it we glimpse the trajectory of 2004 and then 2008 presidential-cycle political communication. We might point out that when the going gets tough, the self-styled "tough"—those who claim to do without Message—in fact revert to its communicational norms. But this is not cause for blame. Rather, such reversion to processual norm comes from the complexity of the process, how many different groups it brings together, each with its own normative ways of operating, each with its own interests that lie behind the way things are, unconsciously, taken to be the natural way of doing business within the order of Message.

To understand political Message, we must remember that American presidential elections are macro-social, mass-institutional forms. They mobilize vast numbers of people who must come together in precise ways in many different functional roles, not just as candidates and voters, instantiating more and less sharply definable interests in the process and its outcomes. The four-yearly cyclic workings of presidential elections are partly a function of constitutional and other statutory stipulation and partly customary practice (for example, that they culminate in a ballot and a new term of office every four years; that the several states, within limits, set qualifications for voting and manage the actual ballot; that there are what in *The Federalist* Mr. Madison called "factions," or what we term political parties, as legitimate and recognized players, monetary supporters of which, including corporations, have, despite congressional attempts, always bankrolled campaigns for election). As well, elections as complex events or happenings consist of normed social practices that, all the while inevitably changing, in fact have a perduring character over historical periods of several electoral cycles. They are only gradually transformed, in interesting innovations of practice, as recurrences of a social institution we can recognize over generations.

Of interest to us in this respect has been campaign political communication as it has been shaped, for example, by the availability of new communicative technologies (television, as opposed to radio, movie-house newsreel, and print media, by 1952; televised face-to-face debates between major party candidates in 1960 and 1968 and since; the digital electoral public sphere, supplementally important from 2004 but definitively so today). Political communication is also constantly being reshaped by new organized political interests making visible their group-invoking participation—for example, commercial corporate interests, companies or industry associations, as sponsors or animators of political communication (Big Oil, Big Pharma; trial lawyers versus the medical insurance industry and their clients, hospitals, and physicians; Rupert Murdoch; *Saturday Night Live*/NBC; David Letterman/CBS). Or the reshaping may be a function of emergently self-conscious voting blocs coming to self-realization as sectorized addressees (economically aspiring small-town unlicensed plumbers named Joe who are iconically caught in CNN's, and thus our, gaze and worked into Senator McCain's and Governor Palin's zingers thereafter in 2008). And, of course, every electoral cycle includes unique historical circumstances. Think of the precipitous meltdown, in autumn 2008, of what is apparently misnamed as the "investment banking" industry, culminating what had started in 2007–2008 in its mortgage-based derivatives bubble. It was against this backdrop, and in relation to it, that the 2008 cyclic presidential process unfolded or wound its way to conclusion.

Of course it is not just political candidates who become enculturated to Message. The very addressees of their communication—we, the potential electorate in the public sphere—also learn how to listen to and look at political communication, and thus we learn what to hear and see, always over the shoulders of media commentators and other shapers of Message. We have to appreciate, then, how political communication in the multilayered jumble of the mass media is like articulate noise shouted into a chasm, a canyon. If it doesn't just dissipate and disappear, it echoes in particular ways as it is picked up and selectively repeated and interpretatively reshaped by a mediating press and other institutions in the public sphere. Political discourse is interdiscursive, meaning it engages other discourse and images circulating among a public that every once in a while will interrupt its distracted noninterest and will want to come to know *who was that who said (or did) that?*[2]

Navigating oneself or being piloted into a position where a public wants to know, where the public pays culturally framed attention to the sociological "whom" who is doing the talking has a technical term among the professionals, of course. It is called getting "on message." Of course, if one does get "on message," there is also the problem of staying there so long as being on Message is doing wonderful things in opinion polls and at the ballot box or its touch-screen equivalent.

Semiotics and the History of Our Brand of Politics

Message, then, is precisely the kind of social fact that can be studied in the field of *semiotics,* the systematic study of how all phenomena can be understood as signs of and for things in implicit as well as explicit events of communication. For example, with all due allowance for the difference of how one might initially think of political personae and consumer goods and services, we must see that in our own days Message is being professionally shaped as an analogue to brand, however Message may have been shaped in earlier periods of U.S. political history.

Brand, remember, is not a physical, psychophysical (perceptual), or other concrete fact about products circulating as commodities on the franker markets of consumerism. Brand is that abstract yet organized set of meaning-images that implicitly surrounds the product or service because of stimulated associations—perhaps what Raymond Williams might well have been gesturing at with the phrase "structures of feeling." Brand implies potential stories, the most important being how people, as potential and actual consumers, project cultural values onto the commodity so as to organize their relationship of use of that commodity. How does this happen? It happens by shaping and contextualizing the product or service in a complex of signs designed to induce that potential story—eventually automatically—once one sees or thinks of the product or service. Message, just like brand, is dynamic and differential, always changing in relation to its field of competition. Yet at any moment it is a structured fact of associations with a degree of coherence, changing as new construals of the product/candidate reconstruct the product/candidate.

Brand is, as the professionals say, "value added" to the mere physical, psychophysical, and so on "stuff" or "service" that packaging, advertising, and distribution professionals try to shape by all kinds of semiotic design. What color should the product be? What color should the packaging feature or should the background be against which the product is displayed, or on which an image of it is displayed in an advertisement? What typeface should appear on the package? Such matters are endlessly thought about in the way of shaping brand semiotics, even more spectacularly in coordinated branding rollout campaigns and other mass-marketing developments.

In fact, the more one starts thinking about it, the more one realizes that Message early on became the real organizing principle of this kind of electoral politics in which we live.[3] It is not the official political history of this country, the one told to us from the time we first had an elementary school civics class, but the history of political communication that still needs to be understood. Communicative reality has constituted and still constitutes the only real experience of electoral political process anyone has. Our polity, our way of organizing ourselves, and sometimes reorganizing ourselves, into social groups with power over property, money, people, services, beliefs, and so forth, differentially determining people's access to these—all of this emerges from the amazing semiotic power to communicate.

Think of what you may have learned of American political campaigns of 50, 100, 150, even 200 years ago, and of how much is now submerged in retrospective interpretative reconstructions of them—"readings" of them is the fancy PoMo term—as "America" (catch the anthropomorphic projection!) deciding on a certain policy issue, or endorsing a certain moral principle, as a collectivity that has spoken through the medium of electoral politics. Then zoom down to the more microscopic level and discover how truly problematic such interpretations are, how completely a function of ideological blinders one uses when looking backward from afar. When we look closely and comprehensively, we find that politics way back when was a free-for-all of local political clubs that put on drink-lubricated spectacles of one sort or another ("infotainments" of their day?), galvanizing to a side very local socioeconomic identity groups and interest groups to the electoral work at hand: ballot boxes needing to be filled, one way or another, and thus determining the consequences for governing and being governed. Floating among all this activity are emergent political slogans, catchwords, and other poetic extractions from discourse by a candidate and by people who, narrating about a candidate, construe a candidate's persona, making it projectable into the public's sensibilities, perhaps even anxieties.

For example, "Tippecanoe and Tyler, too!" is a memorial or mnemonic from 1840, because the Whigs, the more politically conservative party, had just learned how to use Jacksonian Democratic sloganeering, a watershed of Message politics, to their own candidate's Message advantage in drunken rally after drunken rally. Hence the importance of place, as in Tippecanoe, near present-day Lafayette, Indiana, where United States troops under the Whig candidate defeated some desperate, straggling Native Americans in the push west. It became a part of William Henry Harrison's persona on the political stage as it had been for "Old Hickory," General Jackson, the Democrat whose emblem from battle was a Southern hardwood of defined geographical locality. Recall that in this post–Louisiana Purchase period, Native Americans were about the only anxiety-inducing impediment to Euro-American fulfillment of their "Manifest Destiny" to occupy the continent from Atlantic to (near) the Pacific, the U.S.–Mexican War that settled the matter of the coastline being still a few years away. (It was too bad for the party that Harrison was in such fragile health in actual physical reality; recall, he died within a month of his inauguration in 1841.)

The ways are ever changing in how people have circulated such Message messages both directly and by creating artifacts like handbills, direct-mail letters, or e-mails. We must be sensitive to the particular communicative and inscriptional technologies of the time as we study these matters; they have rhythms of circulation and consumption that interact in interesting ways. What we would call the social sites at which and through which political communication—the real work of electoral politics—takes place are as well ever changing. But the necessity remains to understand the processes that lead a public and an electorate to being able to identify political figures' Messages at the heart of the democratic process in ways that are relevant to that politics. We thus get to see that shifting, historically specific dimensions of identity have been made to count in politicians' coming to visibility and audibility—and survival—in the political process.

This is illustrated by two starkly distinct figures in very different eras of political semiotics of Message: Mr. Lincoln and Mr. Bush the Younger (see Silverstein 2003a). Mr. Lincoln's Message moved over the time of his political career from a folksy civil religion of righteous Constitutionalism come-what-may—recall, he started out as a Whig and only later seized the opportunity to affiliate with the brand-new Republican Party—to a chastened and preacherly faith in the mystical work of the Almighty culminating in that second inaugural, shortly before his death, that so richly channels the Old Testament. (Talk about separation of church and state!) In his own biography of image, Lincoln recapitulated the cultural movement of the mass of frontier and Middle America's evangelical folk-Protestant denominationalists. Mr. Bush's 2000 Message was one of trusted, and trustworthy, businesslike CEO Christian practicality (reformed and recovered after a youth of certainly boozy and perhaps druggy high jinks). It was sorely put to an unexpected test by the terrorist incidents that necessitated his becoming commander in chief—the Message-targeted self-descriptor during the 2003–2004 lead-up to reelection was "a war president"—on a world stage that was more sophisticated and unforgiving in combativeness than anything he likely was led to believe he would have to face when being persuaded to run by the RNC powerful. One almost feels sorry for the guy, whose Message in the second, 2004 round came down to the stand-tall Texas sheriff on the lawless terrain, the only protective force between terrorist chaos (identified as from Eye-Wrack, no less!) and your child's nursery.

In this kind of politics of Message, in short, *biographical illusion* is destiny rather than mere anatomy as the good Dr. Freud suggested. The biographical illusion, a plotline moving the politician as character through situations with respect to a whole cast of others, attracts or avoids Issues as it attracts or repels voters, who can imagine a transaction with the illusion and thus can identify with it, can place it with respect to their own interests in Issues. The chief way we come to know our political figures is through the art of their words and other semiotic material that creates and maintains a biographical world in which they can seem to exist—in which, so seeming, they do exist. Political figures have to emerge on the horizon of a tableau and must continue adding to that tableau in ways that are consistent and coherent, or at least not inconsistent or incoherent.

Change of heart as such on this or that issue—what, since the 2004 presidential race, has become known in negative Message as "flip-flopping"—is not what is at issue here. It is perfectly understandable that people grow and develop, just as do characters in the best Bildungsromane, novels of individual character. (Mr. Lincoln's jaw-dropping transformation in 1863–1865 to the identity of racial liberator is a case in point, fixing him in American memory forever. Closer to our time, who can forget how Mr. Nixon's perceived bold move in traveling to the People's Republic of China was milked for Message-worthiness even as part of his semiotic self-redemption after being forced from office in disgrace? He even presumed upon it as essential to his Message in the Oval Office incident we discuss.) But is the change of heart consistent with the biographical construction of one's Message? Therein lies the difference between trust and distrust.

So whatever may have been the modes of Message-ing in Mr. Lincoln's day, when politicians relied on verbatim quotation in newspaper circulation and then many further echoes in popular phraseology for a certain image-building half-life, in Mr. Bush's day a densely crafted use of multiple media that resonate one with another has become de rigueur.[4] Today, as in contemporary branding, a multimodal or cross-modal strategy is necessary to reinforce all the components of a Message in which the political persona—not necessarily the actual individual politician concerned—is to exist in the communicational interface with the public.

The Message in the Bottle: 2004 Vintage

Message being both positive, meaning what you want for yourself, and negative, meaning how you want to brand your opponent, we should consider the thematic intensity of both kinds that became so visible during that electoral cycle. For example, as Senator Kerry got closer to becoming the Democratic presidential candidate, his quiverful of negative Message-ing arrows about President Bush, personifying his administration, was at the ready. The incumbent is *deceptive* (on WMD ["weapons of mass destruction"] and the terrorist connections of the Iraqi government under Saddam Hussein; on Vietnam War–era military service, the future president's own and that of other wealthy and connected reservists drafted to stateside sinecures "through the back door"; on federal programs tilted fully to the right ideologically but running on fiscal empty). The incumbent is *divisive* (cynically pushing the hardest-right Christian agenda of so-called social issues like piety, prayer, parenthood, and U.S.A. Patriot Acts). The incumbent is *dystopic or dystopia-inducing* (losing industry as well as jobs and "off-shoring" corporate wealth; losing medical care; losing the Clinton-era fiscal surplus; losing our friends in the world; losing ordinary Americans our "middle class" hope). Not quite a presidential Nero fiddling as Rome—or Baghdad or lower Manhattan—burned, but clearly someone either cynically devious or just somewhat out of it. (One can recall all the insider-based rumors that Vice President Cheney and Secretary of Defense Rumsfeld were actually running the executive branch.)

Poor judgment. No judgment. Judgment exercised with disastrous results. Worse, a judgment that has been corrupted by the intersection of self-indulgence and strategically manipulative forces.

In fact, that "little Nero" Message matured and became the negative relational counterpart to Mr. Kerry's own propensity toward "policy-wonk-ishness," as, we might note, the Message phrase was rendered when it was used by opponents during the Clinton-Gore administration. (This means a kind of academically, if not senatorial, deliberative public rhetorical style; very middle-management, not the above-it-all boss of silent, or un-wordy power.) During the electoral campaign, both Senator Kerry and Senator John Edwards (running for vice president) stressed poor judgment on the part of the administration, clouded by a lack of, or active brushing aside of, dispassionate fact in favor of wishful ideology. (And note how, therefore, Mr. Bush visibly tried to demonstrate "command of fact" that he cited and recited in his debate appearances—even if perhaps piped into his ear, as conspiracy theorists surmised, from Mr. Rove on radio frequency—though he really kept losing it in the first of the Bush-Kerry debates, seeming out there in cloud cuckoo land a couple of times.) And anyway, who cares about command of fact anymore?

Therefore, too, Mr. Cheney, summoning the dismissive voice of his privileged incumbent's access, admonished—no, laced into—Mr. Edwards, belittling and demeaning him in their one televised encounter for purportedly incorrect facts brought to bear in the vice presidential confrontation. "I wouldn't even know where to begin!" he said time and again, asking for the audience's, the voter's commiserating empathy with his exasperation at the snotty kid.

Already in the primaries, as we noted in our introductory chapter, Senator Kerry's positive Message, which he and his advisers must have thought an end-run around the "War President," was that his heroism as a gunboat commander on the Mekong River during his service in the Vietnam War would trump the pretensions of Mr. Bush. In spite of already widely disseminated negatives countering the Kerry Message, on 29 July 2004 he chose to appear at the podium of the Democratic Party convention as though volunteering with his local 1960s-era draft board: "I'm John Kerry and I'm reporting for duty!" he began with a military salute. Even this cornball appeal to the VFW crowd did nothing to give him the expected post-convention bounce in the polls. Immediately after Super Tuesday the Karl Rove negative Message machine roared into action, with its characteristic way of turning what the Democratic candidate thought was a sure-fire positive into at best, mushy ambiguity, at worst, a lie. The American public repeatedly saw archival footage of then former Lieutenant Kerry's "antiwar"—actually, end-the-war—testimony to the Senate Foreign Relations Committee on 22 July 1971, as a representative of Vietnam Veterans against the War, with its great but now problematic rhetorical question, "How do you ask a man to be the last man to die for a mistake?" The conservative press, such as *National Review,* saw fit to "commemoratively" reprint the testimony in cold, hard type.[5] The negative Message, of course, was designed to draw parallels between 1971 and 2004: how could this man purporting to be a battlefield hero in Vietnam turn around and call the whole thing "a mistake"? It was a traitorous change of heart, fumed the right-leaning commentariat. Could Lincoln's Gettysburg resolve "that these honored dead shall not have died in vain" not give this would-be commander in chief the military-stiff spine to see the current War on Terror through to the end?

It piled on higher and deeper. From March 2004 on we heard that Mr. Kerry voted early and often *against* some weapons system or other (that the Department of Defense, then under Secretary Dick Cheney, it turns out, did not want, either); that he voted to raise taxes again and again and again. (Were there really, as claimed, 660 distinct tax-hike votes in twenty years? That's 33 per year!) We not only heard that the senator changed his mind on what Mr. Bush considered the centerpiece of his War on Terror, the American (and allied) invasion of Iraq initiated on 20 March 2003, but we also actually heard Mr. Kerry himself say that he had reversed himself on supporting it—when he discovered he had been deceived. *Singsong*: "Flip-flopper! Flip-flopper!" Notice that the suggestion of deviousness on the part of the Bush-Cheney administration in the Kerry anti-Bush Message gets turned back in this form of two barrels directed as anti-Kerry Message. Lieutenant Kerry's 1971 change of heart about staying the course in Vietnam must have been opportunistic in the then changing winds of a political career, and his lack of a definitive and fixed position on support of the military (weapons systems), and support of our now militarily focused foreign policy, were of a piece. Unreliable then; unreliable now. The Kerry campaign attempted to justify all this by talking about the subtle contextual inflections and adjustments that policy constantly needs, but this seemed itself to be opportunistic in the instance—more of the same at a kind of "meta" level.

During summer and early autumn, when earlier negatives were not quite working to give President Bush a definitive lead in exceedingly close polling results, weeks of the campaign were taken up by the attempt to push further into negative Message. If the whole earlier campaign was directed to rendering Senator Kerry unreliably a flip-flopper, the later phases went directly to the truth of the very baseline story of his decorated Vietnam service. Again here, note that the negative Message Democrats had been re-excavating concerned the president's dubious Vietnam-era military service. Indeed, what random archival documents the White House apparatus had not succeeded in burying or otherwise making unavailable seemed to reveal a privileged, well-connected young man who was hardly devoted to performing the little stateside service asked of him in the Air National Guard. But coincidentally, a 527(c) independent organization was registered on 23 April 2004, Swift Boat Veterans for Truth, initially funded by Texas Republican power broker Robert J. Perry (who has played a major financial role in the career of Gov. Rick

FIGURE 2.1. Swift Boat Veterans' negative Message taking its toll on Senator Kerry. Cartoon by Rick McKee, *Augusta [Georgia] Chronicle*; reproduced by permission of the artist, ©2004.

Perry), and later richly funded to the tune of some $20 million by such stalwarts as T. Boone Pickens and Harold Simmons. The sole aim was to discredit all of Senator Kerry's claims to heroism during his military service, for which he had been multiply decorated: a Bronze Star, a Silver Star, and a Purple Heart, no less! The Swift Boat organization relied on a complex network of Republican National Committee and Bush administration connections, some of which are still being unraveled, though of course telephone conversations from outside the boundaries of the government as such can now never be traced, nor can Messages passed viva voce as Rove operatives traveled across the country. But the signature Rove style was unmistakable in ascriptions even then. From a Washington, D.C., press conference arranged at the National Press Club on 4 May to the rollout of television spots starting in contested electoral markets in August, all accompanied by dense and continuing press coverage, the aim was to destroy any credibility Senator Kerry still had as a war hero, substituting in the electorate's vision a lying, cheating opportunist as the man now asking for their votes.

FIGURE 2.2. Senator Kerry unable to articulate consistent positions on issues and thus sustaining the negative Message of "flip-flop." Cartoon by Dana Summers, *Orlando [Florida] Sentinel*; reproduced by permission of the artist and Tribune Media Serivces, ©2004.

In combination with the earlier campaign portraying him as a strategic "flip-flopper," the tactic worked: the repeated refrain of quoted voters, of commentators, and others about Mr. Kerry was "I don't know what he stands for." People wanted to see and hear his Message—that is, one articulated not in complex sentences of argumentative prose about findings and issues and programs in shifting contexts of decision making, but in the poetry of ad copy bespeaking identity. What is interesting to note, especially in connection with the Swift Boat caper, is that the various "newspapers of record" (as we term them for their gravitas) and other investigative sources did keep up a continuous exposé on the tissue of connections that kept leading right back toward the suspected orchestrators of this "spontaneous" anti-Kerry Message campaign. Since it was technically extra-governmental, and slickly well done at that, there was no Woodward-and-Bernstein team whipping up indignation beyond already-tuned-in Democrats. Somehow the Kerry campaign could never overcome the one-two negative punch.

By contrast, the positive White House Message about Mr. Bush in 2004 was a mélange of images that superimposed 11 September 2001 and Iraq. Osama = Saddam[a] in the Message equation, for the two had long since blended together in the White House's Message machine. Here was the looming bogeyman from whom Messrs. Bush and Cheney were portrayed to be protecting us, notwithstanding the economy, as earlier the World Trade Center in Manhattan took a hit in late 2003—the first of many from which, even in 2012, we have not yet really recovered. The campaign played itself out on these terms: who will "win" the so-called War on Terror by unbendingly staying the course (not—nah-nah-nah-boo-boo!—"flip-flopping")?

Curiously, on so-called domestic issues, both economic and social, the Republican campaign was just a recycling of all the Message slogans of the 2000 campaign, since, in a sense, the appeal for four more years was to finish that very agenda. And, importantly, the central *agōn* revolved around the protagonists' heroism, leadership, and reliability against the backdrop of global threats. We heard yet again about "the soft bigotry of low expectations" as also about deregulation promising "the ownership society." Once more President Bush could denounce "activist [Massachusetts] judges" and use the phrase "Massachusetts liberal," referencing at once Ted Kennedy and Michael Dukakis along with Senator Kerry, as well as gay marriage and related social "values" issues in and of the Bay State. (Though the case was ill timed for the 2004 cycle, what could be more deliciously ironic in 2012-cycle retrospect than the fact that it was then Republican governor Mitt Romney who, obeying the Massachusetts Supreme Court's 18 November 2003 *Goodridge* decision, ordered town clerks across the state to begin issuing marriage licenses to same-sex couples on 17 May 2004?) All this, of course, was taken up as aspects of "compassionate conservatism" once more, without apology and with a more pointed target in the state's junior senator. No matter how Mr. Kerry emphasized domestic policy and tried drawing Mr. Bush into a contest over it, it never became relational

Message material on Kerry's terms, since the president's people declined to engage it as such.

It seems that what is most telling in showing that we are dealing not with issues as such but with Messages that selectively draw certain issues to them is the more rapid-fire way in which this overall theme of commander-in-chief toughness was played in the final weeks of the 2004 electoral cycle—that is, how it resonated as personal virtue in relation to any issue in the vague conceptual region of Iraq/War on Terror. Recall that in early October 2004, Mr. Kerry used the word sensitive, as in "sensitive *to* [something or other]"—in other words, adjusted or calibrated to it—consistent at least in his attempt at a Message of intelligent, context-sensitive decision making. (The context was that the role of the United States should be "sensitive to" world opinion, to national interests of other states, to the United Nations, and so on.) As a linguistic form, of course, "sensitive [to]" with this meaning is synonymous with another, principally characterological term—one, alas, that is perfect for negative Message-ing. Sensitive applied to a person summons up everything from quiche-eating liberals to "girlie men" (to break into Schwarzeneggerish for a moment), and that is precisely how the White House played the term back as a negative Message operator.

To some in the United States, but especially to those abroad, the Bush-Cheney policies bespoke a United States—and, of course, its emblematic head of state—that behaved like the bully on the playground, not frankly-my-dear-giving-a-damn masculine in that *Gone with the Wind* way (who can forget the president's gloss on swagger? "In Texas we call it walkin'"!). Being "sensitive," the negative Message-ing wanted to suggest, comes out of the femiNazi (Rush Limbaugh) era of the Coalition of the Emasculated, of course.

It was, alas, the same with "[meet the] global test": shifted from a modifier for the *rhetoric* that justifies and rationalizes actions like wars—which ought to be transparently and plausibly truthful, according to Mr. Kerry's somewhat complex sentence structure in one of his debate appearances on national television. It was shifted to seeming to have modified the action of war itself and, hence, to negate the very possibility for unilateral decisiveness of a commander in chief. Heck, was not the very "Bush

FIGURE 2.3. The two Message-worthy senses of "sensitivity" in the
War on Terror. Cartoon by Scott Santis, *Birmingham [Alabama]*
News; reproduced by permission of the artist, ©2004.

Doctrine" a justification for such unilateral—and preemptive—decisiveness of the president as commander in chief? (As you know, in the current
era the constitutional stipulation that Congress "declare" war in explicit
primary performative formality has long since been forgotten. That bunch
have settled for resolutions "authorizing the use of force to 'defend' us"
and then have wrung their collective hands when things have imploded.)

So what "global test?" You mean a president, in Mr. Kerry's view, has to
pass a "global test" of consensus in order to act strategically? Aren't you
man enough to act to defend your wife and young'uns yourself? People
heard echoes of Governor Dukakis's unfortunate Message image that
was projected when he hesitated about delivering summary justice with
a gun, rather than going to court, to an imagined Willy Horton raping his
wife or daughter. (There is another negative Message theme associatively
summoned up here, by the way—namely, Mr. Kerry's marital connection
and other, cultural dispositions toward hated France and Germany, two
prominent foreign states that were not among the Bush "coalition of the

FIGURE 2.4. A plea for a more consultative internationalism becoming a negative
Message image for Senator Kerry. Cartoon by Dana Summers, *Orlando [Florida]
Sentinel*; reproduced by permission of the artist and Tribune Media Services, ©2004.

willing" then fielding troops in Iraq. Any "global test" involving these
unreliable allies puts them ambiguously near to the very "rogue nations"
and "terrorist-sponsoring states" in the somewhat paranoiac and under-
differentiated structure of feeling in the United States that was being
encouraged at that time. Of course, too, "sensitive" internationalists were
last seen in politics when Adlai Stevenson ran for the presidency in 1956,
losing in a landslide.)

Occasionally, for reasons of pique or whatever, members of the press
reveal their sense of how politicians' doings and sayings are—can you
believe it?—Message-driven. Who would have ever imagined? These are
priceless occasions, when the tacit social agreement between politicians
and their press is revealed precisely as the press calls it into question.
Whistle-blowers of Message, at such times they remind us of Toto in
the great film scene in which Dorothy's little dog lifts the curtain on the
real Wizard of Oz, revealed as a mere P. T. Barnum–like humbug who is
running the machine. One suspects that this pique was at work on more

FIGURE 2.5. Early 1970s planning by airman George W. Bush reconstructed
for President Bush's 2004 negative Message campaigning against
Senator Kerry. Cartoon by Pat Oliphant, Universal Press Syndicate;
reproduced by permission of Universal Press Syndicate, ©2004.

than one occasion with respect to the Bush-Cheney administration and
especially with respect to the great Wizard of its Message machine. Not
surprisingly, such eruptions became increasingly familiar precisely as a
function of falling poll numbers among the public, which always embold-
ens the political press corps. Let us recall the press dissection of Mr. Bush's
"Top Gun" caper in the presidential flight suit, landing a plane on the
deck of the USS Abraham Lincoln (no less!) off San Diego to announce
"Mission Accomplished" in Iraq—on 2 May 2003!

The print press just took the scene apart for its lights-action-camera
falseness, lambasting and lampooning the president as they perhaps
hadn't done since Mr. Clinton's "Shampoo" (remember the Warren Beatty movie?) and haircut on the LAX tarmac ("You're so vain!") while Air
Force One held up all passenger travel in and out of Los Angeles.

In this same vein of seeing through the constructedness and frequent
sham quality of negative as well as positive Message, note that by early
September 2004 even the press eventually had had enough of the weeks

of attacks upon Mr. Kerry's service record in the Vietnam War, especially as compared with the public secret acknowledging Mr. Bush's own whereabouts at that period.

If in our form of electoral politics Message will not perish from the political landscape, it certainly was maximally, even overly visible in 2003–2004.

Message is Dead! Long Live Message!

By contrast, let us focus upon the presidential campaign that came to its quadrennial culmination in 2008. How did various types of factors come together in relation to this central armature of the institutional form of American politics? How is it that during the two major party primary campaigns, during which respective party candidates were determined, it seemed that Message was on its last institutional legs, abandoned as otiose by the politically successful, left thus at death's door, while as the country moved into the final phases of the cycle, there emerged (to allude to Lincoln at Gettysburg) a new birth of Message on the political firmament? Is it just an expected function of which particular phase of the campaign cycle we examine? Is it just a singularity, a unique confluence of historical events involving the particular biographical individuals who have been the candidates, or the particular personnel and personalities at all the intersecting planes of complex institutionality? Or is it, as we will suggest, really a function of the strength of institutionally exercised normative expectations that act like an extraordinary inertial pull to the armature of Message as the recurrently emergent social reality, candidates' desires notwithstanding? Could it then be a kind of black hole of institutionalized gravitational force that absorbs everyone's political light because of the way all of the interests come together in a political campaign?

As we have noted in our introduction, there is a huge establishment of professionals for whom Message as communication organizes the very conduct of electoral politics and certainly the economics thereof. It is the presumed-upon communicative framework in terms of which everything is understood, interpreted, planned, and scored. And despite the best efforts of these professionals in campaigns and in the press corps, in 2008 Message seemed at first to be under siege in both parties. Why? Until nearly convention time, this was central to the primary campaigns of both Barack Obama and John McCain in the year of anti-Message style. Each in his own way had built a campaign that challenged the business-as-usual of presidential politics.

Building on his electrifying 2004 Democratic convention address, Senator Obama was reinvigorating a long-unused tradition of great public rhetoric in the tradition of our "civil religion," a kind of secular Protestant-ism deriving from the English Enlightenment and Americanized with King James "plain style" eloquence by Abraham Lincoln (see Cmiel 1990; Silverstein 2003a; Wills 1992). His organization also perfected Web Campaign 2.0, first adumbrated in the insurgent Clean-for-Dr.-Dean primary campaign of 2004 (mobilizing a new generation of the Left, children of those who "clean[ed] for Gene" McCarthy in 1972). The Obama campaign benefited from sophisticated use of the blogosphere, including YouTube, which has been a continuing challenge for the usual soak-wash-spin-rinse campaign wash cycles of the older, pre-web journalism and commentary of print, radio, and TV reportage, since primary documents are forever available, notwithstanding the sometimes urgent need to disappear them for effective "spin."

Senator McCain, too, seemed to challenge the very parameters of Message-ing on his Plain Talk Express, talking as straightforwardly onstage, it appeared, as he did offstage, intimates and non-intimates alike having the privilege of his backstage musings. At first a self-defined outsider— "maverick" became the very much overused (and increasingly inapplica-ble) word—to the Republican National Committee establishment, with its permanent corps of multimedia ad and public relations professionals, it was precisely the Senator-McCain-Goes-to-Washington hokeyness of his whole operation, emblematically summed up in the concept of "straight talk," that appealed to his primary supporters (much as it did to Arkansas governor Mike Huckabee's, factoring out the fundamentalist Christian ideological shadings).

We would suggest that an intentional contrast with the 2004 cycle partly explains the significance of these two attempts to melt Message down during the primary season, at least Message as it had long been understood by their respective political establishments. The critical question to think about is this: were these self-presentations just their subtly calibrated Message in a communicative machine that inevitably shapes candidacy, or had Message indeed reached the limits of its political effectiveness in presidential politics of 2008? Could it be by chance that the two candidates who seemed not to be shaped by traditional Message got to stand against each other in the final 2008 electoral round?

Let's turn to John McCain before he became the Republican presidential nominee. Throughout his career, Senator McCain has been constructed in the image of his Arizona predecessor Barry Goldwater, and by virtue of this he is also someone who recuperates a style of an earlier era. In 1964 the late Senator Goldwater was trounced for the presidency by the incumbent Lyndon Johnson, running for reelection after less than a year in office. Goldwater was unable to escape the negative Cold War–era Message of trigger-happy nuclear nut. The now infamous (but, for professional negative-Message mavens, highly educational) Johnson TV spot that starts with a little girl making wishes on flower petals and ends with a nuclear mushroom cloud fixed Goldwater in the public imagination for good (making visible some of the implications of his own words, it must be admitted.) But by 2008 the cluster of issues that defined political "conservatism" in America had long since moved from 1964's international ones like nuclear war and Soviet containment to advocacy for containment of domestic social—some would say socialistic—progress, the very "social issues" on which the Republican Southern (and Evangelical-focused) Strategy would ride to nearly forty years of dominance (see Perlstein 2008; Phillips 1969). After that electoral defeat, too, Senator Goldwater increasingly took on the role of an opposition figure within the Republican Party, sardonic in his straight-talking antiestablishment stance, a sort of a right-wing Harry Truman, as it were, "giving hell" to establishment types in his own party as frequently as to Democrats.

This, too, has been the stance of Senator McCain, who has been as loved by the political press for his "maverick" and "straight-talking" persona as his ideas about particular issues have been considered nonstarters, or pandering to a public while keeping his faith. During the primary season he kept saying he knows next to nothing about economics, yet he put forth straight-line Bush administration doctrine on the housing and credit crunches that began to seriously squeeze people by spring 2008. He demonstrated he knows next to nothing about the political complexities framing the conflict in Iraq and the wider Middle East, yet he put forth views on U.S. military engagements there that were even more aggressive than those of the Bush administration.

But no one seemed much to care—certainly not to emphasize all of this in secondary media accounts. "The mainstream news media by and large don't cover Mr. McCain; they canonize him," wrote Neal Gabler during the last week of March 2008. Not only does this show a dissociation of the candidate's taking stands on issues with the machinery of a campaign of Message; it also figurates—it constructs a metaphorical image of—someone who is independent of Message altogether. Recall that Senator McCain was incarcerated and tortured in the "Hanoi Hilton" during the Vietnam War. This renders him a surviving hero of a brutal, life-threatening captivity for whom, then, biographically, people projectively understand if he does not take everything else too seriously. This was, for the public, his quasi-crucifixional moment of ritual time-out-of-time, actually about six years in captivity.

Captivity under such duress was an ultimate "truth" inscribed on McCain's body in respect of which all Message-relevant slings and arrows have plausibly become biographically insignificant. McCain was not destroyed by Karl Rove's nasty negative Message campaign in South Carolina in 2000, the sleazy claim of which was that McCain was father to a black child. Although, seeing what was in store beyond that underhanded Bush primary victory, he got out of the presidential race. (So perhaps as Republican Party successions operate, this *was* his "turn.") He may not have been ultimately "Swift Boatable" in the same way as was Senator Kerry in 2004, however, by anyone in this campaign. Even Gen. Wesley Clark became somewhat notorious for what was taken, with delicious Message-driven interdiscursivity, to be an attempt at doing so somewhat later in the campaign, in a CBS *Face the Nation* broadcast of 29 June 2008 that caused a great flare-up in the media.

BOB SCHIEFFER: How can you say that John McCain is untested and untried, General?

CLARK: Because in the matters of national security policy making, it's a matter of understanding risk. It's a matter of gauging your opponents and it's a matter of being held accountable. John McCain's never done any of that in his official positions. I certainly honor his service as a prisoner of war. He was a hero to me and to hundreds of thousands and millions of others in the armed forces as a prisoner of war. . . . [But h]e hasn't been there and ordered the bombs to fall. He hasn't seen what it's like when diplomats come in and say, "I don't know whether we're going to be able to get this point through or not. Do you want to take the risk? What about your reputation? How do we handle this publicly?" He hasn't made th[ose] calls, Bob.

SCHIEFFER: Well, General, maybe—could I just interrupt you?

CLARK: Sure.

SCHIEFFER: I have to say, Barack Obama has not had any of those experiences, either, nor has he ridden in a fighter plane and gotten shot down. I mean . . .

CLARK: Well, I don't think riding in a fighter plane and getting shot down is a qualification to be president.

(The various web accounts of McCain's "singing" to the then North Vietnamese while in captivity also got precisely nowhere, tamped down, in fact, rather than encouraged by the Obama campaign as the kind of negative Message that was beneath them.)

And the point is, *no one* may have been able to "Swift Boat" McCain. He may indeed have rendered himself beyond—really, below—Message as a kind of absolute being, likable in himself, whom reporters protected by declining to report what they observed of the candidate's gaffes, misspeakings, lapses of memory, really far-out views of particular issues, or apparent campaign-stop-to-campaign-stop "flip-flops" (the term of the 2004 campaign that was useful as a negative Message term against Senator Kerry and again in 2008 and even 2012 in the Republican primary campaigns—think Rudy Giuliani in the first and Mitt Romney in both). Thus, McCain's low-key amiability and projection of personal decency may well have played the decisive role in the Republican primary season as the other candidates who were hyped, and hyped-up, by traditional negative Message-ing swung at each other in public so as to reveal the malleable emptiness behind all the Message-driven posturing, while McCain stuck to his I-am-that-I-am self-presentation on and off camera, which was a bit like a stone wall against which the other primary contenders were butting their heads.

There are several extraordinary moments in which this contrast becomes very visible, very apparent to everyone. Take, for example, the multi-candidate Republican debate at the Reagan Library on 30 January 2008 (CNN 2008c). To the initial question by CNN's Anderson Cooper, echoing Ronald Reagan himself in 1980 when running against Jimmy Carter, "So tonight, in terms of the economy, are Americans better off than they were eight years ago?" Governor Romney replied:

> ROMNEY: Well, if you're voting for George Bush, you'd be very interested in knowing the answer to that. If you're voting for Mitt Romney, you'd like to know, "Are you better off in Massachusetts after four years of my term in office?" And the answer would be decidedly yes. I came into a state which was very much in a deep ditch ...

—after which there is a long recitation rattling off gubernatorial accomplishments in a speaking style that can only be called a salesman's pitch, which, periodically, Cooper tries to reorient to the actual question, to no avail:

> COOPER: Let me just interrupt. The question was: Are Americans better off than they were eight years ago? ... How do you feel America is doing?
> ROMNEY: Well, again, I'm pleased with what I do [sic] while I was—as governor and happy to talk about that record.
> COOPER: Are you running for governor or are you running for president, though?
> ROMNEY: But I'm not running on President Bush's record. President Bush can talk about his record.
> Washington is badly broken. I think we recognize that. Washington has not dealt with the problems that we have in this nation.
> . . .
> And as a result, we've got people that feel there needs to be a change in Washington and that's something I represent.

Cooper then turns to the candidate sitting immediately to the right of Governor Romney, Senator McCain:

> COOPER: Senator McCain, are Americans better off than they were eight years ago?
> MCCAIN: I think you could argue that Americans overall are better off, because we have had a pretty good prosperous time, with low unemployment and low inflation and a lot of good things have happened. A lot of jobs have been created. But let's have some straight talk. Things are tough right now. Americans are uncertain

about this housing crisis. Americans are uncertain about the economy, as we see the stock market bounce up and down, but more importantly, the economy particularly in some parts of the country, state of Michigan, Governor Romney and I campaigned, not to my success, I might add, and other parts of the country are probably better off. But I think what we're trying to do to fix this economy is important. We've got to address the housing, subprime housing problem. We need to, obviously, have this package go through the Congress as quickly as possible. We need to make the Bush tax cuts permanent, which I voted for twice to do so. I think we need to eliminate the alternate minimum tax that sits out there and challenges 25 million American families.

COOPER: It sounds like that we're not better off is what you're saying.

MCCAIN: Pardon me?

COOPER: It sounds like you're saying we're not better off.

MCCAIN: I think we are better off overall if you look at the entire eight-year period, when you look at the millions of jobs that have been created, the improvement in the economy, et cetera. What I'm trying to emphasize, Anderson, [is] that we are in a very serious challenge right now, with a lot of Americans very uncertain about their future, and we've got to give them some comfort.

Observe how Senator McCain, speaking in his raspy, tight-throated semi-whisper and at deliberate speed, actually answers the question, with a pointed differentiation of himself from Governor Romney: "[L]et's have some straight talk. Things are tough right now," although the solutions he proposes are straight out of the standard Bush administration rhetoric, essentially to get Congress to lower or abolish taxes and (wink, wink) rein in spending. The effectiveness is clearly not in the tired old proposals; it is all in the pragmatics of contrastive delivery. How starkly McCain's response, equivocating as it is to placate the Bush supporters, points up Romney's blatherish posturing within the confines of his Message as the Mr. Fix-it CEO who moved from industry to public service to excavate Massachusetts from its "deep ditch" (a local Boston phrase for an endless and bedeviled expressway tunnel project), a Washington outsider who wants to appeal to "people that feel there needs to be a change in Washington." (Note how he uses one of Senator Obama's key words, change, though not in the abstract sense of the latter.) But *am I* better or worse off, Governor? McCain just answered the question with, for a candidate, reasonably "straight talk," one of his key phrases: overall in the eight years, yes; right now, no—even if the solutions he proposed are the same-old, same-old.

It was a turning point in isolating Romney right from the first few minutes of the eighty-four-minute broadcast, because each one of the other candidates, Governor Huckabee and Congressman Ron Paul, lined up with lengthy similar "straight talk" and said that things were now bad or worse than eight years ago, leaving Governor Romney's initial Message moment an embarrassingly isolated performance of demonstrable Message-ing that McCain had beautifully made transparent and obvious to the audience.

But this recurs throughout the debate. At another particularly striking anti-Message moment, the topic is the current administration's Iraq War, where the parsing and meaning of terms like "timetables [namely, for withdrawal]" are at issue (CNN 2008c). Janet Hook, of the *Los Angeles Times,* asks Governor Romney:

> JANET HOOK: Obviously, Iraq is still a major issue in this campaign, and over the last few days there's been a real back-and-forth going on here. Senator Mc-Cain has said over and over again that you supported a timetable for a phased withdrawal from Iraq. Is that true?

Now, all during a long disquisition tip-toeing away from "timetables" but embracing stealthy, "phased withdrawal" by Governor Romney, Senator McCain, sitting next to him, begins to develop a broad, sustained grin or smile, which intensifies as his opponent's paragraphs roll on. At the moment when, after a long and contentious back-and-forth, Governor Romney complains that this accusation by Senator McCain is reprehensible, dirty "Washington-style" politics—that is, the politics of negative Message-ing—McCain really goes into high gear as the anti-Message person:

> MCCAIN: And as far as Washington politics is concerned, I think my friend Governor Huckabee, sir, will attest [to] the millions of dollars of attack ads and negative ads you leveled against him in Iowa, the millions of dollars of attack ads you have attacked against me in New Hampshire, and have ever since. A lot of it is your own money. You're free to do with it what you want to. You can spend it all. But the fact is that . . .
> (LAUGHTER)
> . . . your negative ads, my friend, have set the tone, unfortunately, in this campaign. I say to you again: The debate after the election of 2006 was whether we were going to have timetables for withdrawal or not. Timetables were [*sic*] the

buzzword. That was the Iraq Study Group. That was what the Democrats said we wanted to do. Your answer should have been "No."

Boy! The "Plain Talk Express" uses its cow—or bullshit—catcher to effect! In this last segment Romney is shifting in his seat, looking desperately at the moderator, Anderson Cooper, to get him out of this. Senator McCain's stance of identifying Governor Romney with a slick, try-anything, Message-based campaign was the relentless anti-Message-ing by McCain until Romney dropped out. He was defeated by his own Message-ing, as had been Mayor Giuliani, by putting forward subtle, minutely and casuistically parsed positions that, as McCain kept pointing out, gave no cumulative coherence to the communicative stream of Message, both positive for themselves and negative for others, in which they had been swimming away from their actualized political pasts in positions of executive responsibility as governor and mayor, respectively.

But let's turn to the other side of the aisle, as they say in Congress. The Democratic Party primary in 2008 was one of the more interesting because of the two major—and surviving—candidates. Sen. Hillary Rodham Clinton turned out to be all Message all the time, a somewhat predictable campaign style practiced now over twenty years of campaigning at both state and national levels, much of that as the spouse of a candidate and popular officeholder. Sen. Barack Obama, by refreshing contrast, had given a keynote address at the 2004 Democratic convention of such power and appeal that immediately afterward commentators were beginning to ask why he was not the party's nominee instead of Senator Kerry. One must recall that this was even before he was elected to the U.S. Senate as the junior senator from Illinois, where through an extraordinary series of accidents and peccadilloes in the other party he had only token opposition from the fringe right-wing personality Alan Keyes, who briefly moved to Illinois for the purpose. (Because politically he has had, as one says, "the luck of the Irish," he should be Senator [now President] "O'Bama"! This luck recurred during the period of the financial avalanche of post-convention autumn 2008, of course, a great factor in making vivid the choice between Senators Obama and McCain.)

What was extraordinary about Senator Obama is, first, his claim to be, biographically, the apotheosis of a post-Message, post-identity-politics global fusion. This is certainly the theme of his almost mythic autobiography (1995), in which he emerges from black and white, foreign and domestic, Third and First Worlds, poverty and privilege, prejudice and opportunity, ignorance and education, and most of all, the fulfillment— Yes! We can! *Sí! Se puede!*—of the aspirations of "the audacity of hope." In a sense, he is saying, he is the embodiment of an at least official, on-record national civil religious aspiration for a future in which such divisions can be overcome to everyone's advantage. In short, given his actual political resume, he was the candidate of the hope of audacity.

The second extraordinary thing about Obama is that the 2004 keynote address was no fluke; this guy had mastered a rhetorical idiom of extraordinary power. In it are fused two rhetorical registers, as it were. We can identify the best of African American pulpit style, with its images and crescendo/decrescendo cadences and parallelistic phrasal majesty. Think of Dr. Martin Luther King Jr. at the Lincoln Memorial in 1963 ("I have a dream") as the very pinnacle in the modern era of this form of rhetoric brought to our civil religion, which trumped even John F. Kennedy's 1961 inaugural address (Clarke 2004) with its Lincolnesque eucharism, "Ask not what your country can do for you; ask what you can do for your country!" This tradition blends nicely with the great tradition of American civic rhetoric long out of the public's awareness, for it has vanished with Kennedy's "Camelot." Abraham Lincoln, certainly, is the watershed; he brought the plain style of Shakespeare and the King James Bible to a public used to the communicative bombast of a Daniel Webster or a Henry Clay. In Lincoln's image were all the twentieth-century presidential greats: both Roosevelts, but especially FDR; and lastly in the presidential field John F. Kennedy's inspiring 1961 inaugural. (Ronald Reagan's addresses have a kitsch quality, in retrospect, the Hollywood version of public rhetoric. The one example of the Bush-43 administration is the president's admirable memorial sermon at the National Cathedral in October 2001, but this was a sermon, after all.) It is amazing to think that the early 1960s are almost fifty years behind us, and that therefore the electoral torch has been passed to a new generation of Americans who are truly unfamiliar in a sense with these traditions of public rhetoric. Candidate Obama was a "rock star" among politicians precisely because his rhetorical absolute pitch recuperated these great, indeed inspirational, national moments for the old. It also provided the young with something they had not themselves experienced but responded to as a refreshingly different kind of political discourse, given what else is out there: advertising-sized fragments of language used for Message-ing as they are indeed more frankly used for brand.

But who—that is, what—was Senator Obama during the campaign? To be sure, he was a colleague of one of us at the University of Chicago, a senior lecturer in constitutional law in our law school (currently on extended leave). But that seems not to have played any visible role in his own campaign, though many in his administration's technocratic White House corps have been Chicago people. Why play this down? It is not Message-worthy in a positive way, being an "egghead"; the last presidential candidate described in this way was the exceedingly literate and witty Illinois governor Adlai Stevenson, who twice lost by landslide margins to Dwight Eisenhower. In recent elections both Al Gore and John Kerry had tried on a soupçon of eggheadedness in running against President Bush, and the contrast in each contest was telling. But, then, neither one of them could deliver a stirring speech: if Al Gore was considered "wooden," Kerry was positively soporific with his singsong bombast sometimes rivaling W. C. Fields at his most stentorian. In this light, both the Hillary Clinton Democratic primary campaign and the McCain-Palin national campaign attempted to use phrasal fluency, denotational organization, and rhetorical elegance against Senator Obama, suggested by the recurrent Message-relevant descriptor "elite." (At times his detractors have been reduced to negative Message-ing about arugula—*du côté de* Chez Panisse?—on the Obama family's salad plate and Dijon-style—Hey! That's French!—mustard.)

So what about Obama *is* Message-worthy? Here's Sen. Joseph Biden, in announcing his own short-lived candidacy to a reporter in the *New York Observer* on 31 January 2007 (Horowitz 2007). Asked about Senator Obama's then pre-announcement steps toward running, Biden replied:

BIDEN: I mean you got the first sort of mainstream African American—
[REPORTER: Yes]
—who is articulate and bright and clean and a nice-looking guy. I mean, this—
that's a storybook, man.

What a gaffe! (See our chapter on ethno-blooperology.) But how Message-worthy! Intended, let's assume, positively, this comment had a pungently negative effect on his own presidential chances, though apparently, to judge from his subsequent position as Mr. Obama's vice president, he was forgiven. Senator Biden distinguishes Senator Obama from stereotypes of African Americans as the first candidate who can be considered a "mainstream" candidate for office: being "articulate," meaning he speaks fluent, indeed elegantly grammatical and lexical Standard English of a Western U.S. type, without noticeable African American phonological features, except deliberately; being "bright"—you know, Occidental College, then Columbia College and Harvard Law School, *Harvard Law Review* editor in chief, professorial lecturer at the University of Chicago; being "clean and nice-looking," presumably meaning he always wears a currently stylish, custom-tailored, beautifully draping and silhouetting Hart-Schaffner-Marx suit, and even in "accidentally" released beach pictures he looked muscularly trim and buff as though he had been regularly to the health club, and quite handsome, with what some have called (compare JFK, of course) "movie-star looks." Well, if according to Senator Biden, all this sets Senator Obama apart from all previous African American politicians, he is in some sense both ghettoizing him and insulting all other African American politicians at the same time.

Of course, as we noted in our introduction in discussing the expendable surrogate negative-Message bearers, the Clinton campaign had been an unending source of remarks that similarly tried to ghettoize Senator Obama racially. The former president, Bill, Clinton insisted that Senator Obama's victory in the South Carolina primary was nothing more significant than the Rev. Jesse Jackson Jr.'s victory there in the 1988 primary season, supported by African American voters in a politics of—to Mr. Clinton—obviously ethno-racial recognition.

"You are black!" these Message-ing politicians keep saying. "No you can't!" was Senator Obama's anti-Message fusional stance in reply: "Why are you trying to pin an identity on me, a tale—T-A-L-E, as it were—on this [Democratic] donkey?" You can see the bind in which Senator Obama found himself. To respond with a mere denial of the factuality of such negative Message-ings explicit or implied by association would be to allow these others to define his Message, simply putting in play its degree of factual accuracy or imaginative applicability but staying on their strategic semiotic field of contention. (Compare here the flapdoodle caused for his candidacy by the incendiary sermons of Rev. Jeremiah Wright, pastor of Mr. Obama's long-term house of worship in Chicago, ultimately requiring a splendid oration on race strategically delivered in Philadelphia to talk about "perfect[ing the] Union" in the city where the founding documents of the United States were adopted. A true Dr. King moment, solidifying wide support.) A lack of explicit response but a more general repetition of the *post*-racial ideal to which, in reprimand, these others should be held served to disallow others the control of *his* Message.

One can appreciate why the surrogates in the Obama camp did not counter these various charges so much as, with what we term "meta-communication," they criticized and impugned the very acts of intendedly negative Message-ing. In this way they gave the press corps and political professionals who live in the universe of Message a sense of a verbal fight much in the form of those we're familiar with from childhood. A: "Fuck you!" B: "You said a bad word! I'll tell your Mom!" A: "Well, you deserved it! You made me say it because of what *you're* doing!" B: "You're mean!" Etc. Etc. Only in the latter part of the two-party presidential campaign did Senator Obama, with increasingly sardonic tone, use various negative Message epithets of his opponents—as humorous contrasts to his issues or proposals, in the rhetorical mode of "if this be socialism, then we're all for it!" (We should recall here a parallel rhetorical move: the proud turning of the term queer into a rallying cry of the first post–Stonewall, HIV/AIDS generation

FIGURE 2.6. Barack Obama is dressed as a Somali elder by Sheikh Mahmed Hassan in a 2006 visit to Kenya. The photo has become a subject of controversy.

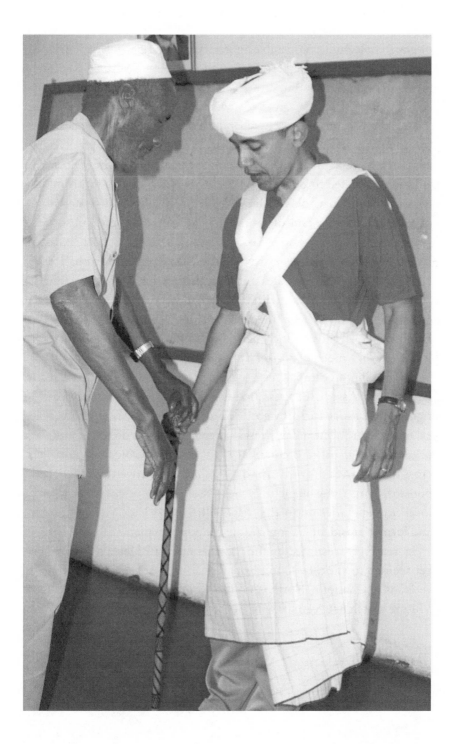

of gay people, and comparable minority-celebrating polarity reversals. And who can forget the presupposition-canceling "We're all Keynsians now!" of Richard Nixon in response to charges of betrayal by economic conservatives for having agreed to government stimulus measures?)

And there is much worse in what developed as a relentless 2008 Clinton campaign of negative Message-ing, taking a cue from the Republicans. Mr. Cunningham, the right-wing Cincinnati talk-show host, you will recall, insisted throughout on calling Senator Obama by his middle name, Hussein, to associate him with an affectively negative stereotype of an Islamic alien, useful, of course, in relation to the context of so many years of Bush administration Message-ing about the late Saddam Hussein. By now, we can presume, everyone knew that Senator Obama's father had come to the United States from Kenya, and that as a young child the senator lived in Indonesia with his mother, who was an anthropologist gone a bit native with a culture she was studying, little Barry in tow (see Dunham 2009). (The political danger of having anthropologist parents?) Indonesia, like much of coastal Kenya, is indeed Muslim.

So the Clinton campaign surrogacy released to the press—or, really, dug up—old Associated Press pictures (fig. 2.6) that first appeared on the right-wing Drudge Report website on 25 February 2004, and in every local newspaper the next day, showing Senator Obama on a visit to Kenya in 2006 in full tribal garb, complete with a head covering that looks like a cross between a Sikh's turban and a Muslim's head covering. (Well, news bureaus, in turn, dug up pictures [fig. 2.7a–c] of all current leaders "going local" as dignitaries on foreign trips—then First Lady Hillary Clinton, and former president George W. Bush among them!)

Increasingly frustrated by the way this negative Message-ing had not yet seemed to stick, by Good Friday, 21 March, speaking to a group of veterans in Charlotte, North Carolina, former president Clinton said of a future match between his wife, Senator Clinton, and Senator McCain:

FIGURE 2.7A-C. Barack Obama isn't the only one to dress up. Top: Hillary Clinton wears a traditional scarf in Eritrea in 1997. Middle: President Clinton dons a royal garment during a visit to Nigeria in 2000. Bottom: President Bush wears traditional Chinese garb in Shanghai in 2001.

I think it would be a great thing if we had an election year where you had two people who loved this country and were devoted to the interest [sic] of this country. And people could actually ask themselves who is right on these issues, instead of all this other stuff that always seems to intrude itself on our politics.

The implication is clear in an environment in which first Senator Obama's wife (having recently said that she was for "the first time" proud of her country in countenancing a black presidential candidate), and then the incendiary Rev. Jeremiah Wright, sounding a bit like radioactive minister Louis Farrakhan, were taken to be close enough to Senator Obama to be counted, in Message politics, as his surrogates or equivalents. While Senator Clinton "loved this country," Senator Obama—who, one must recall, as an exercise of his free speech rights did not early on wear a Bushie American flag lapel pin on his expensive suits—did not. Note the "insinuendo" here of unequivocal negative Message-ing. It is almost but not quite as direct as Governor Romney's blooper moment of autumn 2007 in which he (wink, wink) misspoke, as he addressed the chamber of commerce in Greenwood, South Carolina:

Actually, just look at what Osam—uh—Barack Obama, said just yesterday. Barack Obama calling on radicals, jihadists of all different types, to come together in Iraq. "That is the battlefield. That is the central place," he said. "Come join us under one banner."

(Reporters, as we note in chapter 4, scrambled in vain to find the Obama quote.)

In all of this negative Message-ing, there is no concern for the accuracy of statements. Negative Message-ing works imagistically, by reinforcing stereotypic associations, many of them frank prejudices, seeking to wrap those stereotypes around the opponent, the intent being to create a straitjacket from which he or she cannot escape. Such stereotypes do their work in delegitimating whatever positive Message frames the opponent, and in terms of which the opponent had previously been operating. Each time such a negative Message moment gets an appropriately huffy rise out of the other side—explicitly taking offense, whether directly or through surrogates—such an exchange reinforces the fact that campaigns antagonistically co-construct a Message-centered political communicative environment.

That was a very important part of the Clinton Democratic primary campaign strategy with respect to Senator Obama, who had eschewed Message, by his own account, and one that in every particular the Republican McCain-Palin presidential campaign adopted point by point, in every possible medium. (Republicans worry about the same effect on their candidate of the brutal, scorched-earth negativity of Message framing with which Governor Romney emerges from the 2012 primary campaigns at the hands of Newt Gingrich and Rick Santorum.) And each time the actually intended effect of an insinuendo was registered by a reaction, the offending negative Message lobbers had merely to say, "Gee! It's your problem that you take things in this negative way; they are just innocent gaffes, or innocent sentiments, or truthful even if painful, etc. Thin skin!" (In the instance of Senator Obama, black skin, to be sure!) Note how Bill Cunningham, the "Hussein" guy, innocently asks why using someone's middle name is bad; hey, is he ashamed of it or something? Governor Romney's spokesperson called his elaborate "gaffe" "just a brief mix-up." Howard Wolfson, the point person in the Clinton campaign, was offended that the former president's remarks about patriotic—and not so patriotic—candidates should even have been inferred to have been directed against Senator Obama. (The "Perhaps the shoe fits after all . . . !" ploy; "Why would you think I'm talking about *you*, anyway?" Recall here Carly Simon's 1972 "You're so vain! You must think that this song is about you!") Why, the nerve to accuse a former Democratic president of McCarthyite tactics, of all things! Indeed!

But one must say, the Clinton campaign's strategy was reactive from the first, not having thought that anyone—neither former senator John Edwards, nor Sen. Joseph Biden, nor Gov. Bill Richardson, nor even Senator Obama—could take the long-desired, long-coveted crown from Senator Clinton—the Democratic primaries, in other words, expected to have been a kind of coronation. As the Obamamania, as it has been termed, persisted in early 2008, staying for the most part in its own stylistic register and with a success beyond expectation, the Clinton campaign started to engage in reactive mimicry of Obama slogans and key terms: "Solutions, not speeches!" "Yes, she will!" "Not promises, but solutions!" "Experience, not hope!" "[Ready to be] commander in chief on day one!"

By April the Clinton primary campaign had moved to full-scale negative Message attacks, trying one by one to peel away each potentially damaging demographic or biographical variable of Senator Obama's professed post-Message fusional global selfhood to make it a problem area in Message terms, rather than an asset. It is no wonder that more and more, the "commentariat" press began to conceptualize Senator Clinton's own effective "positive" Message as "rhymes with 'witch,'" to quote Barbara Bush in 1984 on then Democratic vice presidential candidate Geraldine Ferraro. Perhaps even political "spoiler," adding to the unfortunately gendered associations the quality of bad sportsmanship, infuriating feminists associated with the campaign, to be sure. And thus herself delivering to the Republicans the entire structure of their negative autumn campaign Message once it became clear that the positive Message of "mavericks"—"ex-POW" McCain and "hockey mom" Palin—"change"/"reform" was just not working as planned.

This Clintonista spring was understood to be all quite dangerous to anyone of the Democratic side who thought in terms of Message politics, where certain kinds of negativity in the primaries, it was felt, would do irreparable damage to any candidate who was able to survive the onslaught of the internal party battle. For, in the finals, the actual two-party presidential race, the primaries' negative Message becomes what one terms in aesthetic circles "found art," prepared for the other party's candidate or surrogates to pick up and use. Indeed the McCain-Palin campaign did so again and again and again later in 2008, stirring up ethno-racial as well as class and jingoist hatred in abundant evidence at various campaign-stop rallies (the hatred persisting and being relayed to the 2012 presidential campaign).

So when Senators Obama and McCain became the candidates of their respective parties, the issue was this: Could their anti-Message-ing styles survive the channeling force of the massive machine of electoral politics, demanding they fulfill their roles as candidates and—for one of them—as president in the institutionally expected way? Or did the machine of negative Message, once so furiously wielded by the Clinton primary campaign, come back again, though perhaps less effectively than before?

FIGURE 2.8. Jack Higgins's opinion.

FIGURE 2.9. RNC Nevada, North Carolina flyer.

In the view of a Jack Higgins cartoon (fig. 2.8) penned during the seemingly endless Democratic primary season, Senator Obama would have to protect himself from the "kitchen sink" of negative Messages hurled at him by the Clintonites. These very negative Messages were then recycled by the McCain campaign, just as commentators warned during the primaries, though principally by the vice presidential nominee, then Governor Palin of Alaska, who time and again portrayed Senator Obama as a dark-skinned Muslim-in-hiding consorting with terrorists:

> "Our opponent . . . is someone who sees America, it seems, as being so imperfect, imperfect enough, that he's palling around with terrorists who would target their own country. . . . This is not a man who sees America like you and I see America."
>
> —Gov. Sarah Palin to a group of donors in Englewood, Colorado, 3 October 2008 [plus three more stops on 4 October]

Albeit the terrorists in question (fig. 2.9) were WASPy corporate heirs named Ayers in the flush of their under-thirties faux rebellion during the topsy-turvy 1960s (remember Patty Hearst?). And the opponent in question was a peripheral, Hawaiian-grown exotic species, different from "real Americans" in good old continental U.S.A.—'cause, by golly, far-off Hawai'i is separated from the "lower 48" (as Alaskans are wont to say) by a vast expanse of Pacific Ocean, rather than by land (it's Canada, remember?) like Alaska!

Such were the negatives being hurled with increasing intensity in a part of the Republican campaign that seemed increasingly to backfire with all but a fringe of the more general public, even if it temporarily worked at rallying what the party insiders must have come to recognize as its most enthusiastic base, but no longer in any sense the McCain-groupie press corps. (In the otherwise low-turnout 2010 midterm congressional elections, this fringe was mobilized to advantage as "The Tea Party," in the Message image of the anticolonial and extralegal prank of Boston's most zealous patriots in December 1773, leading to a decisive midterm Republican takeover of the House of Representatives.)

But that negative Message would end up, as it were, "'palin' by comparison" to what was arguably the more significant Message space opened up by the ultimate economic meltdown of autumn 2008 that was the culmination of the long-brewing debacle of nth-order mortgage derivatives functioning as phony assets in the capital markets. As all this came to a head at the end of September, just in time for the first presidential debate, Senator McCain's much-vaunted "maverick" qualities started to look loopy, lurch-y, and, well, just plain out of it. The Obama campaign decided to capitalize on Senator McCain's puzzling policy zigzags:

> "Our financial system in turmoil. And John McCain?
> Erratic in a crisis. Out of touch on the economy."
>
> —*Voice-over on Obama TV ad released 5 October 2008*

Already becoming a bit desperate as his post-convention polling bounce evaporated and Governor Palin's disastrous interviews were pilloried in "the liberal press," McCain tried inhabiting the across-the-aisle image of a statesman—excellent on the terrain of foreign policy, of course, where a military Message of patriotic unity is all—in what he finally announced was a national (in fact, international) economic crisis. Alas, this was his weakest suit to play in an area in which, as we saw above, he had little to offer. When the Bush White House hastily arranged an economic "summit" of the two candidates, bipartisan congressional party leaders and Treasury, Federal Reserve, and other executive branch officials, staging it no doubt with the idea that Senator McCain could be seen doing something statesmanlike, the senator sat silently at the margin, contributing nothing positively Message-worthy. (One can only wonder what the internal campaign dynamics were at this time that would leave him so in the lurch.)

But McCain's basic thrust in the home stretch was negative Message campaigning in most respects. As the various positive McCain Message rollouts—"maverick" Palin; his "country first" suspension of campaigning in face of the economic crisis, or at least suspension of David Letterman appearances; and snap populist economic proposals like federal buy-downs of mortgage equity—failed to lift his polling numbers, the campaign in all of its visible and invisible workings went consistently negative as a Message machine. The logic here is this: if the Republicans could give a sufficient number of voters what we might call "cover" along any of the negative Message lines against the opponent, they could be induced to vote *against* the radical socialist non- (and un-)American Muslim black man, Senator Obama—if not enthusiastically *for* Senator McCain—so as to prevent the greater evils dangled before the electorate. One could appeal to fears. These included then Professor William Ayers of the University of Illinois, the Weatherman, as secretary of defense, presumably; giving away our nuclear weapons to fellow "Arab," President Ahmadinejad of Iran; or having, as an upper-middle-class white person, to spend five miserable hours in the waiting room of a governmentally "socialized" medical establishment, instead of the five pleasant hours it takes dealing with an insurance company's HMO waiting room. It all seemed so absurd, given the old-style communicative technologies with which such negative Message-ing was undertaken, with desperate intensity and ubiquity in any state or broadcast market with the slightest chance of Republican electoral victory, and seeming to target those who probably did not have access to—or would not have thought to access—the full range of digital and web media being used by the other party and the Obama campaign.

And meanwhile the most interesting thing is that, save among the faithful—in both senses—of the base of the Republican ticket, exposure of the Republican candidates wound up being devastating to the candidates' positive Message, while for the Democratic ticket, just the opposite was true. While Message is, as we have noted several times, a biographical aura constructed for a candidate, inhabiting that biographical aura as a live character is absolutely essential. Here the advantage went overwhelmingly to the Democratic ticket, both by contrast, which is essential in an *agōn*, and in demeanor in solo appearances. Where the McCain campaign, desperate to distance itself from the sitting Bush administration's Republicanism, had been shouting "maverick, maverick, maverick" on behalf of the good senator, this came dangerously with an undertow of characterological glosses of a less complimentary sort, to be sure: volatile, unreflective, impulsive, unstudied. And sure enough, his debate appearances, his behavior during the Wall Street bailout (oops, world economic rescue) week, and so on indexically screamed "erratic," which is just what the Obama-Biden campaign picked up on and amplified in their own negative Message advertisements (like the one mentioned above), as well as "out of touch," meaning, "rich and old." (Senator McCain's debate

performances were particularly damaging in this respect, where everything from the loose, asyntactic phrases he snapped out to his not being
able to sit quietly and respectfully when not speaking glaringly contrasted
with his opponent's cool-intellectual-dude demeanor.)

Similarly, the McCain campaign, making the best of what we will assume was the impulsive choice of then Governor Palin for vice president,
featured Palin's "hockey-mom enthusiasm" for reform and her great "executive experience," notwithstanding the inevitable seepage of the actual
facts about "bridges to nowhere," "Troopergate," and pipelines, as well as
$150K wardrobes and $1.2M net worth. But it was her disasters of personal
exposure that indexically-iconically solidified the image of "not ready,
if ever, to be 'a heartbeat away from the presidency,'" as the hackneyed
phrase terms it. Tina Fey imitations on *Saturday Night Live* aside (in
which the governor's transcribed speech could be directly incorporated as
satire), one cannot but be struck by the fact that Governor Palin's un-Tel-
e-Prompt-ered™ discourse consists of long, asyntactic strings of ready-
mades that are uttered in assembly-line sequence, with almost random,
if any, connectives between them:

> [From the Katie Couric interview:] "It's very important when you consider even
> national security issues with Russia as Putin rears his head and comes into the air
> space of the United States of America, where—where do they go?"

> [From the Charlie Gibson interview:] "I know that John McCain will do that and I,
> as his vice president, families we are blessed with that vote of the American people
> and are elected to serve and are sworn in on January 20, that will be our top priority
> is to defend the American people."

In terms of topical focus, as for example when a question is asked about
something specific, as instructors of youth we are struck by the fact that
such strings of phrasal ready-mades are what we see on exams and term
papers of people who have been paying only occasional attention at best
in class and beyond. Such students have memorized some few phrases
and can reproduce them fluently as isolated phrases, but their relationship
to any of the other phrases they write shows they know nothing of what
such phrases denote. We might term it 'concept soup,' on the analogy of
a bowl of alphabet soup, where the A-to-Z orderliness of the serial—not
cereal—structure is replaced by a random heap in its watery matrix. For

example, note Governor Palin's remarks below on the vice presidency and Supreme Court decisions. Such statements not only made people of both party affiliations very queasy (and continue to do so, thinking of 2016 and beyond, the enthusiastic fans at auto races and tent revivals notwithstanding), but they also decisively worked against both Republican candidates by emphasizing Senator McCain's impulsiveness and risky choices, such as the very choice of a running mate.

[During the debate with then Senator Biden:] "No, no. Of course, we know what a vice president does. And that's not only to preside over the Senate and will take that position very seriously also. I'm thankful the Constitution would allow a bit more authority given to the vice president if that vice president so chose to exert it in working with the Senate and making sure that we are supportive of the president's policies and making sure too that our president understands what our strengths are."

[Gov. Sarah Palin (R-AK) sat for an interview with KUSA, an NBC affiliate in Colorado. In response to a question sent to the network by a third grader at a local elementary school about what the Vice President does, Palin erroneously argued that the Vice President is "in charge of the United States Senate":]

Q: Brandon Garcia [3rd grader] wants to know, "What does the Vice President do?"

A: Oh! That's somethin' that Piper would ask me as a second grader also! That's a great question, Brandon, and a Vice President has a really great job because not only are they there to support the President's agenda, they're like the team member, the team-mate to that President; but also they're in charge of the U.S. Senate so if they want to they can really get in there with the senators and make a lot of good policy changes that will make life better for Brandon and his family and his classroom and it's a great job and I look forward to havin' that job.

[Katie Couric interview on Supreme Court cases on which she disagrees:]
GOV. PALIN: "Well, let's see . . . (pause) There's, of course in the great history of America there have been rulings, that's never going to be absolute consensus by every American. And there are those issues, again, like *Roe v. Wade*, where I believe are best held on a state level and addressed there. So you know, going through the history of America, there would be others but . . ."
COURIC: "Can you think of any?"
PALIN: "Well, I could think of . . . any again, that could be best dealt with on a more local level. Maybe I would take issue with. But, you know, as mayor, and then as governor and even as a vice president, if I'm so privileged to serve, wouldn't be in a position of changing those things but in supporting the law of the land as it reads today."

By contrast, at least at the top of the Democratic ticket, by resisting the
months-long call by consultants, pundits, contributors, and others to
"fight back," Senator Obama inhabited a positively Message-worthy identity and solidified his image as the strong, silent type—a "cool dude"
if an effete, "elite" intellectual—who simply lets the mud, first Senator
Clinton's and then Senator McCain's and Governor Palin's, fly by and
in so doing avoids being hit by it. In the public stereotype, "socialistic"
and "terroristic" radicals, "angry" black men, anti-American Third World
people do not present this way. Ironically, angry is a term that Governor
Palin and especially Senator McCain constantly used in their public appearances, describing their "friend" Joe the Plumber, on whose behalf
they were irate with "Wall Street" as well as the U.S. government. That
constant refrain indexically gave the impression that it was McCain, not
Obama, who also inhabited that "angry" identity, as became increasingly
clear to the American viewing public. The overall visual contrast between
the two presidential candidates could not have been more stark in their
three debate and other joint appearances—for example, in the Cabinet
Room at the hastily called Executive-Legislative economic summit in late
September. And however studied and practiced Senator Obama's and
Senator Biden's demeanors were in those contrastive settings, to imagine
them as acting out a strategic Message, they would seem to have been successful in giving the lie to the various accusations of negative Message-ing
that the other campaign was increasingly trundling out—straight out of
the conceptual vocabulary of earlier Cold War decades: Message out of
place, as it were.

So Message did indeed come back in the latter phases of the 2008 electoral cycle, as negative Message—in fact, most visibly in the very same
negative Messages of the primary campaigns. (The Republican side even
made some McCarthyite tactical additions from a bygone era in its last,
increasingly desperate phase of "robo-calls" and anonymous mailbox and
windshield flyers.) But what should be learned is that Message is sustained in the completely semiotically saturated communicative milieu of
which political campaigns and incumbencies are made, via mediatization,
to address those at the peripheries of this highly professional milieu, its
addressees or targets among the electorate. From time to time Message

can seem to recede into the background when its unimpeachable "truthiness" (hats off to Stephen Colbert of Comedy Central) projects into and sustains a kind of genuineness, or at least plausibility. When these conditions are strained, even technologically sophisticated Message machinery becomes embarrassingly visible—and less effective precisely for its visibility, as the case study of 2008 following on the heels of 2004 shows.

Three

ADDRESSING "THE ISSUES"

That "The Issues" are a hallowed discursive institution in U.S. electoral politics is suggested by the rote outrage expressed when people fail to address them. The day after the Democratic Party's twenty-first and final primary debate of 2007–2008, held in Philadelphia for finalists Barack Obama and Hillary Clinton, Obama aired this complaint before supporters in North Carolina: "Last night, I think we set a new record because it took us 45 minutes before we even started talking about a single issue that matters to the American people." Irate columnists echoed Obama, like the *Philadelphia Inquirer*'s Trudy Rubin (2008), who railed against the moderators' "'gotcha' questions with no relevance to the problems we face," or Nico Pitney (2008) of the Huffington Post, who, in a bid to convince readers of the new lows to which political debates have sunk, tried his hand at quantification: he sorted "policy" from "non-policy" from "scandal" questions in the debates between Obama and Clinton, arguing that the more recent were scandal-heavy and policy-light.[1] The moderators, concluded *Philadelphia Daily News* columnist Will Bunch, "disgraced the American voters, and in fact even disgraced democracy itself."[2] Unfazed by this reflexive "debate over the debate," as the kerfuffle came to be called, the Annenberg Public Policy Center's stalwart FactCheck.org-ers, unswerving verificationists all, continued to subject the candidate responses to the acid test of truth or falsity: *Did* Obama really say that he wouldn't wear a flag pin? (Yes.) *Did* "people" die from

the Weather Underground's bombing in the 1970s, as Hillary Clinton suggested when she tied Obama to former Underground member William
Ayers? (Yes, but the three who died were group members.)[3]

From laments over The Issues' declining status and complaints that
politicians and debate moderators disrespect them, and from the compensatory proliferation of issue-watching and fact-checking sites and services,[4] it would seem The Issues still do matter. They matter not the least
for the politicians themselves, since it is their behavior toward The Issues
that is taken to reveal their Message. And what matters is not just what reportable things candidates and incumbents say about Issues, like whether
offshore drilling can "help America meet its energy needs" or whether a
"path to legalization" should be offered to undocumented migrants, but
also how they face them: it is their manner of addressing Issues that helps
create candidates' brands.

Which isn't to say that politicians may address Issues as they please,
for there is a certain morally inflected relational etiquette brought to
bear upon their behavior, an etiquette in which the sublime of authenticity looms large. To appreciate this etiquette, we must first take note
of how we encounter this hallowed discursive institution. We must observe a few ways in which The Issues manifest themselves to us and
consider how they matter. The Issues appear, for instance, as legible
design elements on candidate websites, where they are resolved into
lists of named abstract problem areas for deliberation and policymaking,
such as "Health Care" or "Education," each with attached position statements meant to distinguish candidates in a field of competition. In the
forensically framed "debates," The Issues appear as topics of argument
that make up an institutionalized field of stance- and position-taking in
which (1) candidates (again) ought to distinguish themselves, which
(2) the news media and commentators ought to monitor scrupulously,
and in response to such reporting (3) consumer-voters ought to base
their electoral choices.

The Issues are persuasive fictions on several fronts, and on each they
stand as objects of cultural deference, such as national flags or icons of the
Virgin or, perhaps better, like mothers-in-law before sons-in-law (as in cases of in-law avoidance that are familiar in the ethnographic record). If we

consider how fraught The Issues are as objects of address, how their very presence inspires vigilance and fear of missteps, we can consider them on analogy with so-called taboo objects, objects that present hazards—and powers—for politicians by virtue of their strong indexicality.

All of this drama, where candidates and incumbents behave and misbehave before The Issues—"addressing" them, "avoiding" them—is narrated into existence by a chattering class of professional commentators known to some irreverent meta-commentators as the "commentariat." The commentariat's civic virtue consists in helping *you*, the consumer-voter, choose. Through close, critical readings of candidate behavior toward The Issues, they can infer the "implied voter" (compare this with Iser's "implied reader" [1974]), the constituencies that candidates must have really been addressing when they spoke or misspoke or skirted an Issue. They are the color commentators of the oft-bemoaned horse race that is electoral politics, the pace of their reportage quickening before each state-based primary election and the debates leading up to it. They review polls; chart ups and downs; scrutinize slips, gaffes, and peccadilloes. Perhaps these professional commentators are even owed the debt of emplotment, since they mark off time, serializing the campaign cycle by reviewing and previewing episodes, all in a manner and register that, in its most histrionic flourishes, seems parasitic to televised sports commentary shows like *Pardon the Interruption* and wildly popular America-gets-to-vote talent contests like *American Idol* and *So You Think You Can Dance?* If all of this seems terribly irreverent toward The Issues, it is not. For by exposing the stratagems of politicians and magnifying their successes and failures in facing The Issues, the commentariat pays deference to a discursive institution that nobody can seem to respect.

Got Issues?

Campaign websites do try to respect The Issues.[5] Back in October 2008, placed high on John McCain's presidential campaign website, third from the left on the top menu bar, was an [ISSUES] button that revealed a drop-down menu of nineteen links. Subtract the first ("On the Issues") and the last ("Decision Center"), and what remained was a list of McCain's Issue captions: "American Energy," "Economic Plan," "Iraq," "Health Care," "Education," "Climate Change," "National Service," "Homeland Security," "Border Security," "Human Dignity & Life," "Fighting Crime," "Second Amendment," "Veterans," "Judicial Philosophy," "Technology," "Government Reform," "National Security." At the same time, Barack Obama's [ISSUES] button was put in a similar spot—second from the left on the top menu bar. His drop-down menu yielded two columns of Issues, in alphabetical order.[6]

The Issues are enumerable. They can be counted and gathered into a list, but as a whole—as a set that is intersubjectively shared by publics and politicians alike—they are larger than their parts. Like the formidable wholeness and gravity of the world's literary canon, The Issues feel monolithic, but as with the storied canon debates that erupted in the 1980s, there is a whole politics surrounding the question of which Issues get included and excluded. McCain's "Second Amendment" Issue had no analogue in Obama's list of Issues, for instance, while Obama's "Katrina" Issue had no place in McCain's. More often tensions turn on how an Issue is named. Quite a few names for Issues from 2007–2008 could be calibrated across candidate websites ("Government Reform" [McCain] vs. "Cleansing Washington" [Obama]), but differences in Issue nomenclature reveal their shibbolethic nature (e.g., "American Energy" and "Climate Change" [McCain] vs. "Energy Independence & Global Warming" [Obama]). Differences in Issue rubrics can thus be subjected to a kind of membership analysis that discloses Message and permits one to infer the implied voters being courted (McCain's "Human Dignity & Life" = Pro-Life = "The Catholic Vote," among others). Issue captions are Message shibboleths.

And because they are shibboleths designed for an implied voter, presupposed or potential, it is no surprise that these rubrics and their rank order should be responsive to the mercurial dynamics of campaign Message. Their order may be shuffled and their names revised as a campaign unfolds, though Issue captions tend to be added or renamed, not dropped. (Dropping Issues would seem to be bad form, perhaps because potential voters are presumed to care about them, or because abrupt shifts in what candidates care about risk being seen as signs that one cares, deep down, about nothing at all—that one lacks 'conviction.') Hillary Clinton's site added "Reforming our Immigration System" on 8 January 2008, "Improving Our Schools" on 21 January, and "Creating Opportunity in Rural America" on 7 February. Faced with mounting gas prices in the summer of 2007 (this was a vital topic in the June 3 primary debate), Obama's site changed in June from "Energy Independence & Global Warming" to "Meeting Energy Needs," but then late in September 2007 this was changed to "Energy & Environment," just in time to anticipate Al Gore's receipt of the Nobel Peace Prize.

In the forensically oriented "debates," where candidates participate in what is at least supposed to be a zero-sum contest, candidates' positions on The Issues compete. In news media coverage of the debates, Issues and the positions adopted on them are obligatory topics of pre- and post-debate commentary, where they are teased out, compared, and summarized so that consumer-voters can make informed choices. In the 2008 race, for instance, dedicated "Issue trackers," like those of CNN.com, compared candidate positions on Issues from "Abortion" to "Israel" to "Taxes." Sober, putatively disinterested policy reports, like those of the Brookings Institute, compared the tax policies of McCain and Obama. For the past couple presidential campaigns, C-SPAN has supplied topic captions in its televised coverage of presidential (and many primary) debates, captions that remain on the screen as the candidates respond. Sometimes these are captions of the Issue being addressed, or else a direct report or paraphrase of the moderator's question.

Addressivity and the Implied Voter

The Issues circulate through media-scapes as shibbolethic design elements of campaign websites, as discourse topics in televised debates, as objects of coverage by news media and political talk shows, but what we consider below is the way commentators typify candidate behavior in the face of The Issues, this being an important way of constructing the candidates' brands. Akin to taboo objects, The Issues pose certain hazards for those who stand before them, although these hazards apply only to specific categories of social actor (candidates and incumbents), as with in-law avoidance, and they occur only under particular conditions. And, again as with in-law avoidance, the hazards politicians face are very much about addressivity, about who might hear and how these actual or potential (over)hearers will (dis)align with candidates by virtue of the candidates' behavior.

Addressivity, an utterance's "quality of being directed to someone," as Bakhtin (1986, 95) and later writers sweepingly put it, is central to what it means to take a position on an Issue. Addressivity can be polyadic, in the sense that it can involve many forms of directionality and need not mean a simple, dyadic, speaker-to-hearer vector. At minimum, though, addressivity involves a two-place relationship: some utterance in the here-and-now speech event is understood to be 'oriented' toward someone else (a constituency, a critic, a competing candidate), who may be physically there, copresent, or else located in a spatiotemporally distinct event (a past or future time, a near or distant place) as in cases of "interdiscursive" addressivity, address across speech events. While we concern ourselves here with the way the commentariat attributes addressivity to candidate behavior in post-debate coverage, the semiotic means and stratagems by which politicians themselves can invite such readings are many and varied. Addressivity can be conveyed by such familiar resources as pronouns and address terms (think of the diagrammatic chain of role designators, proper names, and titles from the outset of a State of the Union Address, like Bush's from 2002: "Mr. Speaker, Vice President Cheney, members of Congress, distinguished guests, fellow citizens . . ."). More often addressivity is communicated tacitly. In the poetics of stance, for example, cross-turn parallelism (e.g., I don't like those: I don't either [Du Bois 2007]; see chapter 5) can invite us to think that the second stance is oriented to the first because it is felt to resemble it. Gaze direction and bodily orientation are familiar means for selecting addressees and establishing vectors of address, as are pointing gestures.

When it comes to expert readings of candidate behavior, addressivity is less about the way politicians communicate their orientations toward copresent people and groups (compare with the interactionist and conversation-analytic notions of "recipient" and "audience design"), and more about looming "superaddressees," Bakhtin's (1986, 126) term for virtual participants who may never be explicitly addressed but are assumed to be there, who haunt the interaction like a diffuse, abstract overhearing "public," or a "collective consumer witnessing our wants and choices" (Warner 1993, 242), or, indeed, a constituency. Akin to the "implied reader" (Iser 1974) of response theory in literary criticism, we may speak of an "implied voter," a superaddressee whom Message mavens recover through critical readings of candidate text.

In our electoral politics these preoccupations with addressivity are part of a politics of recognition (Taylor 1994), where identities, like demographic categories of identity such as age, sex, class, and religion, deserve and hence vie for equal recognition in the self-consciously multicultural nation-state. Political communication requires "recognizing" and thereby establishing co-membership with some segment of this diversity at the exclusion of others. At a second order of interpretation, regularities of address serve as a sanctioned criterion for distinguishing politicians in the relational field of candidates. Normatively at least, a candidate's recognition of (and hence alignment to) constituencies is diagrammed by his or her position on The Issues, so that Issue watching offers clues as to who the candidate is really "for."

If, like the commentariat, one is attuned to the field of candidates, and if one assumes that when politicians speak they are engaged in differential address to implied voters—reaching some at the expense of others—then the mere presence of an Issue can make candidate behavior highly "indexically entailing."[7] Indexical entailment is simply the way an "index"—a sign (verbal or nonverbal) that points to or indicates some feature of context (smoke to fire, the pronoun "I" to speaker)—does not just passively presuppose the contextual feature, as if that feature were already there before the index; rather, the index helps bring that feature into being. Before that indexical sign occurred, that feature of context was dormant, unnoticed in the background or simply nonexistent. When The Issues are trotted out, a heightened "absorptive aura" (see below) of indexical entailment often gathers around them, an aura that supercharges behavior in the vicinity. Especially in the forensic contexts of the debates, Issues can make us expect that a candidate must be trying to inhabit a position. The Issues can incite a kind of paranoia, a hermeneutics of suspicion, that would have us think that everything in their orbit should be scrutinized for motive and machination—for Message.

What matters is not only "where one stands" (with respect to an Issue) and by implication "for whom one stands" (with respect to an implied voter who cares about an Issue), but also how one orients to both. This *how*, a candidate's manners and bearing before The Issues, in speech and bodily comportment, is constructed by commentators through the aid of quick audiovisual replays and splicings that juxtapose things the candidate said, inciting evaluation and, of course, expert commentary.

Irrespective of a candidate's own manner of engaging an Issue, or even The Issues tout court, there are certain infelicities that all should avoid. There are manners to be minded. There is an etiquette here, though not one that has been written up in any manual of political conduct. On 11 January 2008, for instance, Reuters correspondent Jeff Mason (2008) reports, "Republican presidential rivals John McCain and Romney dueled over economics on Friday." Neither, it would seem, was forthcoming about his plans: "They offered few specifics and focused their attention on the economic situation in Michigan and South Carolina, which hold the next state contests to nominate party candidates for the November election." For Mason, weak information flow ("offered few specifics") reveals the candidates' long-ranged, prospective addressivity. Obscurity before this Issue bespeaks a strategic orientation toward (or "recognition" of) segments of the electorate being courted. Mason reads candidate's stance- and position-taking behavior as addressivity. While he does not go on to typify McCain and Romney as social types by virtue of their addressivity, many forms of commentary do just this. To addressers they attach such incendiary descriptors as "flip-flopping," "pandering," "poll watching," "Issue dodging," opposed to which is a parallel set of positive captions that includes "conviction" and "straight talk." Together, these morally weighted names for good and bad modes of stance- and position-taking—that is, good and bad ways of behaving before The Issues and before the publics who care about them—seem to presuppose a normative figure of the politician, a cardinal, moral dimension of which is authenticity.

Driver's Licenses for Undocumented Migrants?

It is 30 October 2007. In a Democratic primary debate in Philadelphia (*New York Times* 2007),[8] co-moderator Tim Russert cites something front-runner Hillary Clinton recently said to New Hampshire's *Nashua Telegraph:*

> Senator Clinton, Governor of New York Eliot Spitzer has proposed giving driver's licenses to illegal immigrants. You told the Nashua, New Hampshire, Editorial Board it makes a lot of sense. Why does it make a lot of sense to give an illegal immigrant a driver's license?

(Clinton's response to *Telegraph* columnist Eduardo de Oliveria's question of whether she'd support Governor Spitzer's approach wasn't so simple. She was charitable toward Spitzer ["I—I know exactly what Governor Spitzer is trying to do. And it makes a lot of sense, because he's trying to get people out of the shadows . . ."], but warned that "this *can't* work state by state," that immigration "*has* to be looked at comprehensively," and that undocumented immigrants would have "an earned path to legalization" [emphasis mine].[9] For Clinton, Spitzer's proposal makes sense in the absence of a sorely needed federal plan and hence would be imperfect and provisional. She does not simply endorse it. This subtlety was lost on or elided by Russert.)

Just as she did in New Hampshire, Clinton says she understands Spitzer's predicament. Sen. Chris Dodd takes up her sympathy as a tacit endorsement. Chipping in, Clinton rights the record: "I just want to add, I did not say that it should be done, but I certainly recognize why Governor Spitzer is trying to do it." This just roils the waters more, especially given her juxtaposition of epistemic adverb plus verb of cognition ("I certainly recognize") with a strictly negative claim about what she had said ("I did not say that it should be done"), both posing as qualifications (as stipulated by "I just want to add"). Given the blend of delicacy and certainty, surely she must know what she *did* say.

"Wait a minute," snaps Dodd. "No, no, no. You said yes, you thought it made sense to do it." John Edwards and Barack Obama, smelling blood, we presume, join the fray and charge that she is being unclear and dodgy and even self-contradictory—evidence of what, earlier in the debate, they had started to construct as the slick, conviction-less Washington insider, a negative inflection of precisely the branded attribute she had been claiming for herself: Experience.

So what *did* she say?

> RUSSERT: Senator Clinton, I just want to make sure what I heard. Do you, the New York Senator Hillary Clinton, support the New York governor's plan to give illegal immigrants a driver's license? You told the Nashua, New Hampshire, paper it made a lot of sense.

Reasserting himself under the guise of a mediator just wanting clarification, Russert administers a performative on Clinton, swearing her in, as it were: "Do you (hereby) support *p*," with hyperbolically precise person reference, complete with determiner the, state name and role designator (New York Senator), narrowing the indexical focus upon her to the point that no escape is possible—and implying a wish to wriggle free. With several debaters arrayed against her and abetted by Russert, Clinton looks like someone who isn't eager or able to stake out a position on this issue at all.

Which is just how Joe Trippi, senior strategist for the Edwards campaign, frames the matter in post-debate coverage on the political talk show *Hardball* (MSNBC 2007a).

> MATTHEWS: The case you made at the very end, on the issue of driver's licenses in New York State for illegal immigrants, for people in the country illegally, giving driver's licenses, Hillary Clinton seemed to be saying that's an OK idea with her. And then your candidate John Edwards said in the space of a minute she gave two different positions. What are those two positions? Explain the double-talk.
> TRIPPI: Well, I'm still confused, too. I mean—and Obama was confused. I mean, this wasn't just Senator Edwards, that you could not tell where she really was. And by the way, it's clear to me that she'll change her position again on this one within the next week. Probably by tomorrow when her consultants . . .
> MATTHEWS: . . . supporting a driver's license for illegal immigrants by tomorrow? Do you think she's going to dump that position?
> TRIPPI: It depends whether she's in primary mode or general election mode, and I don't think . . .
> MATTHEWS: If she's in a general election mode, where will she go?
> TRIPPI: I think it's going to change.

Trippi says that Clinton's positions depend on whether she is in "primary mode or general election mode"—a matter of who is being addressed and hence addressivity—and he predicts that her position on this is-sue will change yet again once her consultants get hold of her. Trippi is not fastidious about distinguishing types of infelicity ('obscurity,' 'in-consistency'), but lumps them together and fashions them into a form that begins to resemble the figure of the flip-flopper. "Flip-flopper," that derisive epithet for a politician who is "pandering, poll watching or aban-doning long-held views for short-term political gain" (Schulman 2007), is never mentioned by Trippi, but it is this label—and a host of related ones—that is soon pinned to Clinton by antagonists and members of the commentariat, and which subsequently enjoyed tremendous play in the whole 2007–2008 season. Clinton's manner of facing an issue is read as addressivity, and this addressivity betrays attributes of the speaker: a lack of conviction.

It is 31 January 2008. Less than a week before Super Tuesday, when a mass of primary elections had the potential to settle who the Democratic candidate would be, a CNN-sponsored debate was held in Hollywood, California (CNN 2008d). The field of candidates had been narrowed to two: Clinton and Obama.[10] Obama fields a question on the topic of immi-gration, then co-moderator Doyle McManus turns to Clinton: "Senator Clinton, Senator Obama has said that he favors allowing illegal immi-grants to obtain driver's licenses, and you oppose that idea. Why?" Only at the close of her substantial three-and-a-quarter-minute response does Clinton mention the topic of driver's licenses for undocumented immi-grants, and even then she offers no baldly stated position. Co-moderator Wolf Blitzer circles back to settle the matter: "Very quickly, Senator, why not, then, if you're that passionate about it, let them get driver's licenses?" Clinton's reply:

> Well, we disagree on this. I do not think that it is either appropriate to give a driver's license to someone who is here undocumented, putting them, frankly, at risk, because that is clear evidence that they are not here legally, and I believe it is a diversion from what should be the focus at creating a political coalition with the courage to stand up and change the immigration system.

In some post-debate coverage, the distance Clinton put between herself and this Issue was taken up as "avoidance," as an instance of dodging an Issue. And the fact that she eventually staked out a clear position against issuing driver's licenses to undocumented immigrants in response to Blitzer registered to many as a flip-flop. Both are read in terms of addressivity and linked to characterological attributes of the speaker. The following exchange with MSNBC political analyst Craig Crawford took place in coverage of the debate on MSNBC's *Live with Dan Abrams* (MSNBC 2008b):[11]

> CRAWFORD: This is where you saw Obama really playing to the California primary here because he's taking a risk. I mean one reason I think he's feeling less confident than Hillary about Super Tuesday. He took more risks tonight and this is a big one. He signed up for this driver's license program for illegals. He even talked about putting Ted—with Ted Kennedy on immigration reform. Both are efforts to appeal to Latin American voters in California—Latinos, because Hillary has had a lead there. If you take that lead of hers among those Hispanics out of the equation in California, it's a dead heat in California. That's what the whole game is in California. Interestingly, she didn't take the bait. She backed off of that driver's license program, and took, if anything, a more conservative stand and told me she's feeling confident about that vote.
>
> ABRAMS: She tried to avoid answering the question first about driver's—
>
> CRAWFORD: Which is the best thing for Democrats to do, by the way.
>
> ABRAMS: And you know what's interesting, Peter, is they both seemed to recognize—and I was surprised that Obama didn't go in for the kill. I mean Hillary Clinton has clearly changed her position on this. And Obama mentioned it, but he almost seemed like he wanted to put his hand on hers to say, "We don't want to go there. We don't want to go down this road."

Avoidance is read as addressivity, just as Obama's Issue engagement was, the focal constituency with Obama being Latino voters in California, alleges Crawford.

A Question of Principal

We cite these moments from the 2007–2008 primary election cycle to illustrate how perceived infelicities before an Issue, whether judged strategic (Clinton's 31 January 2008 performance) or chalked up to a bad performance (30 October 2007), are read in terms of addressivity and taken to index morally weighted attributes of the speaker. All kinds of dysfluencies and infelicities can be cited as breaches of etiquette, such as false starts and long pauses, odd or brusque topic shifts, dense or overly delicate qualification of propositional content, and of course inter-propositional 'inconsistency' on Issues, which is said to be a canonical symptom of the flip-flop. This is not to say that one can list off objective criteria for each offense as if there were some neat, mechanical rule of law for debate behavior. Most offenses are never registered or are brushed aside, suggesting that additional factors make dysfluencies and infelicities actionable in post-debate commentary. We expose here simply the existence of a relational etiquette imposed on candidates in the presence of The Issues. This etiquette, invoked by the commentariat and campaign antagonists, has moral dimensionalities that involve a sublime of authenticity.

This sublime surely has something to do with the increased cultural salience of the political marketing industry and its commoditization of authenticity. It is hard to overstate just how strident and widespread talk of conviction and flip-flopping has become in electoral politics of late. In the weeks following Clinton's fateful Philadelphia debate in late October 2007, for instance, the charges of flip-flopping increased. The charge was fired among Republican candidates with equal brio, with front-runners Mitt Romney and John McCain repeatedly tagging each other. As testimony to flip-flop's currency, in August 2008 the well-trafficked PolitiFact .com introduced a "Flip-O-Meter" (akin to its earlier Truth-O-Meter), which ranks candidate behavior on issues as "No Flip," "Half Flip," "Full Flop."[12] (Apparently, degrees of flip-flopping now exist, permitting consumer-voters to make finer distinctions.)

As evidenced in Michael Graham's (2007) *Boston Herald* editorial on Clinton's alleged flip-flopping, much of this talk of conviction and flip-flopping, at least from the 2007–2008 campaign cycle, retained an interdiscursive tie to Democratic candidate John Kerry in the 2004 presidential race against incumbent George W. Bush. In that contest flip-flopping was the centerpiece of Bush's characterological argument against Kerry. "How can John Kerry protect us . . . when he doesn't even know where he stands?" So went a Republican campaign attack ad that ran just before the first presidential debate.

In terms of the zero-point, or origo, from which the addresser speaks, flip-flopping typifies allocentric rather than egocentric address. The address originates not from the speaker but from the perspective of some other agent, but to which alter is addressivity transposed? Who speaks to

Issues and to constituents if not the candidate? Professional consultants, perhaps, as Joe Trippi suggested?

Indeed, "flip-flopper," as a derisive epithet for a politician, often speaks to the presence of and suspicion toward political marketing, which has both expanded dramatically as an industry in recent decades and has increased in cultural visibility. Flip-flopping does not describe merely a change of position, but a change often attributed to "pandering" and "poll watching" and, more generally, to subordination to professional strategists. Anti-marketing, anti-brand Message has been on the rise,[13] as attested partly by the fact that charges of inauthenticity and claims to authenticity have become both widespread and strident, contributing to a kind of "histrionic realism" (see chapter 5). How can we forget the garish legibility of the words "Straight Talk Express" blazoned across the side of John McCain's deep blue, star-spangled campaign bus? Or McCain's drumming on his "maverick" sobriquet, reminding Americans that he's bucked his own party (even if the real Mavericks, whose nineteenth-century Texan ancestor refused to brand his cattle and launched the eponym, took offense: "He's [McCain] a Republican . . . He's branded" [Schwartz 2008]). Or Sarah Palin, McCain's vice presidential pick, whose strenuous efforts to be Maverick-y and reinforce McCain's anti-brand brand were mercilessly lampooned by Tina Fey on the late-night television comedy show *Saturday Night Live.*

Irrespective of which constituencies they embrace or eschew, there is a relational etiquette all candidates should respect. This etiquette, which demands deference for The Issues and requires that candidates face them with clarity and conviction, helps explain how commentators can move so fluidly from behavior before The Issues, to addressivity, to morally weighted images of people—that is, how signs of addressivity can trigger readings of candidate character and brand. As "faced" or "avoided" in venues like televised debates, The Issues become in effect ritual sites for authenticating candidates, for verifying whether they are still real.

The suspicion that comes from all of this scrutiny is, of course, that none of the candidates is real. As commentators narrate the strategies of competing political campaigns, candidates tend to be characterized as animators of polled and tested positions on Issues (animators, in the sense of physical bearers of an utterance, as Goffman [1974, 1979] classically put it); their positions are authored by their consultants and advisers. And the real question is whether the candidates can remain the "principal" of what they say, "principal" being Goffman's (1981, 144) term for "someone who is committed to what the words say." The term captions the way speakers can orient toward an utterance in a way that expresses their 'commitment' toward it. Just as the people, the electorate, are understood by default to care about Issues, so candidates should reciprocally be 'care'-full, committed. Candidates are real to the extent that they maintain their reciprocal, bilateral 'commitment' to this discursive institution of The Issues.

Unlike proscriptive regimes that demand strict avoidance (obscenity bans, blasphemy avoidance), candidates are often eager to invite readings of their behavior as branded styles of address, and this may seem quite apart from canonical cases of verbal taboo. To be sure, candidates "*have* issues," too, which should be avoided. Each has a longer list of candidate-relative unmentionables that the opposition strategists they hire (firms that research vulnerabilities in candidates) must identify so that candidates know what not to say. For example, it is unwise for Hillary Clinton to bring up NAFTA on the campaign trail in Michigan (the North America Fair Trade Agreement, passed by President Bill Clinton, which many fault for having gutted industry in the state). And it was downright perilous for her to have brought up the topic of assassination with Obama as the front-runner as she was accused of doing in late May 2008. (Asked to explain why she remained in the race so late, even though she trailed Obama and had little chance of winning, she noted, among other things, the demise of Robert Kennedy late in the 1968 campaign. Her point presumably was that unexpected things can happen.)[14] Obama's middle name, Hussein, was a notorious unmentionable for him during the campaign, too. And so on.

But what makes behavior before The Issues akin to "taboo" phenomena like in-law avoidance is not just that the commentariat polices such behavior in terms of a morally inflected relational etiquette, but that this feverish scrutiny creates an aura of "indexical entailment" around this category of discourse topic.

Consider the peculiar qualities of this aura. A long literature on indexicality has shown how linguistic forms can indicate or pick out features of context, forms like deictic expressions—pronouns such as I and you, tense marking, the demonstratives this and that—whose capacity to point to their surround has been studied most often in sentence-size units. However, as Asif Agha (2007) has painstakingly shown, many forms of "social indexicality" (e.g., the expression of 'deference' and 'politeness') are not the result of a singular signs but rather configurations of signs, what Agha captions as "text-level indexicality." In such cases, the indexical interpretation is not triggered by a few key words but by cross-modal arrays of signs. In the cases described here, we may be tempted to view the indexical readings of 'addressivity' (the way a candidate's utterance is understood to be 'to' and 'for' certain publics and constituencies) as akin to text-level indexicality in discourse, but this would be misleading. A typical case of deference indexicality, for instance, may involve some combination of lexicogrammatical resources (in languages like Tibetan, Japanese, and Korean, for instance), gesture, prosody, sequential order, facts of role inhabitance, and so forth, yielding effects that are gradiently felt as 'deference.' Yet the indexicality of address around The Issues is unlike such cases of text-level indexicality in an important sense: the indexical focus of candidate addressivity is *never* settled in situ through co-occurring signs. It is necessarily an unfinished text to be completed by the social actors who are licensed to finish it, the commentariat.

In this respect, "absorptive" deictic expressions spring to mind. Unlike indexically "focused" deictic expressions (speaker- or addressee-focal expressions like first- and second-person pronouns I and you, which always index specific participant roles, 'speaker' and 'addressee' respectively), absorptive expressions are unspecified for focus. They point, but the forms themselves don't tell us where. In the case of Issue addressivity, what is entailed is merely *that* some focus, some determinate addressee(s), exists, but this addressivity must be worked out—unveiled, really, for it is deep—through hermeneutic labor that the commentariat carries out. There is thus a kind of socially distributed, multiparty interpretive labor required to make sense of candidate addressivity, since the commentariat stands between politician and public in an effort to help consumer-voters decide.

In forensic spectacles like the primary and presidential debates, an intensely absorptive aura of indexical entailment surrounds this institutionalized category of discourse topic. Like iron fillings dragged toward a magnet, nearly any bit of behavior can be adduced as evidence of who the candidate is "really" speaking to and for. In brief, information about who-said-what-to-whom is left blank and filled in by the commentariat in post-event reportage. As guardians of public virtue who ensure that The Issues still matter, it is their self-declared Relevance (Sperber and Wilson 1995) that fashions authoritative interactional texts from candidate behavior, no matter how fragmentary, trivial, or accidental this behavior may seem to noninitiates.

Four

ETHNO-BLOOPEROLOGY

On Tuesday morning, the twenty-third of October 2007, former Massachusetts governor Mitt Romney seemed to some to have done it. Talking to the Greenwood, South Carolina, chamber of commerce on free trade agreements, he digressed to focus on the threat of radical Islam and the "War on Terror." He sharply criticized the opposition of the local Democratic aspirant for the presidential nomination, former senator John Edwards, to Bush administration policies captioned by the phrase <u>the War on Terror</u>. "I think that is a position which is not consistent with the fact," Romney said, presumably intending either "with the facts" or just "with fact." Grammatical error. Slip of the old phrase generator. A minor—a miniscule—dysfluency of *parole,* actualized language. But Romney went on, as long as he was criticizing Senator Edwards, seeming to spread the partisan criticism wider:

> Actually, just look at what Osam—uh—Barack Obama, said just yesterday. Barack Obama calling on radicals, jihadists of all different types, to come together in Iraq. "That is the battlefield. That is the central place," he said. "Come join us under one banner."

Reporters scrambled in vain to find the incendiary quote by then Senator Obama. Whoops! It was actually an *Osama* quote, a summary of Osama bin Laden's call to arms in his then most recently released audiotape.

By midday on Tuesday a report by *New York Times* campaign blogger Michael Luo (2007) had stirred up a hornets' nest: hundreds of angry comments that veered among three positions. The first interpretation is that Romney had made an innocent stumble, presumably stimulated by the most happenstance fact that two somewhat unusual, foreign names rhyme, and one can stumble over the single consonant sound, -*s*- versus -*b*-, that distinguishes them, even though one occurs in a given name, the other in a surname. Early morning speech; Mormons can't drink caffeine to wake up their sleepy brains; innocent confusion that could happen to anyone. (One wag responded to Mr. Luo's report with "Banana-fanna-bo-'bama" we should point out, as if to emphasize the triviality of the incident.) This agrees with Governor Romney's spokesperson's account given to reporters, that "Governor Romney simply misspoke . . . [when] referring to the recently released audiotape of Osama bin Laden. . . . It was just a brief mix-up."

Recurrently posted, however, by anti-Romneyites among these first responders to the verbal disaster was a second interpretation: this must show that Governor Romney cannot keep the concepts of 'Osama bin Laden' and 'Barack Obama' distinct, bespeaking a lack of intelligence so profound as to disqualify him from the presidency of the United States. Tongue in cheek, dripping with sarcasm or not, many commenters responded straightforwardly to this interpretation with a defense, pointing to the governor's not single but double degrees from Harvard—in law and in business administration—and to his previous successes in business and public service as countervailing evidence to inferences of any intelligence deficit.

So if he is not a phonetic doofus and he is not a conceptual moron, there remains a third, very angrily asserted interpretative response. This "misspeaking" was actually a deliberate, if not scripted, attempt by Governor Romney to make explicit the suggestion of similarity between then Senator Obama and the elusive radical fugitive from 11 September—a Joe McCarthyesque smear-by-association in the form of a lame, poorly performed pseudo-gaffe.[1] Several of these commenters—none identifiable as linguistic colleagues in our Rolodexes, by the way—pointed out the unlikelihood of Romney's having merely stumbled over the two rhyming words in just this way. Intending to say "Osama bin Laden," presumably, the governor got out the first two syllables and then choked off the third syllable, hesitating, before starting again, *not* with the other rhyming word, <u>Obama</u>, as one might expect in a purely form-based dysfluency, but with the whole name of the then junior senator from Illinois, "Barack Obama." Continuing on, the governor came to the end of a sentence, and then *repeated* the full, incorrect name once more. No, such observers concluded: this was no flub; it was a somewhat flubbed performance of a "flub," the very flubbing of which gives it away as otherwise deliberate and intended. Courtesy of his handlers and script writers, Mitt Romney was channeling the late Lee Atwater ventriloquated by Karl Rove. Nasty work. "Not nice!" as Midnight the Cat used to intone in falsetto on the *Buster Brown Show.*

So, to use that hip new political term, who's "sliming" whom? Did he or didn't he, and does anyone other than Ronald Reagan's hairdresser know for sure? Doofus, moron, or lowlife (i.e., Gerald Ford, Dubya, or Joe McCarthy), the reactive comments variously proposed: what does this incident tell us about Governor Romney? More importantly, what does this incident and the various ways it is observed, reported on, commented upon, and interpreted tell us about our culture of political communication, in which every slip may be understood to range from the Freudian to the Machiavellian?

Immediately on Thursday the twenty-fifth, just two days later, the newly self-styled "progressive, independent conscience of the city" of Chicago, the *Sun-Times,* editorially opined (2007, 33) on the gaffe with the moron interpretation, it would seem. They tut-tutted away the views of the "conspiracists," those who would see Governor Romney in the slime mold, who "might say Romney deliberately tried to denigrate Obama by [verbally] confusing him with Osama." Instead, they warn, the gaffe

> doesn't speak well of his command of what's happening in the world. And if he's capable of the Obama-Osama slip, how's he going to fare with all the foreign names he'll be expected to get right if he's elected president?
>
> More such miffs from Mitt may be a clue that he's not ready for the big time.

Indeed, in specifically mentioning "foreign names" perhaps the *Sun-Times* editorial board members were still thinking about the hilarious Reuters report (Spetalnick 2007) of 26 September 2007 on the mistaken release of President Bush's actual teleprompter text for his General Assembly address at the United Nations on the previous day. Apparently, Dubya has a heck of a time copin' "with all the foreign names he [was] expected to get right," so the desperate underlings in the West Wing came up with solutions like these that were, embarrassingly, released to the whole General Assembly staff and thence to Reuters:

> [Nicolas] "Sarkozy (sar-KO-zee)"
> [Robert] "Mugabe (moo-GAH-bee)"
> "Kyrgyzstan (KEYR-geez-stan)"
> "Mauritania (moor-EH-tain-ee-a)" [!]
> "Harare (hah-RAR-ray)"

So the president's text comes not with a radio receiver strapped to his back, as was suspected in the televised debates with Senator Kerry in 2004, but with a kind of cheat sheet written in mock phonetics—the kind you give to little kids who cannot be expected to be able to master actual phonetic symbols, let alone just to learn the words they are reading. One gathers that the *Sun-Times* pundits must have figured that two such morons in a row might be dangerous to the country.

Slips of the Tongue: Freudian or Machiavellian?

Governor Romney's gaffe is one of the moments we all love to savor in the spectator sport of an increasingly media-saturated and essentially mediatized American presidential politics: the delicious moment that seems, at least on its face, to have been a misfire or gaffe committed before an audience. When such a moment is recorded in sound and image and disseminated widely and repeatedly by opposing forces dogging one's every syllable, it always circulates along with, and is framed by, evaluative and interpretative commentary, frequently highly partisan. (For example, note that the *Sun-Times* editorial clearly was in defense of the hometown favorite son, Senator Osama—oops, Obama.) This process of mediatized rumination—not, of course, disinterested in nature, one should point out—transforms it from having been merely a "blooper," a term in early broadcast circles (see the appendix at the end of this chapter) for an inadvertent, generally humorous mishap of performance caught in recording as an actor slips, metaphorically, on a banana peel not written into the script. In the best possible case, the mishap can be easily deleted in the edited broadcast version.

In the dialectic of replay and reframing, something in the candidate's recorded performance—whether an obvious "blooper" at the time or, especially, a not-so-obvious one rendered one by opposition bloopermongers—is frequently turned into what we term an indexical of something deeper, an inwardly pointing sign that is revelatory of personality, character, or identity, and thus a diagnostic bit of "truth" that has emerged to public view despite all precautions taken. It thus becomes a negatively valuated symptom of a candidate's negatives in our regime of Message politics. In our post-Freudian universe, recall, a cigar is never just a cigar, nor even a kiss just a kiss, and certainly in our age of total recordability and instant replay no slip-up necessarily winds up on the cutting-room floor of the political process. Under this interpretation, it's like a celebrity *Candid Camera,* in that the bloopering candidate inadvertently reveals something behind or underneath—choose the metaphor—the carefully crafted façade of performance, in which a self, an identity, a biography is performatively achieved for the electorate and broader addressees. And this, both from undisposed-of raw footage and from *Saturday Night Live* caricatures gone viral on YouTube. (The late Gerald Ford tripping while exiting *Air Force One*—the "rube" descending the staircase, as it were—was mercilessly exposed in both media.)

In what we have termed the Machiavellian interpretation of the blooper, it tends to be evaluated as an intentional performance of the unperformable or unmentionable that powerfully ratifies something positive about oneself, something redeeming of an otherwise invisible human quality, or, by contrast, something negative about a political opponent, something that is "in the air" of public opinion, at least in some quarters. A blooper is useful, the Machiavellian sees, since it can communicate someone's affiliation with the otherwise unperformable or unmentionable, one's alignment with particular controversial or negatively valued political perspectives or interests, all the while providing the cover of what has come to be termed in the political field "plausible deniability." Why, in this interpretation Governor Romney merely got caught up in these like-sounding and very exotic—and perhaps (wink, wink), as everyone knows, un-American—names, that's all! The Machiavellian blooper is thus only a blooper when it is rhetorically successful and needs the cover of respectability.[2]

Examples from recent and current presidential political campaigns offer us glimpses into the secret—or, much more to the point, not so secret—life of bloopers. And what we find is quite revealing about political communication, because our entire process of electoral politics operates, as we see it, through the communication of a political figure's Message, a concept that is centrally relevant to understanding the interpretative frames that our American political culture relies upon and continually reproduces. To be sure, electoral politics is not all of politics by any means. In fact, to judge by participation rates of eligible voters, electoral politics may be a decreasingly central realm of how politics is understood to operate in this country, as elsewhere—perhaps an example of the Chicago School econometric model of voter participation costs and citizens' understanding of their resulting benefits in a market. But electoral politics commands our attention as scholars interested in the anthropology of communication in the public sphere.

In this light the study of ethno-blooperology, the data for which being the natives' own interpretative views of blunders, allows us to understand the risks to would-be candidates for office when their bloopers or gaffes, we might say *faults of performance,* are subject to transformation into *performances of faultiness* of one kind or another, one's own endearing humanity or an opponent's off-putting monstrousness. Why should this be happening? What sociocultural framework of institutionalized political communication renders possible this transformability of faults of performance into performances of faultiness? And why should this process of transformation be so potent in bringing highfliers down?

Semiotics and the History of Our Brand of Politics

To understand the potency of this transformability, we must examine political communication through the lens of Message. Message, as we have noted, turns out to be the kind of social fact that can be studied in the field of semiotics, the systematic study of the meanings both explicit and implicit in events of communication, and the norms underlying them. For example, at first you might differentiate political personae on the one hand and consumer goods and services on the other. But as we look systematically at how things work in American politics, we can see that in our own day, a would-be candidate's Message is being professionally shaped as an analogue to a product's brand, regardless of how Message may have been shaped in an earlier period.

For the usual consumerist commodities, let us remind ourselves, brand is, as the professionals say, "value added" to the mere physical, psycho-physical, or other "stuff" or "service" being offered us that packaging, advertising, and distribution professionals try to shape by all kinds of semiotic design. Brand, let us recall, is not a physical, psychophysical (perceptual), or other concrete fact about products circulating as com-modities on the franker markets of consumerism. Brand is that abstract yet organized set of meaning-images that implicitly surrounds the prod-uct or service because of associations that can be stimulated by shape, size, color, packaging and its design, advertising images, and so forth. This structured "story" of a product or service is centrally affective in its workings as a cultural fact, perhaps the best referent in the contemporary world for what the literary critic Raymond Williams (1977, 128–35; Wil-liams and Orrom 1954, 21–22; cf. Filmer 2003) gestured toward in modern culture with the pregnant phrase "structures of feeling." Brand implies potential stories, the most important being how people, as potential and actual consumers, reactively project cultural values onto the commod-ity so as to organize their narratable relationship of use, or avoidance, of that commodity. How does this happen? By shaping and contextual-izing the product or service in a complex of signs designed to induce that potential story, eventually automatically, once one sees or thinks of the product or service, let alone the suggestive advertising text about it.

Such matters are endlessly thought about in the way of shaping "brand" semiotics in the micro-context of packaging, product placement, and so on, and even more spectacularly as macro-contextualizations of a product in coordinated branding rollout campaigns and other multi-mediatized, mass-marketing designs.[3]

The same is true for a political campaign, at the center of which is a candidate and potential officeholder. A political figure's Message, just like brand, is dynamic and differential, always changing in relation to its field of competition, yet at any moment it is a structure of potential associations—biographically imagined ascriptions of outlook, attitude, character—with a degree of coherence. Good professionals seek to transform or change brand/Message by stimulating new construals of the product/ candidate that reconstruct it/him. A political figure's Message is the implicit story that makes sense of how he or she appears to his or her public and especially appeals to his or her adoring, resonating base of the affectively committed. These days, knowing that all such public appearances are matters of product design, we pay attention to what bloopers then reveal to us, who are so culturally conditioned to think in terms of an "inner self" deep down in others as well as within ourselves—you know, the one screaming to get out on the psychoanalyst's couch, or the one we fear will emerge when we let our guard down. Gaffes, or what can be turned into gaffes after the fact, become lenses that sharpen the incompatibilities and incoherences of "the real stuff" in the raw material, the inner person who, through Message, is seeking our understanding—and our vote.

Those who are old enough will remember when pop-semioticians-cum-political-scientists like the reporter Joe McGinniss were able to shock the general public in 1969 with the comparison of Mr. Nixon to a branded political product available for full-press marketing techniques. His *Selling of the President, 1968* was pointedly counterposed to William H. White's *Making of the President* series of books about the JFK and LBJ campaigns of 1960 and 1964, as we noted in chapter 2 (see note 4). But it turns out that Mr. Nixon's brand-like packaging was not the first attempt to use the paraphernalia of marketable commodity "branding" as a way of putting a candidate "on message"; neither is the phenomenon of having a Message in this sense solely a function of the existence of advertising as an industrial-strength applied semiotics of the presidency. Each era's modes of getting "on message" and staying there, or not, use then current semiotic means. That is why Mr. Lincoln was "on message," as pointed out in *Talking Politics* (Silverstein 2003a), no less than Mr. Bush the Younger, even without a Batten, Barton, Durstine & Osborn or J. Walter Thompson agency shaping Civil War–era communication. It is Message that gives significance and reveals the cultural meanings of bloopers on the electoral campaign trail. Recent blooperological data emphasize this for us.

Wanting—and Then Getting a (Blooped)— Message: Howard Dean

Can anyone remember back to early November 2003, when poor Dr. Dean began to succumb to foot-in-mouth attacks from which he ultimately could not recover? He was once and for a long time the so-called front-runner in the pack of Democratic wannabe candidates by a number of measures: enthusiastic volunteers; money in the campaign account; buzz with younger, savvy voters; running a breakthrough start-up Internet campaign that would make now Nobel Laureate Al Gore-Dot-Com proud (as "the inventor of the Internet"—talk about gaffes successfully alleged!); and more. When one achieves such a position in a crowded field, it demands that one move decisively and carefully into the realm of Message, for which, of course, the taking of positions on issues as such is not at all itself what matters.

What *does* matter? What mattered then to Dr. Dean's—or to any candidate's—Message is the way one manages and controls—that is, dominates—the unpleasantness that is created in such situations of agonism, as primary competitions and general elections are set up to be. Primaries are increasingly vicious competitions not so much resting on claims about what is true and false, and candidates' positions on issues, as about whose emblems of identity will be used to wrap around each of the *agonistoi*, the competitors, as the process moves forward to something like or in the image of a presidential election. Emblems of identity are potent signs of who and what one is; they are, let us recall, relational in nature (hence, differentiating characters), and such emblems position people they identify in a structural space of positionalities that defines them publicly as personalities.

So what kind of "stuff" is Dr. Dean—that is, was Dr. Dean's campaign, as a Message-manufacturing enterprise—made of? How could he handle the outburst of a controversy so that it could be read as a Message-defining moment, one that began to afford the public some understanding of who—that is, in identity terms, what—he is? Remember, his whole campaign style was not merely a claim of insurgency—"Hey! I'm not a fed; I'm a governor of an idyllic little state!" (To be sure, Vermont is the idyllic ski resort for the hip and young of the metropolitan northeast, such as, perhaps, Senator Kerry's kin.) His whole campaign was stylistically insurgent, challenging the establishment: "Screw the party hierarchies; I'm taking this to the Clean-for-Dean Deanihackers of the Internet Generation 4.01 Beta!" There were to be no matching federal funds, and a very thin line barely maintained between the Dean campaign and MoveOn .org. The very style of Dean's campaign communicated generational difference as well as class difference; for the Left-leaning young and those older Left-overs who were young at heart, a kind of college or graduate-school practicum about issue politics (but not quite the Naderite cuckoo fringe). But it was not the issues themselves so much as Dean's style of insurgency that not only got the civilian public's attention but also stuck in the craw of the professionals: enthusiasm at the bottom of organized politics is important, even essential (as what is denoted by the phrase "one's 'base'" for the die-hard enthusiasts); enthusiasm at the top is intolerable and bespeaks not being one of us, dear, after all.

Hence, Dr. Dean's opponents' staffs, the press mavens, and of course the party professionals of both RNC and DNC were waiting in autumn 2003 as the primaries drew near. Everyone jumped all over the catchy phrase Governor Dean thought he had been strategically—and ingenuously—repeating among his committed adherents to describe the toughest "sell" for the Democrats in the upcoming national elections of 2004: "guys [repeated as 'rednecks' or 'crackers'] with Confederate flags [elaborated with 'and rifles'] on their pick-up trucks." The rather more professional, Message-centered forces of politics-as-usual extracted it as a blooper, a gaffe on Dean's part, and made *it* a Message issue, to box the not-so-adroit governor into an unintended Message that was not of his own making.

What Dean apparently wanted to communicate to his political troops was this: ever since the Nixon campaign of 1968, the camouflaged but obviously racially focused strategy of the RNC had targeted the electoral votes of the erstwhile Dixiecrat South—the former Confederacy. It had successfully negotiated a particular Message with voters on behalf of its candidates, who, it was thereby suggested, would support the increasingly residual cause of "state's rights," aka Jim Crow.[4] But these very voters, Dr. Dean argued, whom Republican Message politics had formerly approached as resentful, racialized whites, needed to be approached anew. They needed to be redefined by any would-be successful Democratic candidate so that they had a new self-image more in class terms than anything else: as underinsured, poorly served folks screwed by the social welfare system just like the traditionally conceptualized disadvantaged— urban people of color, to be sure, both in popular RNC stereotype and as distinct from those rural "redneck" guys. (This, too, is a dangerous Message stance with an electoral group reflexively imagining itself as perhaps poor but still proudly autonomous. "What do you think we are, welfare queens? Queens! Y'all're insultin' mah masculinity!") In the politics of recognition that is so much at the heart of Message in the intertwined dimensional space of race, class, and gender, it is, to be sure, an inevitably changing and unstable matter as to which of these is or are the usable armature(s) of persuasive communication at any given time.

Now, whatever its possibility for success (not much, probably, as subsequent electoral results have indicated), this dubious plan for a kind of Lefty class-based redefinition of a segment of the electorate is all wonderful when strategizing *about* Message—in private, perhaps in an unrecorded conversation among campaign-staff intimates. Of course, it ought to have remained within the campaign staff meeting: how to transmute, by a kind of communicative alchemy, Southern voter self-identification among the target group of white, working-class males, enough to gain their support in that voter-resonance-with-candidate that Message is designed to generate.

Whatever the case, Dr. Dean's publicly repeated strategy remark became a Message issue, one that, unsurprisingly, folks would just not let
go of. Following its emergence and impact, we can see how demographics
work in such a 'politics of recognition,' as we call it, following Hegel (that's
Georg Wilhelm Friedrich, of course, not Senator Chuck). What this is
all about is the mutual "brand loyalty" of candidate and people—my
"market share"—based on demographic type. Who *was* this Dr. Dean,
and what had *he* done to legitimate a claim to bond with the pickup truck
guys? Fox or quail hunting on Long Island's north shore, or wherever, is
not quite the same thing as the Southern male self-image going back to
Pickett's charge at Gettysburg.

Of course, in the logic of a Message politics of recognition, it was an
incremental blunder of the first order for Dr. Dean to refer to such folks
with the cameras rolling as a "they" whom "we" (we quiche-eaters?) must
not forget about. It's that obvious outsider self-positioning—"I" and "we"
versus "they"—that especially left him open to the double-whammy,
whip-saw charge of slandering/pandering and also neglecting/defecting,
respectively. Slandering by "othering," as he yet sought to pander to the
David Dukeites; and at the same time neglecting the counterposed special sensibilities of the traditional minority constituencies, from whose
special and traditional Democratic loyalties around social welfare issues
he seemed to be defecting, "disrecognizing" them, as it were. He seemed
to want to welcome Southern white men back into, as the Republicans
say, the "big tent." (Elephants—and evangelists—are found in big tents,
of course; Democrats, to be sure, only rarely since the days when they
were Dixiecrats.) But he blundered terribly in creating a marred Message
moment in spite of himself. Message? Neither Dr. Dean nor his people
were sufficiently real-world political professionals to understand what
might happen—indeed, what did happen—in the media echo chamber
where Message reverberates.

This was perhaps one of the more florid instances in the 2004 presidential campaign of a negative Message image that a blooper-prone candidate
fell into like a bear into a fall-trap. And the Message-conscious, Message-
creating media types who feel themselves to be the political professionals

hit on it again and again.[5] Here's the ponderous *Times* editorial from 6 November 2003, titled "Dr. Dean and the Pickup Truck." Sniffing in disdain—compare this with the haughty Upper East Side doorman Eustace Tilly who periodically appears on the cover of the *New Yorker*—that "Dr. Dean was certainly not sounding like a canny [that is, Message-conscious] campaigner," the *Times* goes on to lay out the negative Message as they challenge him to overcome it: "Now Dr. Dean is going to have to demonstrate that his Confederate flag moment was a one-shot, recoverable gaffe and not a symptom of something more haunting, like a pattern of misspeaking or a hardheaded combativeness that makes it impossible to give way with grace." (One presumes that they had turned a deaf ear to the then *current* administration's style straight from the top!) The *Wall Street Journal* on 7 November (2003) is more bluntly cut and dried in an editorial rather more prophetically titled, "Dean's Rebel Yell." Here are their descriptors for Dean and Dean's image-type: "innocent, if clumsy"; "insensitive," directly quoting Rev. Al Sharpton; "[causing] forebodings about [his] 'temperament'"; "beat into submission [by his party]." This last alludes to the widely covered intraparty tension, Dr. Dean reported to have telephoned Mr. McAuliffe, then the Clintonista chairman of the Democratic National Committee, to prevail upon the other Democratic wannabes to cease and desist from encouraging such negative Messageing about him.

But precisely this set of Message images continued to be painted, and they were adorned and embellished before and after the 2004 Iowa caucuses, dialectically mutually reinforced by the other Democratic candidates and the media. If Karl Rove, the Bush White House reelection strategist, had thought early on that Dr. Dean might sweep the Democrats up into a genuinely new, viable, and combative political stance, by this point in the campaign he must have been guffawing about the fact that he was going to have to spend nothing in the general election—except for victory parties.

Then came the 2004 Iowa caucuses on Monday the nineteenth of January. The descriptive adjectives of Message politics took their toll on the country doctor who wanted to be the country's doctor. All the negative Message adjectives came home to roost as, in a clutch of "electability" anxiety, Democratic Iowans moved decisively to caucus with the two then-senators, John Kerry of Massachusetts and John Edwards of North Carolina. Their campaigns had been busy polishing up the positive Message adjectives that party regulars had long been inserting about them into the more conventional Message machines of the campaign: Kerry not so much stolid—as he would prove to be—as solid, "like a rock," to borrow from Chevrolet's positively imaged pickup truck ads (visualize embattled Democrats in the disarray of battle clinging to the craggy-faced, patrician lieutenant like Vietnam-era soldiers under attack—does anyone remember JFK and *PT-109*?); Edwards boyishly charmin' on very traditional sex appeal—recall here the, shall we say, unzipped JFK (if not the unzippered Bill Clinton).[6] Edwards was feeling no personal injury as he felt your pain, yes, ma'am (as only a financially comfortable personal injury lawyer can feel one's pain, perhaps?).

And then came "the blurt heard 'round the world." After the Iowa caucus disaster, in which Dr. Dean came in a trailing third to the senators, he addressed his youthful, enthusiastic precinct workers, ending with a peroration that they would win Michigan, they would win New Hampshire, they would win the whole poetically parallelistic listing of further primary states, and . . . Dr. Dean ended the increasingly loud, rising pitch, and scherzo-to-presto list with an enthusiastic but distinctly out-of-control whoop at the top of his voice and its sonic register. Talk about putting your foot in your mouth when you meant to insert your two fingers for a pep-up-the-team whistle!

Here, indeed, was Dr. Dean's "rebel yell" after all, as blood-curdling as General Pickett's men must have sounded in July 1863 coming up the hill at Gettysburg! It sounded genuine indeed on that January night, instead of crafted and calculated. Everywhere it was instantly replayed as being out of control, and once more it sounded like seemingly defiant—in the circumstances perhaps poignantly misplaced—enthusiasm. It was like cheering on the Yale bulldogs, the Elis, against fiercely fighting Harvard, by inhabiting an affective moment that a desperate football coach with a losing team would surely understand. People took it as the "bad, angry Howard" who really *did* sound—amazingly enough—like the angry Southern white male, the bad counterpart of the "good, very kind, very considerate" New England metrosexual Howard. (Even Dr. Dean's wife, Dr. Steinberg, thought he had lost his temper, as, unfortunately, she soon revealed before Diane Sawyer and tens of millions of television viewers.)

So the "I-have-a-scream" concession in Iowa was yet another moment of inadvertent revelation of an interiority—a *real* passion this—without the hard shell of the soft sell. Its blooper-based message was "enthusiastic amateur; not controlled—that is, in control—enough for national, let alone international, prime time." It just confirmed all the negatives in terms of which an image of Dr. Dean's marginality was earlier constructed by others as the Message that matched his very campaign organization's earlier contemptuous dismissal of the various Democratic Party apparatuses in favor of what we might call the Clean-for-Dean (remembering 1968 and 1972) anti-drug youth brigade. (Imagine their misguided notion that the party apparatuses are actually at the disposal of whoever wins the popularity of "the people," as it were! Imagine how relieved the party apparatus folks were in both parties that January evening that the Democrats, too, in 2004 eventually coalesced on someone to run whose acceptable Message just confirmed the professionals' old-style confidence in him after so many years in the Senate.)

So Dr. Dean totally lost control of his intended Message, which others thus got to fashion for him. Perhaps the governor had not even realized that he was, as a candidate, obligated to be "on message" in any way in the first place, and that he therefore had to keep control of it. But it must be remarked that he had Message problems from the beginning. If we just listen to the voice quality, the manner of pronunciation, the diction, syntactic construction of clauses and sentences, and the paragraphs—the language, in short, around which all the rest wraps—we can see trouble ahead in terms of the Message politics of that particular moment. Dr. Dean cuts a vocal figure straight out of educated, committed, enthusiastic but privileged preppy culture: slightly over-resonant voice tonality; vowels like [ɛow] in words like home; complex, deverbal nominalizations as the arguments of propositions; lengthy paragraphing; and so forth.[7] Contrast the entire vocal self-presentation of Senator Kerry (a YouTube or equivalent video archive search can assist us in remembering back to that seemingly now ancient time): even at his most stentorian moments

Kerry sounds almost like a W. C. Fields parody of the political hack, replete with stage-volume stereotypes of candidate's speech.[8] The whispers of 'patricianism' in his background—with a grandfather originally named Kohn?—were set to become slyly positive Message comparisons with the earlier wealthy Massachusetts war hero, Senator *P.T. 109*. Of course, only here the new JFK has wedded across party lines, if not to an Auchincloss stepchild, at least to H. J. Heinz (and one wonders if he "relishes" the connection). It all adds great Message interest, and you will recall that there were placements of human interest articles profiling the stylish Mrs. Heinz Kerry as a kind of country squiresse of Fox Chapel, the toney Pittsburgh suburb, in all the women's magazines.

So Dr. Dean's cumulative bloopers worked decisively against his having any of his own Message traction in the uphill slog that was his campaign from the outset. The bloopers allowed opponents, aided by the construing media, to construct his Message for him, notwithstanding any positions on issues big and small that the naïve think are what electoral politics in the United States is centered on.

Message as Branded Celebrity

We thus must again point to the convergence, in the political public sphere of Message, of the narrative legibility of celebrity through the public's familiarity with the plotlines of soap opera, our dominant and pervasive narrative art because semiotically appealing to deep-seated affective responses in us. Real-life—if we can use the term—celebrities have been rendered soap-operatic grotesques so that the public can take account of them; the cyclic ups and downs of their "private" lives (and even of their actually private ones, when revealed) are as central to their celebrity status as artistic or other achievement. The one realm is permeable to the other for true celebrities, giving them a strange, almost astigmatic partially double image coming into and going out of focus in no matter what context celebrities are encountered. Skillfully managed, the professional/"private"/private divides can be a source of heightened celebrity. One thinks of such figures as the film star and torch singer Judy Garland, born Frances Ethel Gumm, who by mid-career could attract standing-room-only, in-the-know audiences to her concerts, all attending in anxious rapture, waiting for moments when her heartbreaking, if well publicized, soap-operatic private life materialized on stage. As for later generations' dead-at-twenty-seven pop music stars, Garland's professional art gained the communicable emotional depth of fictive verisimilitude at the always risky intersection of these partly superimposed worlds—worlds essential to her continuing stardom.

Garland's case is, perhaps, an extreme of how the focus of a celebrity's public has come to be shaped in just this way, the fans emotionally connected because they are ever anxious about tidbits of revelation that the hyper-produced "product" has airbrushed out of the picture. In current times there is no dearth of celebrities in all walks of professional endeavor where semiotic laminations that are similar in type, if not as well actualized, provide the very basis for celebrity. Carlos Irwin Estévez, aka Charlie Sheen, formerly of the television show *Two and a Half Men*? The cloying Kardashians, Kim Kourtney, and Khloé? (The Kim Kardashian–Kris [note the K!] Humphries wedding/divorce reminds one of nothing so much as the classic ad for Memorex™ audio products: "Is it live or is it Memorex?")

Communication—Message—centered on the stage of electoral politics, too, is perforce assimilated to the dominant modes of comprehensibility in public interpretation. Given the permeability of figuration across a parallel set of worlds through which we experience and imagine political candidates and incumbents, as characters on this stage they hold our interest precisely to the degree to which we can put them in such duplex and interacting plotlines.[9] Achieving this state of being as an emotion-focusing icon—and bad boys and girls keep our interest no less than goody-goody ones!—is what a political figure strives for. It is what the veritable army of consultants, designers, press agents, and so forth are being paid to bring about.

The Messengers of Message

The professionals in the political press corps certainly also play an essential role in this. Privy to various degrees to the workings of campaigns and of administrations, reporters and commentators certainly understand the nature of the partials of Message that are oriented to achieving and maintaining political celebrity for a figure. Such Message partials become the stuff of political reporting, operating completely within an envelope of trade professionalism as the press construes and evaluates the effectiveness of this or that new Message-idea actualized, perhaps as a test or "trial balloon," to gauge reaction.[10] Whether engaged in providing a stream of *personalia* and gossip from deep inside a political organization, or covering issues newly emergent as the vehicle for agonistic posturing across camps, the press corps positions itself between politicians and their would-be publics. In this interstitial position, members of the political press play their role in a mutually negotiated institutional form—"politics-as-usual," let's call it. In respect of political organizations, their continued status as almost-insiders privy to happenings compels them to tread with measured aggressiveness, lest they find themselves being denied access and hence of lesser value within their press organizations. In respect of the reading, hearing, or viewing political public attuned to the universe of celebrity we've just pointed to, they must promise information and analysis getting "behind," "underneath," "inside of"—choose your metaphor—the front-stage or externally presented doings and sayings of the characters of the professional world. Here is a wonderfully compelling, internally functional overall social system of checks and balances: the press learns to live more or less in the parameters that the current system of Message-ing offers to them, and in which, indeed, they play a vital role even in attemptedly objective reportage.

Within this social system of Message, opponents' agents as well as reporters pounce on bloopers and render them material for interrogating and criticizing Message, because they impugn the "truthiness" (again using Stephen Colbert's word) of the falsities that are, by common presumption in this universe, proffered as Message in the first place. That is the essence of the success of the "Swift Boat Veterans for Truth[iness]" caper, of course, that Republicans used with such effectiveness against Senator Kerry in the general election, as of so much of the Bush reelection campaign in 2004. It invoked a hidden, deliberately suppressed counter-reality to the Kerry campaign's explicit positive Message about the senator's long ago, Vietnam War–era heroism in combat. In the first instance this attack on Senator Kerry rendered his campaign's account a merely self-serving *Rashomon* partial truth, but ultimately it rendered the whole story a plausible metaphor of a quality of the senator already in play in 2004—in other words, Vietnam-era military "cutting-and-running" as a species of malleable "flip-flopping" even in time of war. The strategy of giving the press and its public a hidden "truth" worked. It seems to have been designed as a counter to Democratic attacks on President Bush, to deflect press and electorate interest in Mr. Bush's own youthful record beyond the Message of his then current role as "war president/commander in chief," against whom Senator Kerry was running. (Recall the jumble of evasions, bureaucratic document suppressions, and obfuscations about Bush's recruitment to and tenure in the Air National Guard during the Vietnam War, making it impossible even to gauge "truthiness.") Such strategies can be found among the many results of our politics of Message, but they are very interesting ones to use to analyze the nature of our system of political communication.

When one is being taken seriously, then, bloopers count as part of the currency of the process of uncovering the fault lines between the on-stage and off-stage stories; when one is understood not to be in contention, they do not. When then Sen. George Allen of Virginia was caught on video addressing an opponent's campaign operative of color with "Hey, Macaca!" it was the end of the line for him as a serious contender, in his widely presumed pre-presidential run for reelection to the Senate. A senator campaigning in the now Republican Old South seemed not to limit his hostility to the presence of an electoral opponent, but to express a racializing hostility by calling the man a monkey. Bloop!

By contrast, recall from our earlier discussion then Sen. Joseph Biden's announcement of his candidacy for the presidency in a *New York Observer* interview on 31 January 2007 (Horowitz 2007). His interview included the following about one of his not yet formally announced opponents:

I mean you got the first sort of mainstream African American—

[REPORTER: Yes]

—who is articulate and bright and clean and a nice-looking guy. I mean, this—
that's a storybook, man.

But this description of Senator Obama was not taken to be blooperish evidence of Senator Biden's actual attitudes toward African American political figures of the recent past and the present—even if it *might be* his actual appraisal—since he was just not taken to be a serious candidate for whom Message can do anything: Biden has long been considered to be all blooper, all the time. Surely, then, he would prove to be a safe choice for vice president under the very "storybook man" he had been contrasting with earlier African American political figures.

But it is precisely the press's and the public's framing of electoral politics by communicable Message that renders anything a candidate says or does always potentially blooper-worthy in one or another mode. "Freudian" bloopers—or ones taken so to be, like the "Macaca" moment—always trump the candidate's carefully engineered, sought-after projective identifiability offered to his or her electorate by one that seems, in one sense or another, to originate elsewhere, inside. These bloopers communicate Message more powerfully as they are augmented in rippling media waves that are difficult to counteract. By contrast, a "Machiavellian" blooper—a blooper implant to attract press-gazeworthiness—is a double-voiced ('polyphonic') performance, very difficult to carry off (as with some of the imputations against former governor Romney), that plays with the great pragmatic fall-back strategy of plausible deniability at the same time it attracts or reassures those in unembraceable realms that dare not speak their names.

Appendix: On the Etymology of the Term <u>Blooper</u>

The term <u>blooper</u>, a noun used more or less as a synonym of <u>error</u> in the expression type <u>make an error</u> or of <u>boner</u> in <u>pull a boner</u>, seems to have entered television discourse from that of radio and motion-picture sound engineering, with contamination of at least two other register streams of vernacular, those of baseball and euphemistic cursing. The

OED (*s.v.*, sense 2) understands the term to denote a "blunder or howler, esp. of a public or politically embarrassing kind," and its earliest citation in this sense is from 1947, on the cusp of dominance of commercial network television. (A citation from the journal *American Speech* [Simonini 1956] as well explicitly identifies this site of usage: "In radio and television broadcasting, where the spoken word is of utmost interest and importance, lapses are known as *bloopers, fluffs, slips* and *boners.*") Here, note the -<u>er</u> suffix, one of the widened vernacular uses of the noun of agency to indicate something done (rather than someone doing), the emergent result of an action characterized in terms of whatever the word stem indicates.

Semantically, bloopers and boners are negatively evaluated as mistakes, revealed to those monitoring or addressed by one's actions as consequences of one's engaging in such action on a particular occasion. For example, the boner leaves people with the impression of one's bone(headedness). In the case of the <u>blooper</u>, whatever gaffe one has made brings about the need for editorial remedy. Metaphorically, then, its occurrence in the "audio track" of life requires a <u>bloop[ing patch]</u> (or requires the recording engineer <u>to bloop</u> it from the record)—that is, from early "talkies" (*OED, s.vv.*), "to cover a splice on a sound-track with a . . . triangular or oval black section introduced over a splice in the positive sound track, to prevent the noise ["bloop!"] which the splice would otherwise cause" (technical citation from 1931). Observe that a splice is indicated because whatever error was committed would necessitate cutting and editing a film or tape recording of the performance. So the <u>blooper</u> denotes that which would, in the best of editorial worlds, necessitate someone's dealing with the potentially embarrassing "bloop," the verb <u>to bloop</u> being one of those zero-derivation ("conversion") denominals in English like <u>to bag</u>, meaning 'to do whatever is normative and customary with a bag or sack, *viz.*, put [things] into; to wrap for carrying'; or <u>to pen</u>, meaning 'to do what is customarily done with a pen as writing instrument, *viz.*, to write; metonymically widened, to author' (also 'to put [*sc.*, living things] into an enclosure' based on another denotational sense of the noun). What is customarily done to a <u>bloop</u> is editing it out of the record by cutting and splicing and then covering over the potential noisy signal of elision with, at first, mechanical means, as in the 1931 technical manual, and later by electronic means.

Observe, too, the parallel usage in the register of baseball. Here, the blooper, attested in the OED from 1937, is a pitch (and sometimes a batted ball) making the trajectory of a slow, high parabolic curve (rather than a fast, linear power ball), giving a kind of synesthetic image of roundedness and what this sounds like. Note the bl- onset and counterpoised labial stop final -p, and the long, high, back, rounded vowel they flank. There are parallels among the "ideophonic" words of English and other languages that suggest the quasi-affective and quasi-delocutionary origins of the form. So the blooper here is that which results in a "bloop!"—very much like the media sense, though seemingly independent of it in origin.

Finally, both of these have that characteristic slangy use of the -er nominalizer, which is, as noted above, widened from the "noun of agency" derivation that describes the ascriptive 'agent' of some predicable action. In such slang registers, these words seem to denote the action itself, in fact, built on word stems that are derived from or just sliced out of expressions an eyewitness or auditing evaluator might descriptively use in reaction to what has been done. Hence, a boner is something done by an ascriptively boneheaded agent, in "pulling [one]." A blooper is something done that ascriptively—and metaphorically, in the media case—requires follow-up blooping after being edited out of the record. Similarly, a baseball blooper, watched from the field, makes one want to exclaim in synesthetic reaction, "[bluːp!]." The term blooper in this understanding is very much parallel to the slang term bloomer 'a great mistake,' as in the phrase—note parallels above—to make a bloomer where its equivalence to mistake is obvious. The OED (s.v., sense 3) cites it from 1889 as Australian prison slang, "[a]bbreviated from the expression 'a blooming error.'" Of course, bloomin[g] is a deformation, a euphemism, for bleedin[g], itself a euphemism for bloody, each of the three an increasingly unacceptable vulgar affective adjective bordering on blasphemous curse. So something that one does is a bloomer—also describable as a "bloomin' error" or equivalent—when what one has done would cause others to think of the perpetrator as a bloomin,' bleedin,' or even bloody idiot! A bonehead, even.

Five

UNFLIPPING THE FLOP

CHERYL OTIS: Senator Kerry, after talking with several co-workers and family
and friends, I asked the ones who said they were not voting for you, "Why?"
They said that you were too wishy-washy. Do you have a reply for them?
JOHN KERRY: Yes, I certainly do. (laughter)

—*8 October 2004. Second presidential debate, held at
Washington University in St. Louis, Missouri*

Reminiscing Kerry

On 30 October 2007, more than two months before the primaries began,
the Democratic Party held a televised debate in Philadelphia for seven
of its presidential hopefuls, which included then front-runner New York
senator Hillary Clinton (*New York Times* 2007). At a certain moment, as
recounted in chapter 3, Clinton was pressed about her view on governor
of New York Eliot Spitzer's beleaguered proposal to issue driver's licenses
to illegal immigrants. "It makes a lot of sense," she was quoted as saying of
his plan in New Hampshire. In response to the debate's co-moderator Tim
Russert, her answer this time around seemed more measured: two parts
sympathy ("what Governor Spitzer is trying to do is to fill the vacuum")
and one part disapproval ("we need to get back to comprehensive immigration reform because no state, no matter how well-intentioned, can fill

this gap"). Sen. Chris Dodd, one of the seven candidates on stage, read Clinton's sympathy as tacit agreement with Spitzer's position, and she swiftly corrected him: "I just want to add, I did not say that it should be done, but I certainly recognize why Governor Spitzer is trying to do it." With this John Edwards and Barack Obama resumed the evening's grating refrain: that Clinton was inconsistent, that her inconsistency bespoke a lack of conviction. This was arguably what people in the industry call a "moment," a turning point in a candidate's fortunes. In post-debate coverage on the political talk show *Hardball,* Joe Trippi, senior strategist for the Edwards campaign, ratcheted up the criticism, attributing Clinton's shifting positions to whether she was in "primary mode or general election mode" and predicting that her position would change again once she spoke with her consultants (MSNBC 2007a). It was left to the commentariat to name the charge against Clinton, as editorialist Michael Graham (2007) of the *Boston Herald* did in an uncharitable opinion piece published two days after the debate:

> Hillary Rodham Clinton may have achieved the politically impossible: She has managed to out-Kerry John Kerry himself. Sen. Flip-Flop, you recall, famously claimed that, on the issue of funding U.S. troops, he voted "for the $87 billion before I voted against it." Clinton, on the other hand, managed to declare herself both for and against driver's licenses for illegal aliens at the same time. When it comes to illegal immigration, Hillary is FORGAINST!

Likened to the unsuccessful 2004 presidential candidate John Kerry, Clinton was cast as the grotesque "flip-flopper." In the weeks that followed, the trade in accusations of flip-flopping quickened, enough for *New York Times* commentator Jim Rutenberg (2007) to call this the "season of the 'flip-flop'" on 4 November, or as Reuter's Steve Holland (2007) augured back in June, "It's the year of the flip-flop in U.S. politics."

A few observations: a candidate's infelicitous stance-taking on an Issue (from dysfluencies to excessive qualification to the extreme of self-contradiction) is read in terms of addressivity, indicating the speaker's alleged efforts to reach certain absent others (segments of the electorate being courted, as Trippi suggested); addressivity, in turn, reveals morally inflected attributes of the speaker (lack of conviction); and having such attributes classifies the candidate as a social type (flip-flopper).

Observe how fluidly this post-debate commentary moves from the interpretation of speech, to addressivity, to characterological attributes, to full-blown political persona. Why should a speaker's fumbling around the Issues be attributed to machinations involving campaign strategy and spectral publics? Why should these misfires be read characterologically, as if they betrayed what qualities and kind of person, and politician, speaks? While we have touched on some of the assumptions about electoral politics that seem to condition these interpretive reflexes, let us now see how candidates try to manage—even harness—these reflexes, how they try to use signs to get "on message" in discursive events like debate. How, in particular, might one get back on Message after a charge as grave as flip-flopping, where suspicion has been leveled at the very style in which one orients toward The Issues? By returning to the first presidential debate of 2004, we shall see how John Kerry tried to counter the charge of flip-flopping by performing its opposite: conviction. Through a close reading of certain moments of this debate, we will see how Kerry tried to achieve this self-presentational feat partly through the poetic fashion in which he qualified—took stances on—what he said, even if, at the end of the day, like some gymnast who tries in vain to stop and correct himself in midair, Kerry found that it wasn't so easy to unflip.

Stance-Taking in Debate

"Stances" may be distinguished from "positions." "Positions" are relatively durable Issue-centered policy statements (in speech or print) that purport to commit candidates to future courses of action, suggesting how they'd behave as an incumbent. As official vehicles of Message, positions are crafted with care; trotted out on campaign websites under Issue rubrics like "economy," "education," and "defense"; aired at campaign events; disseminated to the press and their publics through "talking points"; and, of course, re-invoked, clarified, and defended by the politicians themselves in debate.

Positions ought to last, too, at least for the duration of the electoral cycle, lest the changes risk drawing scrutiny. Stances are more evanescent, if by this useful term we mean the diverse ways people use signs to assess or evaluate things communicated. In research on language use, *stance* often refers to a speaker's evaluations of the propositional content expressed by an utterance: "the lexical and grammatical expression of attitudes, feelings, judgments, or commitment concerning the propositional content of a message," as Douglas Biber and Edward Finegan (1989) put it some two decades ago. Stances can be affective, based on verbs like <u>fear</u>, <u>regret</u>, <u>love</u>, and <u>hate</u>. They can be epistemic, involving verbs of cognition like <u>think</u>, <u>believe</u>, <u>know</u>. And there are many other kinds of stance, some of which do not rely on discrete words and expressions at all.

"Stance" has been used more expansively as well, where it means not only linguistic assessments and evaluations of people, events, and things, but also interpersonal orientations—stances toward others. Scott Kiesling (2005, 96) includes both senses when he speaks of stance as "a person's expression of their relationship to their talk (e.g., certain about what they are saying) and to their interlocutors (e.g., friendly or dominating)." And Asif Agha (2007) captions these two senses elegantly by contrasting "propositional stance" with "interactional stance"; the first is about orientations toward the content of speech, the second about social orientations among people. Stance, in short, would seem to offer a window onto how candidates orient toward Issues and toward each other. And in our electoral politics, stance *itself* has become an object of critical reflection and a vehicle for Message. After all, isn't stance-taking on The Issues a canonical way in which flip-floppers diverge from mavericks? The former are fickle, because they pander and slavishly follow the directives of their marketing-savvy consultants; unlike mavericks, flip-floppers have no conviction and say whatever is expedient, which makes their stances shifty, unable to support positions.

A simple way to see how interlocutors orient toward each other is to compare their propositional stances, to scan their stances for formal similarities and differences, to attend, that is, to their "poetics" (Jakobson 1960). In his research on stance-taking in conversational interaction, John Du Bois (2007) speaks of poetics through the notion of "resonance." Poetic structures, like the myriad forms of repetition and parallelism that are familiar in the metrical poetries of the world, help people construct and interpret interpersonal stance-taking, for "[a]s stances build on each other dialogically," writes Du Bois (2007, 140), "the analogy implied by their structural parallelism triggers a series of interpretive and interactional consequences," as illustrated in this simple case:

(1) SAM;   I don't like those
(2)   (0.2)
(3) ANGELA; I don't either. (159)

That Angela aligns with Sam is made evident to Sam, and to analysts who study the transcript afterward, partly through the design of her response. Through parallelism, "[a]nalogical relations are established between the juxtaposed stances (I don't like those: I don't either)," such that "[t]he foregrounding of this dialogic relation potentially invites inferences based on the comparison" (159). Compare propositional stances, and we can identify interactional stances—that is, "emergent alignments and stances among participants" (Agha 2007, 96). Or consider an example of cross-turn repetition and parallelism in Kathleen Ferrara's (1994) case study of a psychotherapeutic encounter. Ferrara found two recurrent poetic response types, what she captioned as "echoing" and "mirroring"; the former is client-initiated, the second therapist-initiated, and both involve cross-turn repetition and parallelism. Here is an example of mirroring (the "fall" indicates terminal falling pitch):

> Sharon (client): when I went home last week I made a discovery [fall]
> Marian (therapist): a discovery [fall] (75).

Ferrara found that mirroring tended to function as an indirect request for the client to elaborate, but notice that there's also something about the design of the therapist's response that seems to harmonize well with the tacit norms of psychotherapeutic intervention. (Technically put, we say that there is a "motivated," rather than arbitrary, relationship between discursive form and pragmatic function. The form of the therapist's response isn't just an arbitrary convention but has qualities that seem intimately related to what it is meant to "do.") To sense this, consider how our impression of the therapist would likely change were she to have overlapped the client's speech and ended with a terminal rise in pitch, a pitch used for asking questions. Consider how that would dial up our sense of the therapist's 'intrusiveness,' perhaps to the point that it alters our sense of what *kind* of questioning and intervention she is doing. In contrast, through mirroring, the therapist plucks delicately at a thread of talk, gently working on and with what the client says. The very parsimony of the therapist's contribution—a single, pregnant word, "discovery," lifted from the client's own speech—also seems to contribute to this sense of her delicacy and nonintrusiveness.

Compare this delicate, therapeutic cross-turn poetics with the aggravated parallelism of two boys hurling directives at each other on the streets of Philadelphia. Here is a moment from Goodwin's (1990) classic study of African American youth:

> Tony: Why don't you get out my yard.
> Chopper: Why don' you *m*ake me get out the yard. (240)

Move-wise, Chopper's utterance is what conversation analysts call a "counter," for he doesn't respond to the directive to get out of the yard but instead fires it back at the source, Tony. He issues a counter-directive. Part of what makes this counter recognizable as a counter is, again, its poetic properties. Chopper's response exhibits tight, cross-turn parallelism with Tony's, which conveniently spotlights Chopper's novel element: the causative make me). These kinds of exchanges, explain Goodwin, "display their status as escalations of prior actions—by making use of the talk of prior speaker and transforming it to their advantage; in essence, they turn the prior action on its head." Indeed, in literally building on Tony's utterance by means of parallelism, Chopper figures a kind of adversarial escalation of tension. The poetic properties contribute to our sense of what Chopper is doing to Tony.

All of this suggests that poetic structure—felt likenesses and anti-likenesses across speaking turns—does not just help us figure out how people differentially evaluate speech in terms of right or wrong, true or false, good or bad, and so forth. These likenesses can also help interlocutors "act out" and exhibit to each other social and cultural relationships, like the way therapists should interact with clients, or the gendered way in which male sociality plays out through verbal duels and jockeying for position in the fluid hierarchies of the peer group.

Stances in face-to-face interaction need not be responsive strictly to things said in that immediate encounter. Mediatized events like televised political debates resound with all sorts of shadow dialogues and echoes of past encounters, where candidates say things that are responses to nobody in the room. Indeed, Du Bois speaks of resonance in stance-taking as the "dialogic" articulation of stance effects—the way one stance seems to 'speak' to another, prior stance—and by dialogue he rightly does not mean only the simple and familiar case in which people swap "speaker" and "hearer" roles across turns of talk. "*Dialogicality*," writes Du Bois (2007, 140), "makes its presence felt to the extent that a stancetaker's words derive from, and further engage with, the words of those who have spoken before—whether immediately within the current exchange of stance utterances, or more remotely along the horizons of language and prior text as projected by the community of discourse." Distant stance objects, objects evaluated but not mentioned in the here-and-now speech event, would certainly be included here; so, too, would distant subjects, absent others to whom one aligns or dis-aligns.

In a trivial sense, all speech is "interdiscursive" in the sense that it has ties to other contexts (Bakhtin 1981, 293 et passim). The question is, how does an utterance "formulate . . . its own connection to other events" (Agha 2007, 72–73)? In terms of stance, how does one take a stance that (dis)aligns with participants in a speech event other than the present one? This question may be restated, more fundamentally, as a question of addressivity. Like the post-debate coverage of Clinton cited at the outset of this chapter, infelicities in information flow can be read as betraying the candidates' strategic orientation to—their "recognition" of—segments of the electorate. The journalist, that is, reads the candidates' stance-taking as addressivity, inferring the implied voter by figuring out "to whom" and "for whom" their utterances were truly addressed. Addressivity in such cases is not a feat achieved by the stance-taker per se but is the result of subsequent interpretation—addressivity by uptake.

Kerry, by contrast, is anything but passive. He does not leave it in the hands of commentators to get his Message right. He speaks in a way that invites us to see what he says as interdiscursive, as oriented toward speech events other than the here and now. As we shall see, Kerry's conspicuous performance of 'conviction,' an impression that owes much to the poetics of epistemic stance-taking, suggests through its very stridency and histrionic qualities that it is designed as a response to critics, just not critics on the stage or in the studio audience.

Kerry's 'Conviction' as Anti-Flip-Flopping in the First Presidential Debate of 2004

The televised 30 September 2004 presidential debate featured three primary participants: the Republican incumbent (President Bush), the Democratic challenger (Sen. John Kerry), and the moderator (television journalist Jim Lehrer). Others participated in different capacities, such as the studio audience, the mass of television viewers, and those who missed the event and encountered it piecemeal through post-event audio and video clips, and through reports and editorials in the news media. If we consider the battle for defining the debate's outcome (who "won"), which begins even while the debate is in progress as party operatives feed the press favorable reports on what their candidate just said, in a certain sense debates are not what transpire on stage.

When Kerry strode onto the stage at the University of Miami in Coral Gables to debate Bush, he was shadowed by criticism that he lacked (among other things) decisiveness, resolve, and conviction—a cluster of valued attributes linked to the ideal of "strong" leadership. Purported inconsistencies in Kerry's positions and voting record had been paraded before the public, all evidence of a pernicious character flaw. Kerry, in his critics' hands, was fashioned into a mirror image of Bush, whose earnest, tough, "stay the course" demeanor had been showcased as the right stuff for a nation still reeling from 9/11 and kept on edge about future terrorist threats. The negative caption for Kerry as a social type—one that enjoyed wide circulation in the 2007–2008 election season—was the *flip-flopper*.

In one tracking poll that asked respondents to rank the appropriateness of the word "steady" for Bush and Kerry using a 0–10 scale, a precipitous drop for Kerry began at the end of August and stretched into September.

For "says one thing but does another," Kerry polled low from roughly 12 September till the general election (Jamieson 2006, 18–19). At no point did he poll on par with Bush on either question. In the third week in September, the Bush campaign unleashed its notorious "windsurfing" attack ad. With summer footage of Kerry tacking back and forth in Nantucket to the tune of Strauss's "Blue Danube" waltz, a voice-over inquires, "In which direction would John Kerry lead?" In response comes a crush of inconsistencies:

> Kerry voted for the Iraq War, opposed it, supported it, and now opposes it again. He bragged about voting for the $87 billion to support our troops before he voted against it. He voted for education reform and now opposes it. He claims he is against increasing Medicare premiums but voted five times to do so. John Kerry, whichever way the wind blows.

Three days before the first debate, the Bush campaign aired an attack ad that harped again on Kerry's alleged flip-flopping, leaving the audience with this doubt: "How can John Kerry protect us . . . when he doesn't even know where he stands?"

Trained as it was on the issue of foreign policy, the first presidential debate offered Kerry an opportunity to deflect such criticism, and for many viewers, that's precisely what he did. Speaking for those who witnessed Kerry's performance on 30 September, his then running mate, John Edwards, had this to say in the following week's vice presidential debate with Dick Cheney (CNN 2004): "They saw a man who was strong, who had conviction, who is resolute, who made it very clear that he will do everything that has to be done to find terrorists, to keep the American people safe." About both Edwards and Kerry, Cheney countered:

> You're not credible on Iraq because of the enormous inconsistencies that John Kerry and you have cited time after time after time during the course of the campaign. Whatever the political pressures of the moment requires, that's where you're at. But you've not been consistent, and there's no indication at all that John Kerry has the conviction to successfully carry through on the war on terror.

And a bit later, continues Cheney:

> The problem we have is that, if you look at his [Kerry's] record, he doesn't display the qualities of somebody who has conviction.

Both Edwards and Cheney attend to the question of "resolve" and especially "conviction," and it is especially this latter characterological attribute that Kerry pins to himself and exhibits at the outset of the 30 September debate.

As for the debate's sanctioned procedures, Lehrer poses a question to a candidate; the candidate responds (two minutes); the response is followed by the opponent's rebuttal (ninety seconds); and, at Lehrer's discretion, candidates are permitted a one-minute "discussion extension." No time is reserved for opening statements, but two-minute "closing statements" are permitted. Lehrer addresses Kerry first, inviting him to speak of his beliefs about his ability to safeguard America against a future terrorist attack: "Do you believe you could do a better job than President Bush in preventing another 9/11-type terrorist attack on the United States?" Kerry's response is telegraphic at first, "Yes, I do." After thanking the organizers and conveying his sympathy to the Floridians who endured a harrowing hurricane season, he begins his answer proper. Transcript Segment 1 below (see table 5.1) highlights parallelism, since the speaking turn as a whole is densely poetic relative to other turns in the debate, and since the repetition of personalized epistemic phrases (e.g., I believe, I know) is relevant to the performance of Kerry's Message.

Let us begin by noting a few tacit forms of addressivity and by suggesting how these contribute to Message. In lines 15–28, Kerry announces a "plan," a "better plan." Than what, than whom? the comparative prods. Than "this president" (line 10), whom Kerry charges with having shattered alliances and dragged the United States into the debacle of the Iraq War. While superficially self-focal, save for the parting shot at Bush for not "reaching out to the Muslim world" (line 21), the comparative better sets Kerry against the current administration. The mere fact of having such a plan interdiscursively evokes, for many at least, the familiar charge that it was precisely a failure of planning that contributed to the setbacks in Iraq, that Bush invaded "without a plan to win the peace," as Kerry would soon argue in this very debate. Insofar as these valorized attributes of self are recognized as inverse attributes of Bush and his administration, they serve as a critical moment of contrast. Plan is what Kerry has and Bush lacks.

Table 5.1. Transcript Segment 1

Lehrer: Do you believe			you could do	a better job than President Bush in preventing another 9/11-type terrorist attack on the United States?		
Kerry:			yes, I do.			
[...]						
1						
2	and	**I believe**	I can	make America safer than President Bush has made us.		
3	but		President Bush and I both love our country equally			
4		**I believe**	we just have	a different set of convictions about how you make America	America is	safe.
5						safest and
6						strongest when
7						we are leading the world and
						we are leading strong alliances.
8			I'll never give	a veto to any country over our security		
9	but	**I also know**		how to lead those alliances.		
10			this president	has left them in shatters across the globe.		
11	and		we're	now 90 percent of the casualties in Iraq		
12	and			90 percent of the costs.		
13		**I think**		that's wrong,		
14	and	**I think**	we can	do better.		
15			I have	a better plan	for homeland security.	
16			I have	a better plan	to be able to fight the war on terror	
17					by strengthening our military,	
18					strengthening our intelligence,	
19					by going after the financing more authoritatively,	
20					by doing what we need to do to rebuild the alliances,	
21					by reaching out to the Muslim world,	
22					which the president has almost not done,	
23	and				beginning to isolate the radical Islamic Muslims,	
24					not have them isolate the United States of America	

Table 5.1. Transcript Segment 1, continued

25	I know	I can	do a better job		in Iraq.	
26		I have	do a better job	a	to have a summit with all of the allies,	
27				plan	something this president has	not yet achieved,
28						not yet been able to do to bring people to the table
29		we can	do a better job		of training the Iraqi forces to defend themselves,	
30	and	I know that we can	do a better job		of preparing for elections.	
31	all of these, and especially homeland security, which we'll talk about a little bit later.					

A second self-focal interdiscursive moment, "I'll never give a veto to any country over our security" (line 8), is independently recognizable as a charge leveled at Kerry by his critics and invoked by Bush later in the debate. This is, again, self-focal—it is trained on him—but by implication it is "directed at" or "addressed to" the voice of certain distant critics.

A third moment occurs in line 2, where Kerry declares that he, like Bush, "love[s] [his] country." Here, Kerry ascribes to himself an attribute that some of his most vitriolic critics had said he lacks: patriotism (recall the attack ads that questioned Kerry's war medals and his turn of opinion against the Vietnam War, and criticized him for his decision to vote against a $87 billion resolution to supply emergency funds for the troops in Iraq and to support reconstruction there and in Afghanistan). That is, Kerry ascribes to himself a disputed attribute: patriotism. For those acquainted with this criticism of Kerry, his professed love of country reads as an instance of what we might call "characterological antithesis." Though self-focused, it is tacitly addressed "to" critics who charged the opposite at some earlier, unspecified point in time, and it is "for" the overhearing electorate, the virtual superaddressees who are invited to witness the sting of Kerry's rejoinder.

And so it is with <u>conviction</u>. Kerry says he has conviction early in the speaking turn ("we [President Bush and I] just have a different set of <u>convictions</u> about how you make America safe"; *conviction*'s second syllable is also strongly stressed, just so that we don't miss the word), and does so right as he begins to deliver the first of a series of epistemic phrases in parallelistic fashion.

As a whole, Kerry's first turn to speak is densely parallelistic relative to his other turns in the debate, with the exception of the end of his closing statement. Of special interest is his striking repetition of first-person-singular subject-predicate frames. Besides the string of personalized epistemic phrases <u>I believe</u> (lines 2, 4), <u>I think</u> (lines 13, 14), <u>I know</u> (lines 9, 25, 30), observe the parallel set of first-person-singular frames with the predicates <u>have</u> (lines 15, 16, 26) and <u>can do</u> (lines 1, 25, 29, 30). The first-person-singular frame predominates. (Compare with Silverstein's [2003a, 51] discussion of "cantillation with tremolo" in the Gettysburg Address, where Lincoln repeatedly strikes certain rhetorical notes, as it were.) By sheer force of repetition, Kerry's epistemic phrases almost seem to figurate 'conviction,' the attribute he ascribed to himself early in the speaking turn; the "steadiness" quality of conviction seems modeled iconically by the repetition of epistemic phrases.[1]

This series of epistemic phrases seems amplified by the chorus of <u>I have, I can do</u>, whose complements denote Kerry's foreign-policy-related capabilities, strengths, and objectives. Even within the epistemic set alone (<u>believe, think, know</u>), three of the verb-of-cognition predicates have complement clauses that speak to Kerry's competence. So we are presented with copious signs of two attributes, "conviction" and "competence," yoked by the parallelistic iteration of *I*, the pronoun into which these qualities converge, becoming one: Kerry. Kerry counters the charge of being a flip-flopper through characterological antithesis. He invites us to see himself as a candidate in possession of the branded attribute of 'conviction' partly through the ascription of <u>conviction</u> to self, through the repetition of personalized, lexically denoted expressions of epistemic stance, and through a battery of *I*'s. Against the criticism of flip-flopping, Kerry's "I" seems remarkably—conspicuously—stable, hardly evidence of a politician whose positions shift "whichever way the wind blows"![2]

An objection could be raised that surely the epistemically oriented design of Lehrer's question ("do you <u>believe</u> that") spurred Kerry to mention <u>conviction</u> and resort to epistemic stance-taking, just as it invited him to contrast himself with Bush ("you can do a <u>better job than</u> President Bush."). Though Kerry's responses do partially resonate with Lehrer's question, question design alone doesn't explain Kerry's behavior well. It is telling, for instance, that an analogous litany of personalized epistemic phrases occurs in Kerry's last turn to speak in the debate, and, like turn one, these phrases are accompanied by the self-ascription of <u>conviction</u>, yet this closing turn is *not* a response to a question by Lehrer; it is a "closing statement." Kerry begins his closing statement by referencing his first speaking turn and by putting on record his patriotism and conviction, just as he did in his first turn:

> From Kerry's first speaking turn:
> "I believe President Bush and I both love our country equally, but we just have a different set of convictions about how you make America safe."

From Kerry's closing remarks:
"My fellow Americans, as I've said at the very beginning of this debate, both President Bush and I love this country very much. There's no doubt, I think, about that. But we have a different set of convictions about how we make our country stronger here at home and respected again in the world."

In his closing statement (see Transcript Segment 2 [table 5.2]), as in his first turn to speak, Kerry's declaration of <u>conviction</u> is followed (albeit not immediately as in turn one) by a string of epistemic phrases. In terms of the density per turn of personalized epistemic phrases (specifically, <u>I think, I believe, I know</u>), Kerry's opening turn had the highest density (7 epistemic phrases out of 340 words), and his final turn had the second-highest density (6 out of 360).[3] Together, the first and final speaking turns contain no less than 24 percent (13 out of 54) of all of Kerry's personalized epistemic phrases based on <u>know, think, believe</u> (this includes phrases with negated <u>do</u> [e.g., <u>I don't think</u>]). At the debate's beginning and end—memorable moments, moments that are ripe for self-presentational Message—Kerry ascribes to himself a key disputed attribute, 'conviction,' and exhibits this quality partly through the poetic organization of epistemic stance.[4]

Evidence for this interpretation may also be found by briefly comparing Kerry's behavior with Bush's. Bush's first opportunity to speak is a rebuttal to Kerry's first turn. While Bush's turn, like Kerry's, is dense in poetic structure relative to his other speaking turns, there is no attempt to predicate <u>conviction</u> of himself, no high density of epistemic phrases, no preponderance of <u>I</u>. Only two tokens of "I" occur. Instead, Bush produces three tokens of <u>our</u>, nine of <u>we</u> and one of <u>us</u>, and only two verbs of cognition occur, <u>realize</u> and <u>understand</u> (only the latter is personalized with <u>I</u>). Bush uses his first turn to list off and laud his administration's accomplishments (no surprise for an incumbent, perhaps, but he could have touted his own role in these accomplishments).

Finally, consider Lehrer's first question to Bush, which is just as epistemically oriented and contrastive as the question he asked Kerry: "<u>Do you believe</u> the election of Senator Kerry on November the 2nd would increase the chances of the U.S. being hit by another 9/11-type terrorist attack?" Question design influences how people respond, and as we

would predict, Bush does begin by responding with <u>believe</u>, which reso-
nates with Lehrer's question: "No, I don't believe it's going to happen.
I believe I'm going to win, because the American people know I know
how to lead. I've shown the American people I know how to lead." This
initial resonance is fleeting, though, because <u>I</u> gives way to <u>we</u>, <u>us</u>, and
<u>our</u>, exhibiting a pattern similar to Bush's first speaking turn. (In his sec-
ond turn, Bush says things like, "We have a duty to defeat this enemy,"
"We have a duty to protect our children," and "if we lose our will, we lose.
But if we remain strong and resolute, we will defeat this enemy.") After
this brief moment at the turn's outset, no personalized, clause-initial
epistemic phrases occur.

While Bush does not perform or *exhibit* "conviction" through epistemic stance-taking, as Kerry does, he does speak quite explicitly *about*
this branded attribute, and how he does so is revealing. Bush concedes
that not everyone agrees with his "tough" decisions and then reminds his
audience, "But people know where I stand," "people out there listening
know what I believe." "And," continues Bush, "that's how best it is to keep
the peace." Here, Bush all but restates the parting question from the attack
ad aired three days before the debate: "How can John Kerry protect us . . .
when he doesn't even know where he stands?" Indeed, Bush presses this
claim repeatedly in this debate, painting Kerry as a weak leader and a flip-
flopper. Unlike Kerry, Bush does not try to exhibit or perform conviction.
He doesn't need to. He just nods to public opinion: "people know where
I stand." So while Bush's response also speaks to candidate "conviction,"
a move partly motivated by Lehrer's epistemically oriented question and
by Kerry's earlier speaking turn, it differs markedly from Kerry's.

Stance-Taking beyond the Speech Event

If we were to try to analyze Kerry's interactional stance-taking only by in-
specting local, dialogic resonances among utterances that occur on stage,
we'd catch just a little fleeting cross-turn parallelism between Kerry's
utterances and Lehrer's question. Again, no such resonance with Lehrer
occurs in the final turn, because Lehrer poses no question. What we see
here, instead, is robust turn-internal parallelism of epistemic phrases, and

Table 5.2. Transcript Segment 2

[. . .]

but	**I believe**	I have	a difference with this president.
			we're strongest when we reach out and lead the world
			and build strong alliances.
	I believe	I have	a plan for Iraq.
		we can	be successful.
		I'm not talking	about leaving.
		I'm talking	about winning.
and		we need	a fresh start,
			a new credibility,
			a president who can bring allies to our side.
		I also have	a plan to win the war on terror,
			funding homeland security,
			strengthening our military,
			cutting our finances,
			reaching out to the world,
			again building strong alliances.
because	**I believe**		America's best days are ahead of us
not	**I believe**		that the future belongs to freedom,
			to fear.
			that's the country that I'm going to fight for.

Table 5.2. Transcript Segment 2, *continued*

and	I ask you	to give me the opportunity to make you proud.
	I ask you	to give me the opportunity to lead this great nation,
		so that we can be stronger here at home,
		respected again in the world,
and		have responsible leadership that we deserve.

Thank you, and God bless America.

these phrases resonate not primarily with the epistemic stances of any copresent interactant but with the speech of absent others—of Message antagonists. As viewers who are familiar with the media coverage leading up to this debate will sense, Kerry's response in turn one seems addressed neither to Lehrer nor Bush nor anyone present, but to the voice of critics who had called him a flip-flopper—a social type who lacks precisely what Kerry here displays in great measure: "conviction."

Kerry's dense, hypertrophied poetic arrangement of personalized epistemic phrases, accompanied by the self-ascription of conviction and situated in this particular interdiscursive surround, helps make epistemic stance into an index of presidential persona—a sign of a candidate with "conviction," itself a rejoinder in an large-scale character contest.[5] It is a "rejoinder"—not unlike Chopper's—insofar as the response is apprehended as a mirror image of an attribute (*lack* of conviction, the stereotypic failing of flip-floppers) ascribed to Kerry by critics at an earlier point. In sum, these patterns involving epistemic stance-taking help perform a kind of characterological antithesis across speech events, and it is only under conditions of interdiscursivity that the branded, characterological attribute of "conviction" becomes manifest. "Conviction" isn't signaled directly by the word conviction or by the personalized epistemic phrases and their poetic arrangement. It is only when these patterns are understood as forming a "response" to distant critics—critics who had pegged Kerry as a flip-flopper—that "conviction," as *anti*-flip-flopping, becomes readable. Interdiscursive addressivity helps us read Message off of stance-taking behavior.

Though political commentators may talk as if one could read Message directly off of a politician's signs, it should be obvious from the amount of contextualization supplied here that the branded, characterological attribute of "conviction" cannot be inferred directly from stance-taking in sentence-sized units. Kerry's stance-taking must be understood in relation to a multiplex configuration of signs, only some parts of which can be found in the transcript. To recount some of the evidence: (1) conviction is ascribed to self in both first and final turns, forming part of the co-text and motivating the relevance of the characterological attribute of "conviction" by way of denotation; (2) the first and final turns, where this high density of personalized epistemic phrases occurs, are understood to be critical moments in debate and hence phases in which self-presentational Message is expected; (3) the question of Kerry's "conviction" had already been an object of media attention in the days and weeks leading up to the debate, and Bush himself rapidly re-invoked this in the debate; (4) the poetic structure, extremely dense relative to other turns in the debate, foregrounds the stretch of discourse containing the epistemic phrases, making it something of note; and, most generally, (5) presidential debates are widely understood as (among other things) character contests, which primes viewers to read speech behavior in terms of what it reveals about the speaker.

All of this reminds us of just how poor typical debate transcripts are when it comes to studying Message. Transcription itself is no pen-to-paper capture technology, as students of language know well; it is inherently selective and incapable of exhaustively representing the details of interaction. Standard journalistic play-script transcription leaves out "dysfluent" signs like filled pauses (uh, um) and cut-off speech (b—but), omits pregnant pauses, fails to highlight discursive phenomena like repetition and parallelism. It risks missing critical discursive details that people use to infer what Message stratagems are in play. But it is especially the interdiscursivity of Message, charted here, that reminds us of how porous the boundaries of events like political debates are, that the written debate transcripts that are produced and circulated after the fact are such poor artifacts for understanding Message politics. Some things never show up in a transcript, at least not directly: the recirculation of some new bit of positive Message introduced days or weeks earlier; a rebuttal directed at a recent negative television ad; the downplaying of bad news—a dip in the polls, the loss of an endorsement, a month of poor fund-raising, the sudden departure of a key staff member. All such moves are very much where the action is, and yet transcripts register only traces of these acts, sometimes very faint ones. Insofar as speech indexes an event from a day prior, a month prior, a generation past, a bygone era—at whatever degree of spatial or temporal remove—it suggests that we must look beyond the close quarters of this ninety-minute speech event to see Message through the narrow aperture of the transcript.

Kerry's Epistemic Pose: Who the Stance-Taker Really Is

That Kerry's stance-taking behavior may be understood partly as a counter to absent critics will not surprise those who are acquainted with the dynamics of Message, but it is not so simple to say what Kerry has done. Dramaturgical tropes spring to mind: "display," "strategy," "self-presentation," "performance." We are primed to call Kerry's move an "act," a "scripted" act, part of the "theater" that is televised political debate. (Remember Jon Stewart's famous hijacking of CNN's political debate show *Crossfire*? By turns funny and serious, Stewart ripped into the show for being "theater"—like pro-wrestling—not a venue for sorely needed substantive debate. On the theatrics charge, he drew gales of laughter when he poked fun at Tucker Carlson's necktie: "How old are you?" Carlson: "Thirty-five." Stewart: "And you wear a *bow-tie.*")

But when there's a convergence between our dramaturgical metalanguage (the terms analysts use to describe what's happening ["display," "posing," etc.]) and the ethno-dramaturgical metalanguage of the politicians we study, we need to exercise care. In this case—even here, in this very chapter—we do often speak in remarkably similar terms, so let us pause to reflect on this convergence.

In his essay on "response cries," Erving Goffman (1978) explored how seemingly spontaneous expressions of inner states like <u>ouch</u> (speaker 'pain') or <u>yuck</u> (speaker 'disgust') tend to be uttered for those in earshot—a signal for an audience as much as for self—and with a keen sensitivity to the categories of overhearer who are present. ("If women and children are present, your male self-communicator is quite likely to censor his cries accordingly: a man who utters *Fuck!* when he stumbles in a foundry is likely to avoid that particular expletive if he trips in a day nursery" [799].) Even if this kind of recipient design—this attentiveness to hearers and overhearers—were stretched to include far-flung interdiscursive phenomena—that is, non-copresent interlocutors, people who aren't physically there—there is still the question of *who* the stance-taker qua speaking subject is. That is, we are forced to confront issues that dogged Goffman's discussions of self-presentation and related phenomena from the start, including the question of what model of the speaking subject he seems to assume. For the unsympathetic, Goffman had a specific so-ciohistorical model of the fractionated self—a self split into inner and outer—which he naïvely assumed to be universal. To recall Gouldner's (1971) influential (if somewhat unfair) critique, the actors in Goffman's dramaturgical microsociology, those "busy contrivers of the illusion of self," as Gouldner put it, were really just a portrait of one sociohistorical category of person: the late capitalist bourgeois subject who has experi-enced a "transition from an older economy centered on production to a new one centered on mass marketing and promotion, including the mar-keting of the self" (381). This is no place to revisit Goffman's theory of the person. We only wish to register a concern that we not rely uncritically on a dramaturgical metalanguage here, since that metalanguage merits study in its own right. That metalanguage, which involves a preoccupation with dissimulation and dramaturgy, is, in fact, central to the empirical story here, for stance itself has become an object of reflection in U.S. electoral politics: stance is something talked about and used to read Message. The preoccupations with "conviction" and "flip-flopping" suggest that talk about stance-taking—and not just the turn-by-turn dynamics of stance-taking itself—demands attention, that it isn't enough to study stance strictly in terms of how people orient to propositions and orient to each other, no matter how expansive we take the scale of the encounter to be.

Histrionic Realism and the Flip-Flopper Grotesque

On the Saturday evening following the 30 October Philadelphia debate, Senator Obama brought the criticism of Clinton to another stage, to the late-night television comedy show *Saturday Night Live*. He showed up at a fictive Halloween party at the Clintons' house, dressed as himself. "Who is under there?" pried Hillary (played by Amy Poehler). Peeling back a mask of his own face, Obama dug into Clinton: "Well, you know, Hillary, I have nothing to hide. I enjoy being myself. I am not going to change who I am just because it's Halloween."

The charge of flip-flopping wasn't limited to the Democrats. During the 2007–2008 primary season, Republican front-runners Mitt Rom-ney and Sen. John McCain turned on each other and traded charges of flip-flopping, often with allusions to the attacks on Kerry from 2004. In the lead-up to the 5 February 2008 Republican primary contests, each issued a video recalling the 2004 anti-Kerry windsurfing ad. In Romney's video, stills of McCain were set to the "Blue Danube" waltz as viewers were led to the acerbic punch line: "John McCain. Always for Tax Cuts . . . Except when he's against them." But the moniker stuck to Romney because of his stunning reversals on Issues like abortion, gay rights, and immigration. And in the present 2011–2012 primary cycle, Romney has again been in the crosshairs. An op-ed piece from the *Daily Beast* reads in part: Romney's "policy reversals makes 2004's whipping boy, John 'I voted for it before I voted against it' Kerry, look like an exemplar of political consistency" (Latimer 2011). In autumn 2011, Romney's then rivals—Gov. Rick Perry and Rep. Michele Bachmann—resumed the flip-flop chant, with Democrats cheering them on. In one attack ad, Rick Perry likened "Obamacare" and "Romneycare," treating the two as one and the same, and included a cameo by the late journalist Tim Russert, who was shown waving yellow-and-orange flip-flops in Romney's face during an interview from 2007. A website devoted to Romney's flip-flops (mittromneyflipflops.com) offered a greatest hits of contradictory statements, each pair of quotes set in large font against a stark white background (e.g., "I don't line up with the NRA," "I'm a member of the [NRA]"), each with a hyperlink to the news source that reported it and a Facebook "like" button for viewers to register and share their derision. Another site, WhichMitt.com—this one sponsored by the Democratic National Committee—invited viewers to jeer at Romney in a multiple-choice quiz format. ("Multiple choice" being the barb Sen. Ted Kennedy famously directed at Romney in 1994 debate for the Massachusetts senate race. Kennedy: "I have supported the Roe V. Wade. I am pro-choice. My opponent is multiple-choice.") Against a similarly stark white background (the facts being in black-and-white), was an Issue name and then a question: "Which of the following statements has Mitt made?" In each of the quiz's six questions, options 1 and 2 were statements that expressed contradictory positions, while 3 read "all of above." The answer for each was, of course, 3; click it—or even click a wrong answer—and you got treated to a video clip that documented Romney's Janus face. "With Mitt," the quiz concluded, "the answer's always 'all of the above.'"

As a term of derogation for politicians who change positions, *flip-flop* may be traced to the late nineteenth-century United States, as the *Oxford English Dictionary* suggests, but of what moral offense does this characterological term now speak? First, flip-flopping, as a moral offense, cannot be placed on a scale that runs from dissimulation at one end to sincerity on the other, for all such acts involve disjoining or aligning inner states from outer signs. In failing to take a stand, the flip-flopper calibrates signs outwardly, not inwardly, with respect to some determinate mental state ("conviction") that drives discursive action. Recalling Goffman's familiar decomposition of "speaker" into finer participant roles (the "animator" who physically produces the message, the "author" who composed the message, etc.), the flip-flopper suffers from a chronic failure of "principal"-ship, an inability to be committed to what he or she says.

As a word, the career of flip-flop could be traced and its social distribution charted. And there are histories here, to be sure. Perhaps this moral transgression should be understood in light of the old Protestant-inflected ideal of "sincerity" (Trilling 1972; Keane 2002), or in relation to registers of "direct" or "plain" speech (Bauman 1983). Perhaps this figure is just one more symptom of the postmodern depthless subject, which Fredric Jameson (1991) famously tied to conditions of late capitalism. Although the figure of the flip-flopper may be placed in one or more of these histories and narratives of change, we would like to close by focusing, if speculatively, on a much narrower sociohistorical context to which both conviction and flip-flopping seem to speak, and that involves political marketing and candidate branding in particular.

Both "conviction" and "flip-flopping" reflexively typify stance- and position-taking behavior. They bend back and comment on styles of orientation toward The Issues. Unlike the kinds of personal attributes a campaign might poll for, like "strength" or "likeability," "conviction" and "flip-flopping" speak to the presence of (and, crucially, suspicion toward) professional political consultancy, marketing, and polling. Many remarks about flip-flopping and cognate terms explicitly suggest this. Flip-flopping does not merely describe some gross and sudden change of position for private gain but a change that comes from trying strategically to please voters—through "poll watching" and "pandering"—and, more generally, through blindly following the dictates of one's strategists. Much has been made of the importance of professional consultancy, polling, and marketing firms in electoral politics today, as attested partly by a small industry of books, opinion pieces, and films decrying their purportedly corrosive effects on the democratic process. Although polling, for instance, can be traced to the early nineteenth century in the U.S. context, its regular use for governing is only a few decades old. Equally striking has been the application of marketing principles and techniques to political campaigns, forming what is captioned as "political marketing."

In this respect, flip-flop is part of a family of characterological terms for candidate (in)authenticity. On the valorized end of the slide are "uncandidate" and "uncampaign," for instance, both of which appear to draw on 7-Up's influential "uncola" campaign that was first launched in the late 1960s. (As for the lexico-semantic artistry of this trope, the negative prefix un- attaches unexpectedly to a concrete, count-noun stem, a stem that denotes a generic class member, cola. Cola [at least for many American-English speakers] is a superordinate term for branded varieties like Coke, Pepsi, Sprite, Fanta, and when used as an epithet for the brand name 7-Up, it motivates the metaphoric reading of 'not'-class member, i.e., 'unconventional.') A famous piece of anti-brand branding, the uncola has found some life in talk about campaign politics. ("The Uncandidate" moniker, for instance, is attested in the 1980s with Democratic congressman and senator Paul Simon of Illinois; with Democratic senator of Massachusetts Paul Tsongas, who competed with Clinton for the presidential bid in 1992; and especially with independent candidates Ross Perot in 1992 and Ralph Nader in 2000.)

Whatever else this figure of the flip-flopper may signify, for many today it speaks to the commoditization of political personhood.[6] It registers and moralizes the incursion of market(ing) principles into the preserve of "authentic" selfhood. Conviction—being real, being above the "permanent campaign" (Blumenthal 1980), where even incumbents enjoy no respite from message—has become a sublime. How can the stance-taking subject calibrate "inner" states with "outer" signs so as to lay bare one's soul—one's "character"—when these stances are increasingly suspected of being tested, polled, and scripted, and where there is even an emerging connoisseurship for distinguishing real from ersatz subjectivity? (Remember the bloggers who tried to enlighten readers about the "fake" tears that Hillary Clinton shed just before the New Hampshire primary contest—tears credited by some as important for her win in that state—when a woman from the audience asked her how she keeps going under the pressure?) Real conviction is soteriological: having it would mean transcending the electoral market and its web of professional strategists and consultants; it would require un-branding. Though un-branding is unattainable, commoditized, small-c "conviction"—an anti-brand brand—is available to all candidates, though it requires finding ever new ways to exhibit it and prove that one's opponents lack it.

This is not to wax nostalgic for some waning Real, as if there had once been an earlier Message-free era of political authenticity, a time when politicians really were sincere and communicated transparently. It is simply to note how anti-brand, anti-marketing Message has been on the rise in U.S. electoral politics, a period we have captioned as late democracy. Message turns back on itself, reflexively problematizing its own mediatization. It tries to appropriate for its own ends the various "crises" of media representation that are so familiar in the public sphere. Mediation itself—the "filter," those who "come between" politicians and their publics—becomes a means of constructing Message. Cutting through the filter, performing "im-mediacy," breaking out, becomes critical to crafting a positive Message in late democracy. One ironic result of this reflexivity may be something of a treadmill effect in political performance. For viewer-consumers who are inundated with signs of conviction and charges of its absence, conviction may register only through increasingly strident and hyperbolic acts of baring one's soul, as in Obama's *Saturday Night Live* appearance. The result may be such an intensification of the grotesque that it pushes presidential performance into the realm of the burlesque. The figure of the depraved flip-flopper, and the sublime state of conviction from which he has fallen, may be symptomatic of a new "histrionic realism" that requires ever more explosive feats of authenticity, role distance, register breaks—anything that can rediscover life in the grotesque, or at least the semblance of a pulse.

Six

THE MESSAGE IN HAND

That politicians can sway audiences through gesture is an old conceit, as the writings of the first-century Roman rhetorician Quintilian, for instance, attest. Quintilian offered copious advice on how orators should use their hands and manage their bodies, and made it sound as if these signs had stable meanings and predictable effects: "To strike the thigh, a gesture which Cleon is supposed to have first practiced at Athens, is not only common, but suits the expression of indignant feeling and excites the attention of the audience" (Book 11: 374). The contemporary scholarly literature on gesture has had precious little to say about this venerable subject, and what has been said has been eclipsed by a mass of op-ed-styled musings by journalists and political commentators, with the occasional cameo played by the more sober, if often dubiously trained, "body language expert." These musings range from the waggish (e.g., a shot at Sen. John McCain's "twitchy finger air quotes" [Muller 2008]) to the incendiary (e.g., accusations that Obama slyly flipped off Hillary Clinton in April 2008 when he scratched his cheek with his middle finger [Malcolm 2008]). And there's always ample satire, like the Huffington Post's Matt Mendelsohn's piece from late October 2008, which poked fun at McCain's proclivity for air quotes: "McCain Injures Fingers Making Quotation Marks Sign, Suspends Campaign." "Today," complains Jürgen Streeck in one of the few, careful case studies of political gesture, "most publicized pronouncements on the matter have the quality of pop psychology or pop ethology: Unconscious motives or psychological dispositions are attributed, often on the basis of a single photograph, and universal meanings of isolated behaviors are invoked, in statements that are sometimes witty, but rarely enlightening" (2008, 155).

These musings belong to an industry of media commentary in which no facet of candidate behavior is safe from scrutiny, for, as we have seen, even verbal slips and gaffes can be treated as signs revelatory of character, thoughts, and machinations. Apply this to gesture, and the result is a caricatured version of a familiar view, "that gesture 'leaks,' betraying a speaker's true feelings and thoughts, perhaps in opposition to more treacherous (because more conscious?) words which may try to conceal them" (Haviland 2006, 67). If anything, the commentariat's relentless pursuit of deep meanings betrays something about its own dispositions: its suspicion that candidates are opaque, dissimulated creatures whose signals, like public-relations copy and clever ads—caveat emptor!—demand critical readings, so that consumer-voters can see who candidates "really" are and make informed, market-driven choices.

How *does* gesture figure into Message craft? Rather than treat candidate gestures as if they were direct, unmediated expressions of Message, let us follow the long, sinuous semiotic pathways that run from co-speech gesture to candidate brand. We will trace just a few of Barack Obama's gestures, beginning with an off-Message moment from the first Democratic primary debate in April 2007 and ending with an on-Message moment from the first presidential debate against Republican nominee John McCain in October 2008. Through this exercise in gestural exegesis, we shall see that gesture cannot directly index candidate brand, although it can participate in projects of candidate branding in complex ways.

Looking Sharp: Barack Obama's Precision-Grip Gestures (2007–2008)

Barack Obama did not look sharp at all in the first Democratic primary debate of 2007. The debate was held in South Carolina on 26 April and featured eight candidates and the two moderators, Brian Williams (NBC News) and David Stanton (Columbia, South Carolina's WIS News). A question about terrorism tripped Obama up. As described in chapter 1, Williams had presented a hypothetical scenario in which another 9/11-style attack occurs while the current debate is in progress, and asked how he would respond. Obama got the question first.

> Senator Obama, if God forbid a thousand times we learned that two American cities had been hit simultaneously by terrorists and we further learned beyond the shadow of a doubt it had been the work of Al Qaida. How would you change the U.S. military stance overseas as a result?

Obama's response:

> Well, the first thing we'd have to do is make sure that we've got an effective emergency response, something that this administration failed to do when we had a hurricane in New Orleans. And I think that we have to review how we operate in the event of not only a natural disaster, but also a terrorist attack. The second thing is to make sure that we've got good intelligence, *a.*, to find out that we don't have other threats and attacks potentially out there, and *b.*, to find out, do we have any intelligence on who might have carried it out, so that we can take potentially some action to dismantle that network. But what we can't do is then alienate the world community based on faulty intelligence, based on bluster and bombast. Instead, the next thing we would have to do, in addition to talking to the American people, is making sure that we are talking to the international community. Because as already been stated, we're not going to defeat terrorists on our own. We've got to strengthen our intelligence relationships with them, and they've got to feel a stake in our security by recognizing that we have mutual security interests at stake. (MSNBC 2007b)

After Obama's turn-initial <u>Well</u>, he begins ordinarily with a "first," promising order—a concrete plan, perhaps? But if a plan is being unfurled, then it is an awfully long one, delicately organized into two hierarchically nested layers. There is a "first" step and a "second," the second consisting of two substeps, "a" and "b." Buried several layers deep is the line about what he'd concretely do. To many observers, and campaign antagonists like the Clinton campaign, Obama's response sounded wonkish and weak—weak on the War on Terror.

Obama veered off Message and knew it, especially since John Edwards and Hillary Clinton—the two other candidates who got the chance to field this question after he did—answered with the promise of swift retaliation. Obama tried to get back on Message, but his next chance to speak was in response to a question that had nothing to do with terrorism and defense. It was trained on his personal life, on what he's doing to help improve the environment. Obama fielded the question by saying, "we've also been working to install lightbulbs that last longer and save energy," then seemed to feel compelled to double back to the last question, to get the Message right this time.

In Transcript Segment 1 (see table 6.1), where Obama doubles back, observe the series of what we shall refer to as his "precision-grip gestures" (indicated by the "P" and "p" below the line of transcribed words; see note 1 for a full explanation of transcription conventions). As explained below, this is a gesture in which the hand looks like it is grasping something small. It is shaped so that the tips of the thumb and index finger are held in contact, the other fingers curled under to be in contact with the palm of the hand (see fig. 6.1).[1]

This time Obama delivers the tough, respond-to-terror-with-manly-decisiveness Message, but it's late and strident, suggestive of a candidate who is trying too hard, and who may have leaked how he "really" felt during his first shot at the question (which is how some commentators read that moment): the candidate doth assert too much. Notice the succession of precision-grip gestures here—his longest stretch of precision grip in this debate.[2] Obama produced no precision-grip gestures whatsoever when he answered this question the first time.

Why now? As Obama tries to recover from his botched answer and get back on Message, he seems eager to demonstrate that he *has* a sharp, effective point to make, and it is in this environment that precision grip occurs robustly.

This moment offers evidence of the way precision grip has accumulated additional indexical meaning in debate contexts. Through examining how Obama used this hand shape in gestures in televised debates (2007–2008), let us tease apart distinct effects of co-speech gesture to see how these effects build on each other. We will see that (1) precision-grip gesture highlights information in speech, providing, more technically, what is called "focus"; that (2) this gesture has undergone a degree of conventionalization and has reemerged as a resource for doing the argumentative act we gloss colloquially as "making a 'sharp,' effective point"; and that (3) repetitions of precision grip in debate can invite one to infer

Table 6.1. Transcript Segment 1

Obama	and that's something
	that I'm trying to teach my daughters
	uh
	eight year old Malia
	and- and-
	five year old Sasha
	uh

but

one thing that I do have to [go back on
                   P p   p

uh on this issue of terrorism (1.1)
      P   P

we have genuine enemies out there (.7)
   P   P   p p

that have to be hunted down (1.3)
              P

networks have to be dismantled (.7)
        P   p p   p

°uh° there is no contradiction
          P p p P

between us
P

uh us-

intelligently using our military (.5)
 P   P   P

and in some cases
      P

lethal force
P   P

to take out (.4) terrorists]
P   P

Table 6.1. Transcript Segment 1, *continued*

and at the same time

building the sort of alliances

and trust

around the world (.5)

that has been so lacking over the laf-

uh last six years

not just that one is *making* a sharp point, but that one *has* a sharp point to make, or even that one *is* sharp, argumentatively speaking. All this means that—under certain conditions, and in an indirect fashion, traced below—gesture can come to exhibit qualities of a politician and from there may even contribute to the candidate's brand.[3]

Obama's Precision-Grip Gestures: An Overview

"Precision grip" refers to a family of gestures ("groupings of gestural expressions that have in common one or more kinesic or formational characteristics" [Kendon 2004, 227]) named for the prehensile motion in which something small appears to be grasped. Distinct subfamilies of precision grip can and have been distinguished (see Kendon 1992, 2004), which vary along such key dimensions as hand shape and hand movement. We focus here not on precision grip tout court, but on a subfamily involving index finger to thumb, hereafter labeled "IFT," since these are the precision-grip forms that Obama used in the material studies, this form also being used by most of his Democratic rivals from 2007 to 2008.[4]

Public pronouncements on candidate gesture tend to fixate on highly conventionalized gestures that, like words, are easy to cite in post-event reportage. Obama's precision-grip gestures are not of this sort—that is, they are not gestures that have been termed "emblems" (Efron 1972;

Ekman and Friesen 1969) or "quotable" gestures (Kendon 1990, 1992), which are highly conventionalized, easily reportable manual gestures, which sometimes have names, such as the "OK sign" or "thumbs-up." Gestural emblems have more language-like properties than the more frequent, improvisational, and idiosyncratic forms of gesticulation (see especially McNeill 1992, 2005; Kendon 2004); they can occur in the absence of speech and count as a meaningful utterance by themselves; and they may have widespread and easily reportable glosses, as in the case of "thumbs-up" often glossed as "good," "fine," and so forth, or the "OK sign," which can be considered a kinesic equivalent of the expression "OK." When Obama drums on Message themes in his talk, he offers no gestural emblems. It is not as if Obama flashes certain gestures when he invokes Hope or Change or rails against Hillary Clinton for allegedly being a Washington insider. It is not as if there are gestural equivalents to, say, the rugged Carhartt jacket worn during a hunting photo op, or the red or blue necktie worn as accessory totems of Republican and Democratic Party affiliation. Message does not appear to have been transduced into gesture, even if some commentators talk as if it had. Still, conventionalization and emblematization are not all-or-nothing but rather gradient processes— admitting of degrees—and while precision grip has not developed into a full-blown quotable gesture, it has become a device for showing that one is doing what we call "making a point." And under certain conditions, making a point can even help make candidate brand.

A few major dimensions of IFT precision-grip variation can be distinguished based on recurrent forms of the gesture (see fig. 6.1). In terms of form, the canonical IFT for Obama in the 2007–2008 material is one in which the thumb tip touches either the forefinger's tip—the distal phalange—or the distal interphalangeal joint (illustrated in [b])[5] with fingertips curled in and touching the palm ([a] in fig. 6.1) Obama produces IFT precision grip with either right or left hand, or, much more rarely, left and right hand together (though not necessarily with the same hand shape, as illustrated in [c]). Rare, too, are IFTs in which Obama's fingers are spread out rather than curled in toward the palm; illustrated in [d]. Movement-wise, the vast majority of his precision-grip gestures involve

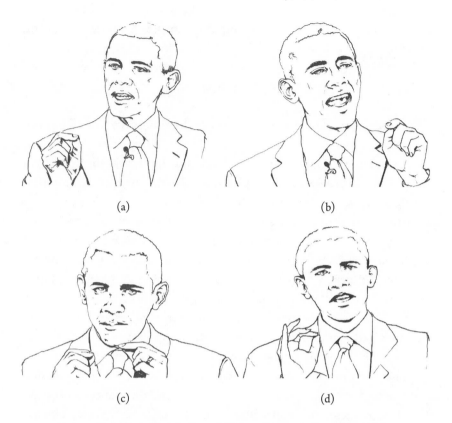

(a) (b)

(c) (d)

FIGURE 6.1A-D. Variation in Barack Obama's IFT precision-grip shape during debates (2004–2008)

(a) thumb touches forefinger distal phalange, fingers curled toward palm (23 July 2007)

(b) thumb touches forefinger distal interphalangeal joint, fingers curled toward palm (23 July 2007)

(c) two-handed stroke with varied thumb position, fingers curled toward palm (15 Nov. 2007)

(d) thumb touches forefinger's distal phalange, fingers spread (21 Oct. 2004)

Artist renderings.

forearm action that produce low-amplitude thrusts either downward, or, more frequently, downward and outward, away from the speaker.[6]

Precision Grip's Basic Meaning: "Focus"

Desmond Morris (1977, 58) suggested in the mid-1970s that IFT precision grip "reflects an urge on the part of the speaker to express himself delicately and with great exactness. His hand emphasizes the fineness of the points he is stressing." Adam Kendon, drawing on careful, empirical "context-of-use" studies, observed that for the IFT precision grip, "the semantic theme that they share is related to ideas of exactness, making something precise, or making prominent some specific fact or idea" (Kendon 2004, 240).[7] In Obama's case, precision grip's basic meaning has to do with information structure. It singles out chunks of information in the flow of speech, creating an effect that in linguistics is often broadly called "focus." It helps make certain elements in speech stand out and can be conceived as a kind of gestural "highlighting" of discourse. Consider a moment from the first presidential debate of 2008 shown in table 6.2.

What kind of focus does precision grip create here? IFT precision grip alone does not unambiguously express any one subtype of focus. It can yield a wide range of information-based "focus" effects, depending on context. Consider, for example, the gesture's "stroke" phase—the phase of a gesture involving "the peak of effort" (McNeill 1992, 83). This is the phase that expresses the gesture's meaning through its form and movement and through its co-expressivity with speech. In the case of line 8's "three hundred billion dollars" (table 6.1), the stroke coincides with and seems to help create an effect we could call "contrastive focus" (it singles out $300 billion as opposed to the $18 billion in earmarks mentioned by McCain.) However, in the same stretch of discourse, IFT precision grip also coincides with the introduction of a new entity in discourse. In Prince's (1981) terms, the second two tokens of "three hundred billion dollars here" (lines 13 and 18) are "textually evoked entities," entities already mentioned in prior discourse, neither of which receives precision-grip highlighting. This means that even in one line—line 8—we cannot say that IFT precision grip expresses one type of "focus." On other

Table 6.2. Transcript Segment 2

Obama	1	but [let's be clear] (.6)
		P p p
	2	uh [earmarks account for eighteen]
		P P P P p p
	3	billion dollars
	4	in last year's budget (.7)
	5	Senator McCain is proposing
	6	and this is a fundamental difference between us (.7)
	7	uh
	8	[three hundred billion dollars] (.7)
		P p P p pp
	9	[in tax cuts] (.6)
		P P P p
	10	to some of the wealthiest (.5)
	11	corporations
	12	and individuals in the country
	13	three hundred billion dollars (.6)
	14	now
	15	eighteen billion
	16	uh
	17	is important
	18	three hundred billion dollars
	19	[is really important]
		P

occasions, precision-grip strokes may also occur with focus-related opera-
tors in language like <u>but</u> and <u>not only</u>. In brief, by itself IFT precision grip
creates a diffuse focus effect; it does not signal any one kind of focus.[8]

It would also be incorrect to say that precision grip highlights only
information in speech. It also has interactional dimensions, as suggested
by the fact that onset strokes (the first stroke in a series of similar, successive strokes) tend to occur in environments in which the speaker is
trying to draw attention—"secure recipiency," as we say—of an interlocutor through gaze direction.[9] Obama tends to shift his gaze toward an
interlocutor around the time that he starts doing precision grip, which
suggests that precision grip tends to be directed or "addressed" toward
others. It seems to express a degree of addressivity, an addressivity not
specified through precision grip alone—this gesture is unlike "deictic,"
that is, pointing gestures (which can, indeed, pick out addressees)—but
through other communicative means, such as gaze direction and linguistic (e.g., the pronoun *you*) and gestural deixis (sometimes jointly). Precision grip may therefore be said to have an "addressive" focus as part of its
basic meaning. And in many cases—perhaps most, insofar as the event
is understood as a debate—some degree of interpersonal 'opposition' is
presumed. Precision grip highlights information that is understood by
default to be directed not just 'to' but 'against' someone else.

Precision Grip in Debate: What It Looks Like to "Make a Point"

Again, why should Obama have resorted to precision grip when he tried
to recover from that botched answer in his first 2007 debate? When the
need for an 'effective' response became relevant, we saw an increased
density in precision grip. This occurred because precision grip, simply
put, has become part of what it "looks like," in terms of gestural demeanor, to do the argumentative thing we term "making a 'sharp' point,"
a rhetorically 'effective' move issued in an environment of contention.[10]

Precision grip has become a gestural ready-made, a stock gesture in the
repertoire of candidates.[11] Evidence of this can be sensed, if only crudely
and indirectly, through noting an association of precision grip with debate

Table 6.3. Transcript Segment 3

Obama	1	I don't-
	2	I don't know where John's getting his figures
	3	[l- l- le- let's just be clear] P
	4	what I do is I close
	5	corporate (.6) loopholes

contexts. Indeed, Obama's precision grip tends to occur more frequently in televised debates than in non-debate settings like speeches delivered to sympathetic audiences at campaign events.[12] Discursively, clues to precision grip's value can be found in the way candidates sometimes use precision grip to signpost that something new, argumentatively, is under way or about to start. In line 1 of Transcript Segment 2, note how the precision-grip onset occurs with "but let's be clear," and that the stroke syncs with <u>let's</u> rather than <u>but</u> (as one might expect if information alone were being foregrounded). Consider, likewise, the following examples from the same debate—the first presidential debate of 2008 (see tables 3–5):

In Transcript Segments (TS) 3–5, Obama's onset of precision grip—that is, the moment when the first stroke of the succession of IFT precision-grip strokes occurs—coincides with a reflexive caption that typifies his argumentative behavior: "let's just be clear" (TS3 line 3; see also TS2 line 1); "I just have to make this point Jim" (TS4 line 2); "let's get back to the core issue here" (TS5 lines 2–3). Each of these captions—being clear, making a point, getting back to the core issue—describes positive argumentative moves and is followed by stance-taking in which Obama disagrees with McCain. (In TS5 the seeming concession in line 5, which concerns apparent military progress in Iraq, gives way to criticism of McCain's position.) The fact that precision grip is part of what it looks like to make a point helps us sense why Obama relied on this gesture when he tried to recover from his weak, off-Message answer.

Table 6.4. Transcript Segment 4

Obama	1	but I- I j- I j-

	2	I just have to make this [point Jim
		P

	3	°uh°

	4	John
		P

	5	it's been (.) your President
		P p p

	6	whom you said you agreed with
		P P

	7	ninety percent of the time
		P P P

	8	who presided] over
		P

	9	this increase in spending (.7)

	10	this orgy of spending

Table 6.5. Transcript Segment 5

Obama	1	but that's (.) senate inside baseball

	2	l- l- [l- let's get back
		P P p p
	3	to the core issue here]
		P

	4	uh

	5	[Senator McCain is] absolutely right
		P p

We also feel inclined to read 'sharpness' of speaker off of Obama's precision-grip gestures, because precision grip has become a conventionalized device for making a sharp, effective point. And while it is possible that a single precision-grip stroke could trigger such a reading, surely it is Obama's copious application of precision grip to his discourse that invites us to read his conduct as evidence of debating prowess—a prowess that has just been cast into doubt, both by his weak answer and by Clinton's and Edwards's more "decisive," on-Message responses to the same question. Obama's precision-grip strokes seem hyperbolic and compensatory. Through repetitions and parallelisms of the gesture, he draws attention to the gesture's conventional use in debate—that of 'making a point'— and invites us to see his precision grips as *speaker*-focal indexicals, signs that are revelatory of the speaker's qualities. He doesn't explicitly ascribe valorized attributes like 'decisive'-ness to himself—that would have been brash, and likely unconvincing. Instead, Obama acts out these qualities, as if through pantomime (see Silverstein 2003a). He exhibits them cross-modally through speech and gesture. Densely poetic precision-grip gestures invite us to infer that Obama has a sharp, effective point to make, and perhaps that he, too, *is* sharp.

Precision Grip in Message

He may have tried to look sharp, but Obama's attempt to get back on Message after the terrorism question failed. Commentators largely disregarded his second try, focusing instead on his first, which they evaluated in relation to front-runner Clinton's. Here, for instance, are members of *The McLaughlin Group* (2007) in post-debate commentary on 27 April:

> MR. MCLAUGHLIN: The big question of the night was, how will Obama measure up to Clinton? Here's Clinton on how she would respond, if president, to a major terrorist attack.
>
> SEN. HILLARY CLINTON: (From videotape.) I think a president must move as swiftly as is prudent to retaliate. If we are attacked and we can determine who was behind that attack, and if there were nations that supported or gave material aid to those who attacked us, I believe we should quickly respond.[13]
>
> MR. MCLAUGHLIN: Here's Obama.

SEN. BARACK OBAMA: (From videotape.) Well, the first thing we'd have to do is make sure that we've got an effective emergency response, something that this administration failed to do when we had a hurricane in New Orleans. And I think that we have to review how we operate in the event of not only a natural disaster, but also a terrorist attack.

MR. MCLAUGHLIN: Question: How did the two front-runners measure up in the first Democratic debate? I ask you, Eleanor.

MS. CLIFT: I think they both more than held their own, but Hillary Clinton in particular was very decisive in that answer. In fairness, Obama got the question—he was first to get it, so the others did have a chance to think through their thoughts. And you saw him really thinking on his feet. But he tends to talk more in abstractions. She's much better on specifics. And she was really commanding and she was warm. I don't think her front-runner status was threatened in the least.

MR. BUCHANAN: I think her front-runner status is more secure than ever. I think she was excellent in that answer. Her answers were crisp and sharp in the whole debate. She was presidential, John. And frankly, the general consensus is that Barack Obama was gauzy, abstract. He's taking pieces out of his speech and delivering them. And he really performed far below expectations. And I think his momentum has been slowed, if not stopped.

"Gauzy, abstract," says Buchanan. "Tends to talk more in abstractions," says Clift. Clinton, by contrast, is judged "crisp and sharp" and "very decisive." Other commentators tended to agree.

The negative Message aired on McLaughlin's show was no isolated incident but represented a kind of running criticism of Obama: that he's good at inspirational speeches but weak on details and substance. Such criticism had been aired before April 2007 but became acute in the wake of Obama's early debate performances, between 26 April and August 2007 especially. Obama came to be plagued by criticism that he is weak on details, on specifics (criticism that targeted, interdiscursively, Obama's reputation of being a gifted, inspiring orator). Some campaign insiders suggested that this off-Message period for Obama was due in part to his campaign's own miscalculation, debate strategy gone awry. Obama's initial strategy in the 2007–2008 Democratic primary debates was reported to have been this: he had planned to go "thematic" to set himself apart from then front-runner Hillary Clinton.

What made it worse was that Obama knew he'd helped build this box himself; that he'd left himself open to, and even invited, the charges of insubstantiality that were bedeviling him. He had signed on to the strategy of stressing thematics over specifics, on the grounds that waging a battle with Clinton on the policy margins would pay paltry dividends. (Heilemann and Halperin 2010, 111–12)[14]

Clinton would reign over policy detail, Obama would push "thematics." After the first few debates, though, it became clear that Clinton's quick, sharp, lucid responses made Obama's look anemic and insubstantial. "All sizzle and no steak." That's how *Game Change* authors John Heilemann and Mark Halperin (2010, 111) put it, summarizing negative Message about Obama at the time. In their insider account of the Obama campaign, they briefly discussed this off-Message period in 2007 when Obama struggled with the debates. Heilemann and Halperin also reported on a self-conscious attempt by the Obama campaign to turn back this criticism in the late spring and early summer of 2007. A concerted effort was made to be more substantive and sharper, to be, dare we say, more 'precise'? "He wanted to be seen as substantive. He *was* substantive. And not being viewed that way was hurting his chances, he thought. I've spent my whole life caring about policy, he told his staff. I want to have new ideas, I want them to be specific. I want to make sure that no one can say they're not specific enough" (Heilemann and Halperin 2010, 112). The *Game Change* authors did not reveal the exact timing of this reported effort to retool Obama's debate strategy, but it likely occurred in the June-July window, and it is noteworthy that at the end of June, in the 28 June debate, a spike in Obama's precision-grip density occurs.[15]

Obama didn't use much precision grip in the four Illinois senate debates against Alan Keyes in 2004 (the density averaged less than 1 percent and ranged from.03 to 2.5).[16] In the first two debates of 2007, the densities were higher than 2004 but still rather modest (7.7 on 26 April, 5.2 on 3 June). But on 28 June 2007 the density increased (and there was no corresponding increase in precision-grip density in non-debate contexts for the same period) nearly threefold, from 5.2 percent to 14.7 percent, and with just two exceptions, for the remainder of the debates it remained consistently high, never falling below 14.5. This increase in density early in the debate season of 2007 appears to have coincided with a period in which the Obama campaign took stock of the first couple of debate performances and tried to readjust.

Precision-grip density is a crude measure—a hint, at best—and it is unlikely that this means Obama's consultants coached him on precision grip or tried to transform Message into co-speech gesture in a project of characterological antithesis, as if the task was to have him argue that he is *not* gauzy and abstract through exhibiting the very opposite qualities. If this shift in density betrays anything, it reveals subtle changes in Obama's gestural habits. These embodied habits may be *responsive* to the interdiscursive dynamics of Message politics, but they are not, properly speaking, "transductions" of Message into gestural form, "transductions" meaning conversions of signs from one semiotic modality to another, often in a bid to generate power (Keane, forthcoming). In product design and branding procedures, one often tries to convert abstractions that are first verbalized—for example, abstract nouns like "strength," denoting a desired brand attribute—into palpable semiotic form (a color or texture, a kind of attire, etc.) so that these forms can then serve as design elements that suggest or point back to the brand. Gestural transductions of Message would mean that precision grip has become a brand-emblem for some social domain of people, but there is no evidence that it has.

And even if precision grip *had* become an emblem, it would still be incapable of indexing candidate brand directly, first, because brand is interdiscursive. It is interdiscursive in the sense that a candidate brand's distinctiveness rests on comparison; brands become recognizable only in a relational field of competition, figured typically as a "market," in which each jostles and vies for consumer-voter attention. Second, candidate brand is interdiscursive in character because mass-media commentary by professional journalists and pundits mediates Message, interpreting it "for" the electorate.

Speaking for Main Street: Gesture and Gaze in Cross-Modal Message Craft

Obama may have stumbled out of the gate in 2007, but by the presidential debates of fall 2008, he had improved a lot. He certainly sounded on Message in his first speaking turn of the first presidential debate of 2008, held by the University of Mississippi on 26 September.

As the cascade of alarming financial news began in September 2008—the storied investment bank Lehman Brothers filing for bankruptcy; Merrill Lynch selling itself to Bank of America; the bailouts of Fannie Mae and Freddie Mac, AIG, the auto industry; the massive "Emergency Economic Stabilization Act of 2008"—the whole ground of the electoral contest shifted. In just two months the economy displaced the Iraq War as the central Issue for Message craft. It also arguably helped dampen buzz around Sarah Palin, McCain's surprise VP pick, who, at least until late September, hadn't been hurt by disastrous interviews and stinging parodies on *Saturday Night Live.* The shift ended up being in Obama's favor, thanks in no small measure to McCain gaffes and Message misfires.

So pressing was the economic crisis that the first debate, which was supposed to have been trained on the topics of foreign policy and national security, was expanded to include critical domestic matters (NewYork Times.com 2008). Wasting no time, journalist and moderator Jim Lehrer addressed the crisis in the very first question:

> Let me begin with something General Eisenhower said in his 1952 presidential campaign. Quote, "We must achieve both security and solvency. In fact, the foundation of military strength is economic strength," end quote. With that in mind, the first lead question. Gentlemen, at this very moment tonight, where do you stand on the financial recovery plan?

Obama got the question first. His response featured a number of key nonverbal accompaniments. Besides IFT precision-grip gestures, there's a series of gestural forms that we can call "count" or "list" gestures. Typically used when a speaker counts off items in some cardinally or ordinally structured list—"one," "two," "three"; or "first," "second," "third"; or "a," "b," "c"—or else some unnumbered but otherwise parallelistically structured sequence, these gestures' strokes occur with each new item being counted off (see fig. 6.2; while not discussed here, variation in hand shape exists in Obama's list/count gestures). The thumb may be extended on saying "one," thumb and index finger extended on saying "two," thumb, index, and middle finger on "three," and so forth. Or, with two hands, the index finger of the right hand may strike and depress the left hand's little finger on saying "one," the ring finger on "two," and so on, ticking off each item while moving across the hand's digits.

FIGURE 6.2A-B. Examples of Count/List Gestures, Democratic Primary Debate, 4 August 2007.

More pronounced than gesture in this turn is Obama's gaze, for he does something here that he didn't do during the primary debates, and that is to initiate "direct" gazes at the camera for long stretches of time. It's as if he were looking "at" us, the American people. He strikes up this gaze behavior early in his first speaking turn, and maintains this gaze for almost all of it; he does this again in a couple turns early in the debate, and then again in his closing statement (see table 6.6).

In addition to direct gaze, observe how Obama presents us with an elaborate, fourfold list. This is unusually expansive, for Obama had produced plenty of threefold lists during the primary debates, but not fourfold ones. Obama's intricate list makes him seem awfully 'orderly.' A candidate with a serious *plan*, perhaps, which is just the kind of "direct-reassurance"-to-the-American-people Message that McCain—being "out of it," as the Obama campaign charged—wouldn't be able to offer as president. By re-transcribing lines 26–34 in a manner that draws out the heightened parallelism, let us now inspect what is arguably a key Message moment (see table 6.7).

Who speaks in lines 28 to 34? Obama, of course, yet he purports to be just animating the utterance. He physically conveys it—utters it—but attributes authorship to someone else, since <u>wonder</u> and <u>you</u> frame

Table 6.6. Transcript Segment 6

12	we are at a defining moment (.5) << initiates and maintains 'direct' gaze at camera>>
13	in our history (.8)
14	our nation
15	is involved in two wars
16	and we are going through the worst financial crisis
17	since the Great Depression (.8)
18	a::nd
19	although we've heard a lot about Wall Street
20	uh those of you on Main Street
21	I think
22	have been struggling for a while
23	and you (.) recognize that
24	this could have an impact
25	on all sectors of the economy (.8)
26	a::nd
27	you're [wondering
	P p
28	how's it going to affect (.) me?
	P P
29	how's it going to affect my job
	P
30	how's it going to affect] my house
	P
31	how's it going to affect my retirement savings
32	or my ability
33	to send (.)
34	my children to college (.5)
35	so we have to move (.) swiftly
36	[and we have to move (.) wisely]
	P
37	and I've put forward
38	a series of proposals that make sure
39	that we protect (.5)
40	taxpayers as we engage
41	in (.) this important rescue effort
42	[number one
	L
43	we've got to make sure that] we've got oversight
	L l l
44	over this whole process
45	$700 billion dollars
46	potentially is a lot of money
47	[number two
	L

Table 6.6. Transcript Segment 6, *continued*

48	we've got to make sure] (.) that ta:xpayers
	L
49	when they are putting their money at risk
50	have (.) the possibility of getting that money back
51	and gains
52	if the market
53	and when the market uh returns
54	[number three]
	L l
55	[we've got to make sure that
	P
56	none of that money (.5)
	P P P p
57	is going to pad
	P P
58	CEO (.) bank accounts
	P
59	o:::r]
	P
60	to promote golden parachutes (.7)
61	[and number four]
	L
62	we've got to make sure that we're helping homeowners
63	because the root
64	problem here
65	has to do with the foreclosures
66	that are taking place all across the country

Table 6.7. Transcript Segment 7

26	a::nd
27	you're [wondering
	P p
28	how's it going to affect (.) me?
	P P
29	how's it going to affect my jo:b
	P
30	how's it going to affect] my house
	P
31	how's it going to affect my retirement savings
32–33	or my ability to se:nd
34	my children to college

the message as reported, as something someone *else* thinks. Who "wonders," then, if not Obama? "Those on Main Street"—a voice Obama had conjured up moments earlier.

As Webb Keane (2001, 268) explains, "The concept of voice, meaning the linguistic construction of social personae, addresses the question 'Who is speaking?' in any stretch of discourse." This is a "social voice" (Agha 2005), a broad category of social actor rather than a biographically specific individual to whom we can pin a proper name. The metonym "Main Street" is a counter-metonym to "Wall Street," and Main Street here stands for "middle class." Both are shibboleths, naturally, not mere labels for objective classes of people; they are rhetorical design elements meant to appeal to all those who feel the "middle class" should be championed. Message-wise, it is middle-class Americans whom Obama says he'll defend as president—in contrast to McCain, whom Obama tries to position as their antagonist. Here Obama draws on Democratic-Party-centered stereotypes about the Republican brand (pro–big business, anti-labor), and does so at a time when there was popular outrage against Wall Street for its role in the financial crisis.

As for McCain, it didn't help that in late August 2008, in an interview, the poor guy couldn't remember how many homes he owned: "I think—I'll have my staff get to you." If he wasn't having a senior moment—which would have fueled fears that McCain was too old and enfeebled to take the reins as commander in chief—then it meant he was "out of it" in a worse sense: that of being so moneyed and patrician that as president he'd be deaf to the needs of ordinary folk. In what was surely a tit-for-tat against the McCain campaign's earlier attacks, which had accused Obama of being out of it—not in terms of wealth but in the sense of being elitist, a celeb with a grossly inflated ego—the Obama campaign preyed on McCain's off-Message moment with a television attack ad called "Seven," referring to the number of homes it said McCain owned. The ad began with a domestic scene. A boy with a backpack steps off his bike and heads toward the front steps of a modest, brick single-family home. His mother waits at the door. The school day, we imagine, is over. The lighting is soft, and the boy's steps are in slow motion, so that, with the lilting piano notes in the background, we feel an emotive wash of "small town," "family"

nostalgia. A male voice-over shatters the scene's serenity by giving expression to the mother's—and by extension all homeowners'—anxiety:
"Maybe you're struggling to pay the mortgage on your home," it begins,
then ends with a callous statement by John McCain: "but recently John
McCain said that the fundamentals of the economy are strong." The ad
then cuts to another home, this one grander but marred by a red foreclo-
sure sign that glowers at us from a white wooden post in the foreground.
Next comes a second statement by John McCain, who, speaking on the
same day he uttered the first quote, can't recall how many houses he owns.
Seven, the ad responds for him, and closes with a fade-in to a third house,
the White House, where it delivers its cutting coda: "And here's one house
that America can't afford to let John McCain move into."

When Obama invokes the middle class in his first turn of the debate,
he vents their concerns in their own words. Lines 28–34 represent their
speech and thought. Formally, the lines look like a straightforward "direct" report (e.g., "Bill said, *'I'm hungry'*" as opposed to indirect: "Bill
said that he was hungry"), as if Obama were being faithful to the form
and content of some originary utterance—in this case, the speech and
thought of the middle class. As with all directly reported speech, the
quote's deictic expressions—such as the pronouns I and you, and, in
lines 28–34, the me and my's—get their value not by pointing to the
immediate context—to Obama, who is doing the reporting. In direct
reports, transposition occurs, in the sense that the reference point for
these expressions is no longer the here-and-now reporting event, the very
occasion of Obama quoting these words; in this case, the perspective is
shifted to members of the middle class, who express their own worries
and frustrations by way of Obama.

Obama has become Main Street's cipher, echoing its concerns, but
what of the gestural, precision-grip overlays? To whom do *those* signs belong? Not to those on Main Street, but to Obama, who acts as if he were
there not just to convey their concerns but also to argue and advocate on
their behalf. He is *for* them, represents them. In Transcript Segment 7 we
have, in short, a cross-modal case of Bakhtinian double voicing. Locked
in an intimate dialogue here are two voices, the one being represented
(those on Main Street), and the one doing the representing (Obama).

And if we weigh aspects of context like Obama's elaborate list making and direct gaze, on balance the dialogue leans toward Obama's own voice as future CEO in chief. It is Obama who takes their side, feels their pain, advocates on their behalf. We sense his agency. In laminating precision grip over this stretch of reported speech, Obama inhabits the lifeways of the middle class—who, if we are to take the final line of his first speaking turn seriously, are the very reason he seeks the presidency.

> I think that the fundamentals of the economy have to be measured by whether or not the middle class is getting a fair shake. That's why I'm running for president. That's what I hope we're going to be talking about tonight.

Obama looks solidly on Message here—no surprise, for this was his first turn, and we expect what he says to be relatively scripted—but that doesn't ensure that the legions of professional commentators will respond favorably.

Keith Olbermann, for one, didn't appear to have been moved by Obama's efforts to reassure an anxious middle class and set himself off from McCain.

> He [Obama] never talked about the reality confronting the working guy out there, the working woman out there. If he wants their votes, why doesn't he talk about the world they live in, why doesn't he talk about the fact that they're losing their pensions? (MSNBC 2008a)

Some did get the Message. Some picked up on Obama's striking "direct" gaze and contrasted that with McCain's behavior.

> John McCain tended not to look either at his opponent, Barack Obama, or at the camera. He tended to address Jim Lehrer. So he wasn't looking at the camera. Look at Barack Obama. He looks straight at the camera. He also was willing to engage John McCain again and again and again. And I think that he got the advantage there. (ABC 2008)

McCain did occasionally glance directly at the camera, but only fleetingly, never for long. His longest stretch was barely more than a second. Obama resorted to this marked gaze behavior for considerable lengths of time, and in environments—"character zones," Bakhtin (1981) would say—in which the voice of the middle class was present. Tellingly, Obama's gaze behavior was most pronounced in his first and last speaking turns, the last being the closing statement. First and last turns are renowned as high Message moments, as we saw with Kerry's attempt at anti-flip-flopping, and both feature Obama's longest stretches of direct gaze. (No less than 89 percent of Obama's first turn, nearly all two minutes of it, was spent in direct gaze, and the part that wasn't was at the beginning, when Obama was busy thanking the moderator, the commission, and the university for hosting the event. The second-longest stretch—a roughly twenty-second-long segment—occurred in his closing statement, and the last time he had made a direct gaze was some fifty-three minutes earlier in the debate.) He was clearly turning on direct gaze at the debate's beginning and end, with Message in mind.

In reading candidate behavior in terms of Message, some commentators attended not to the body but to speech, scanning the candidates' discourse for key words. They performed, in effect, a kind of makeshift "content analysis."

> Number of minutes in a debate, 90. Number of times John McCain mentioned the middle class—zero. McCain doesn't get it. Barack Obama does. (CNN 2008b)

And two days earlier:

> What I did hear Barack Obama say, was in order to get the economy moving again, we've got to deal with reinstating the middle class so they can have money to spend. I watched John McCain talk about how he's going to give $300 billion more to corporate America as well as the very wealthy. And Barack Obama says, look, give it to the people who need it, the people who in fact are in the middle class, that's going to move the economy. Also this. John McCain, how dare you come and give a debate and you don't even say the word middle class? (CNN 2008a)

This sample of post-debate commentary reminds us, once again, that candidate brand depends on the critical mediation of the commentariat—the "filter," as Dubya used to say. It reminds us, too, that all sorts of verbal and nonverbal signs can contribute to readings of Message without these semiotic elements being singled out and cited as Message partials; no surprise, since these elements are not ordinarily experienced as a collection of separate elements but rather as a dense mesh of signs.

Decoding "Body Language," Uncovering Message

Gestures *do* get singled out and mused on from time to time, often with the aid of "body language experts," and this genre of commentary merits attention in its own right. These musings cannot be dismissed offhand as bad science; they are that, of course, but not to the extent they play a role in fashioning and disseminating Message. Consider, for instance, remarks made about John McCain's "tense," "stiff," "choppy" gestures and rather narrow gesture space—the fact that he doesn't seem to be able lift his arms very high—which remind many of the torture he endured as a POW at the infamous Hanoi Hilton. In a 24 October 2008 episode of *The O'Reilly Factor*, Bill O'Reilly brought out "body language expert" Tonya Reiman, but before inviting her to comment on a video clip of McCain, he was careful to offer a preemptive contextualization that was sympathetic to McCain: "We want to always tell the audience that we are very, very cognizant of his war wounds and that he can't do with his upper body what most people can do because he had his arms and shoulders broken and things like that" (Fox News Network 2008b). McCain's body bears traces of his military past, we are told, traces that can, in turn, index strength and steely resolve—all potentially positive facets of his "brand." To be sure, this past poses Message risks for McCain, too. A whisper campaign cut into McCain's Message during the 1999–2000 Republican primaries, when rival George W. Bush's campaign insinuated that McCain's POW years helped explain his oft-mentioned "temper" and spread poisonous rumors about his mental scars and volatility and general lack of fitness for office. In 2008, though, this negative Message about his POW years was no longer salient, and McCain instead was simply a veteran who had served and suffered for country, unlike Obama, who never served and, who knows, may not even be American, as the "birthers" maintained.

In the same 24 October show, after rolling a clip of McCain talking about William Ayers, O'Reilly asked Reiman about a McCain gesture that caught his eye:

O'REILLY: What's the karate chop? What's that?
REIMAN: That's the absolute nonverbal swipe. Definitive. I'm not swaying on this.
O'REILLY: I'm not going to change my mind . . .

REIMAN: I'm not changing my mind.
O'REILLY: . . . no matter how much money you give me.
REIMAN: My position is solid. That's it. (Fox News Network 2008b)

As far as gesture commentary goes, the exchange feels fairly typical, and we should observe how Message—perhaps not surprisingly—gets insinuated into these purportedly disinterested readings of gesture as the commentary unfolds. O'Reilly's colorful "karate chop" descriptor preserves—or at least doesn't disrupt—associations we likely already have about what kind of person and politician McCain is: 'tough'? a little too 'aggressive' maybe? Some of these associations were probably activated through discourse, just through O'Reilly's reminding us of McCain's wartime wounds. There is something about McCain that makes this descriptor a more natural choice than, say, "stiffness" and "awkwardness" in delivery, which, incidentally, were often said of John Kerry's gestures in his 2004 debate performances. (Some snarky viewers said Kerry looked, and sounded, like a "haunted tree.") While O'Reilly's "karate chop" typification may seem consistent—or, again, at least not inconsistent—with our image of McCain, if we follow the flow of gestural descriptions, the consistency builds till McCain sounds like he's squarely on Message.

First Reiman substitutes O'Reilly's "karate chop" with a more authoritative sounding "the absolute nonverbal swipe" (note the definite article and register upgrade; she's the expert). Like O'Reilly, she implies that McCain's gesture was strategic and aggressive, as "swipes" usually are. Reiman goes further. She traces the gesture's trail back to McCain's mind, revealing his internal state as being one of "not swaying" on an issue. (She does this by paraphrasing McCain's inner speech with a direct quote, though there's no matrix clause used to frame it as a quote—for example, a frame like, "He was {thinking, wondering, etc.}.") "Chops" and "swipes" may have sounded a tad too aggressive, having strayed a little too close to that old gossip about McCain's temper and the whisper campaign that had linked such alleged volatility to his POW years. While these descriptions risked nudging McCain off Message, "not swaying" and "not changing"—sticking to one's guns, as they say—sound positive and awfully familiar, do they not? They sound like things politicians ought to do, and something mavericks always do. In a matter of seconds, our commentators have settled into familiar grooves and produced, in effect, a charitable on-Message reading of McCain's hands. They have seen the hands of a maverick.

Take yet another step back and witness the tacit Freudian-style logic at work here, where verbal and nonverbal signs allegedly leak inner states. (Think of *Lie to Me,* a television series [now cancelled] that drew inspiration from the research of Paul Ekman. The show featured a firm of deception experts who scrutinize involuntary micro-expressions to separate truths from lies. Many political "body language" decoders maintain a similar sensibility toward how signs function.) Other musings on body language seem to rest on Machiavellian-style principles, where signs deployed by politicians are understood to be deliberate, strategic means of getting addressees to infer that one has certain inner states, irrespective of whether one really has them.

In some cases, we find a blend of Freudian- and Machiavellian-styled critical readings. Consider, for instance, another exchange involving O'Reilly and Reiman, this one about a moment in the vice presidential debate between Sarah Palin and Joe Biden. In the video clip that O'Reilly shows (Fox News Network 2008a), Biden gets choked up when he mentions his son, who was serving in the military. "Why is he looking down?" asks O'Reilly, to which Reiman replies:

> That's where we grab our emotions from. Whenever we get very emotional, we look down. And he was. The catch in the throat, that's you know, an involuntary muscle. It just gets caught. And you get your throat caught and you hear in the voice. And then you look down, and you see the corners of the mouth go down. And that's a true emotional response. And this actually was where I think Sarah Palin lost points, because at the end of this she saw a very emotional Joe Biden. And instead of looking at him making eye contact, which would have been very powerful. Instead she chose to basically keep that smile pasted on her face and ignore that.

Reiman casts Biden's physiological responses as direct, natural indexes of his emotional state—"a true emotional response"—whereas she judges Palin's behavior as strategic and off-Message: Palin "chose" to maintain a smile and "ignore" Biden's emotional response. Reiman swings between a view of political communication as made up of signs that "give" Message (the Machiavellian mode) and that "give off" Message (the Freudian mode). O'Reilly doesn't let Biden's authenticity escape scrutiny, however. He scratches at the patina by asking Reiman about Biden's frozen forehead, a forehead curiously unresponsive to his tender emotional state. Tell-tale signs of repeated, unmanly Botox injections? O'Reilly mischievously asks. ("I don't know why guys do that, I guess.") Biden's emotions may be real, just not the tautness of his skin.

—

We must admit to a qualm about the very premise of this chapter's exercise. If candidate branding is multimodal, isn't it wrong to privilege gesture and inquire into its role in Message craft? Speech commands attention in debates and stump speeches and town hall discussions, and a vast range of semiotic materials—nearly anything, it would seem—can be exploited to serve as vehicles for Message. So isn't it misguided, then, to tease out one strand, manual gesture, and then ask about its role in holding this cross-modal fabric of candidate brand together? In abstracting out gesture and speculating about its role in candidate branding, do we not risk committing a metonymic fallacy, where we ascribe Message to a part—gesture—that is not experienced as a part, that carries no meaning as a part, that cannot convey Message as a lone sign? Don't we risk doing just what the body-language decoders do, and that is to strip out signs, isolate them, and read them as direct indexicals of Message, or of speaker's minds, or both?

The exercise of abstraction performed here, which asks about the meanings and Message relevance of co-speech gesture, does carry this risk, but it may also be precisely the kind of exercise that can put to rest exaggerated claims made about what gesture does in political oratory and debate. The exaggerations—and there are many—include that of *pervasive emblematicity* (as if most, if not all, political gestures were strongly conventionalized and engineered to achieve rhetorical effects) and *indexical im-mediacy* (as if the indexical path from sign-vehicle to object were 'direct'). In showing how these intuitions break down, this exercise can deter us from trying to jump straight from tokens of gesture to qualities of politician—a jump that is familiar in popular pronouncements on political gesture but also in classic writings like that of Quintilian. Effective though these exaggerations may be in terms of shaping Message about candidates through mediatized commentary, they make it seem as if gesture could index qualities of politicians in as unmediated and rigid a manner as smoke to fire or brand names to their proprietary source. In a sense, such habits of decoding political gesture resemble a neo-physiognomics—physiognomy being that old science of gleaning hidden facts about people from observable qualities of their bodies, moral attributes from the morphology of the face or skull, or, in this case, qualities of politicians from the shape and movement of their hands. In teasing apart the layers of semiotic mediation involved in interpreting gesture, it becomes possible for us to address with more care the old question of how gestural signs participate in the art—or applied science, as the political marketing industry would now have it—of political persuasion.

Seven

WHAT GOES AROUND . . .

How much of what a candidate or incumbent says and does makes it through the concentric layers of media filtration to reach at least a segment or sector of the public? And in what form do the doings and sayings as they are represented by media reports advance or counter the Message intended by the occasion of those doings and sayings? Here we deal with the *circulation of Message*—that is, with the chains of reports of reports of reports of . . . happenings or events the apparent movement of which through social space-time is controlled, in our political public sphere, by the organized political press across a variety of media.

Reporting a prior event, in print journalism or elsewhere, is never merely a report, never a passive, disinterested relay of narrated event in the past to addressees in the present. It is well known that one's personal or organizationally derived attitude toward how a prior event should or should not become newsworthy colors how we report it, and that this coloring can have consequences—"media effects" as students of communication are wont to say. Less obvious is the fact that our very sense that we can follow the principals of a reportable political event by tracking the circulation of their Message-worthy images in social space-time depends on many such events of reporting. As prior events get reported and re-reported, extended *chains of interdiscursivity* form, and these chains across events of reporting events that themselves report events . . . elaborate a network across which we feel the palpable illusion of Message-in-motion. Understanding the crystallization of Message requires that we break up this illusion, especially, as in this extraordinary example, when there are competing Messages sent through the highly reticulated institutional structure of the White House press corps and its sponsoring press organizations.

So let us consider in this light that most important mode of circulation: the circulation, via mass media, of news of happenings and doings that will affect us as members of society and participants in one or more levels of polity. In the mass democratic polities, such as the United States, complex structures of circulation across the socio-spatiotemporal trajectories of communication via print, radio, television, websites, and other media give the citizenry a deferred and vicarious glimpse into the workings of government (itself a complex organizational structure of differentiated powers exercised by those who are incumbent in its various offices). In particular, politicians in the institutional order of mass electoral politics have always had an interdependent relationship to "the press" or "the media," precisely because of their utility in publicity, tantalizingly available for strategically attempting to shape reportage on behalf of a political interest, group, or figure.[1]

The modern American presidency in particular, and all fractally lower-tier orders of electoral office, have increasingly depended on the fact that in such polities it is understood to be an obligation of the media to report the doings, sayings, and other goings-on of any candidate for high office as it is for the incumbent of such office. Political folk learn the rhythms of production of such reports and benefit from study of them and of the wider effect of them on the consumers of media: the electoral populace. Political professionals shape and reshape the doings and sayings of political figures to aid their efforts to get into or stay effective in office. Such professionals speak in their own technical discourse of a political figure's Message, which, as we have seen, is an intentionally stimulated public-sphere imaginary of a sustained, circulating biographical or character image that allows the populace to frame and understand the doings and sayings of the politician. Message in this sense is, as we have said, a cultural concept akin to "brand" in the more general field of marketing, an auratic *je ne sais quoi* that in many cases differentiates one otherwise chemically or functionally same or similar product line from a competing one.[2] The semiotics of brand involve packaging, and it is useful to think of the modalities through which a political figure is thus packaged for Message, both by presentation in certain ways and by avoiding other kinds of presentation that would be deleterious to the coherence of the Message already in process. In politics, with its presumptive default connection to policy and thus to issues relative to which governmental policy is made, a great deal of Message involves at least suggesting a value relationship to certain issues through the complex *son et lumière* of occasion, of staged governmental ritual, designed and carried off just so—even if a specific policy on such Message-relevant issues is not explicitly articulated on such an occasion so much as gestured toward, as in the example we treat.

What we are concerned with here, then, is the way that presidential Message, seemingly strategically organized on a ritual occasion for news media, is threatened, potentially overshadowed, by what are reported as highly negative doings and sayings during the ceremonial event—creating a negative Message that relates to a very different area of issues and that thus threatens the effectiveness of the planned one in its focal area. We are particularly concerned with the way that print news media treated these two Message-relevant events seemingly framed in a single occasion, revealing for us something of the workings of institutionalized socio-spatiotemporal trajectories of circulation on which, certainly, the American presidency has always depended.

Contextualizing the Event That Precipitated the Text

Let's go back to 6 August 1973. Washington, D.C., and with it the rest of the country, was burning not so much from the summer heat as from the daily revelations, broadcast live on network television, of witness after witness who came before the Senate Select Committee on Presidential Campaign Activities, chaired by Sen. Sam Ervin Jr. The scandal was becoming ever more visible, revealing both the Nixon administration's and Richard Nixon's personal involvement in planning, carrying out, and then attempting to cover up the bungled burglary of the Democratic National Committee headquarters in the Watergate Complex on 17 June 1972, during the previous year's presidential election season.[3] On the sixth of August, for example, as the next day's *New York Times* reveals on its front page, the Ervin Committee heard testimony from Patrick Gray, the former CIA director, who, realizing that the White House had been invoking his agency to try to put a stop to FBI investigation of the matter, had told Mr. Nixon to cease and desist—unsuccessfully, it turned out.

In fact the *Times* of 7 August has numerous stories of bad news for Mr. Nixon (fig. 7.1), including a page-one report of another separate investigation revealing that $10 million of public funds had been spent on his estate in San Clemente, California—justifiably and exclusively, the White House maintained in the face of deep public skepticism, for security upgrades for the president. Mr. Nixon's vice president, Spiro T. Agnew, former governor of Maryland and Baltimore County executive, was notified that he was the target of an FBI investigation on suspected acts of "extortion, bribery, and tax evasion."[4] The Vietnam War was still raging its way toward its "peace with [dis]honor" dénouement. Things were not going well for the guy in the Oval Office on any front, to say the least. It was almost precisely a year to the day before Mr. Nixon would be forced by his own party to tender his resignation as president.

But there was one bright spot for Mr. Nixon on the sixth, pictorially reported in a nice United Press International photograph at the bottom of page one in the next day's paper (fig. 7.2). He held a bill-signing ceremony for legislation in one of his signature policy areas—one with which he captivated much of so-called middle America in both the tumultuous 1968 election and certainly in his landslide 1972 reelection: law enforcement. Given that part of Mr. Nixon's Message was (irony of ironies) toughness on crime and beefing up of police powers as the "law and order" answer to 1960s anti–Vietnam War, drugged-out hippiedom, here was a bill originating in Rep. Peter Rodino's House Judiciary Committee (another irony) that would give the beleaguered president a bit of positive publicity. On Friday the third of August, both the House and Senate voted final adoption of a bill for supplementary funds and new powers to the Law Enforcement Assistance Administration, an executive branch agency that had been established in 1968 under Lyndon Johnson. Accordingly, on the following Monday afternoon, the White House mounted one of

"All the News
That's Fit to Print"

The New York Times

LATE CITY EDITION

Weather: Sunny, but today, fair and warm tonight and tomorrow. Temp. range today 79-92. Monday 89-75. Temp-Hum. Index yesterday 79. Full U.S. report on Page 71.

VOL. CXXII . No. 42,199   NEW YORK, TUESDAY, AUGUST 7, 1973   15 CENTS

CAMBODIAN TOWN HIT IN U.S. ERROR; 25 TO 65 KILLED

American Pravda Figures
—Other Reports Indicate Battle Killed More

AN INVESTIGATION BEGUN

Survivors Flock to Capital
—Raid Apparently Worst Accident of War

PHNOM PENH, Cambodia, Aug. 6—An American bomb strike on a large Cambodian town this morning killed and wounded hundreds of people, many Government soldiers and their families.

BURGER PROPOSES LIMIT ON APPEALS: Chief Justice Warren E. Burger, right, being applauded by Justices Harry A. Blackmun, left, and Byron R. White after speech to the American Bar Association. He urged screening of appeals. Details on Page 17.

2 Skylab Astronauts Set Record for Space 'Walks'

By JOHN NOBLE WILFORD

ISRAEL PRODDED BY U.S. ON PEACE

State Department Begins an Effort to Generate New Mideast Ideas

By BERNARD GWERTZMAN

Brooklyn Union Granted 15-Million Gas-Rate Rise

By WOLFGANG SAXON

U.S. Army's Plan In Germany Fights Dissenters in Ranks

By CRAIG R. WHITNEY

AGNEW IS UNDER U.S. INVESTIGATION IN 'POSSIBLE' CRIMINAL VIOLATIONS; INNOCENT OF WRONGDOING, HE SAYS

Gray Says Nixon Seemed To Ignore Warning in '72

By JAMES M. NAUGHTON

Vice President Agnew

CASE IN BALTIMORE

It Is Reportedly Linked to an Alleged Scheme Involving Kickbacks

By R. W. APPLE Jr.

WASHINGTON, Tuesday, Aug. 7—Vice President Agnew announced today that he had been informed that he was under investigation for possible violations of criminal law.

Wheat Tops $4 a Bushel To Reach a Price Record

By H. J. MAIDENBERG

10-MILLION SPENT AT NIXON HOUSES

Security Is Cited as Reason for Outlays—Account ing Pledged by President

By WALLACE TURNER

Violence Flares in South Jamaica As Policeman Kills a Black Man

By ROBERT D. McFADDEN

NIXON EXTENDS AID FOR LAW ENFORCEMENT: The President gestures after signing bill to extend Law Enforcement Assistance Administration three years, at rear, from left are Clarence M. Kelley, F.B.I. director, Attorney General Elliot L. Richardson, and Representative Peter W. Rodino Jr. of New Jersey. Details are on Page 31.

NEWS INDEX

NIXON EXTENDS AID FOR LAW ENFORCEMENT: The President gestures after signing bill to extend Law Enforcement Assistance Administration three years. At rear, from left are Clarence M. Kelley, F.B.I. director; Attorney General Elliot L. Richardson, and Representative Peter W. Rodino Jr. of New Jersey. Details are on Page 31.

FIGURES 7.1 AND 7.2. From The New York Times, August 7, 1973 © 1973 *The New York Times*. All rights reserved. Used by permission and protected by the Copyright Laws of the United States. The printing, copying, redistribution, or retransmission of this Content without express written permission is prohibited.

those moments of high presidential ritual, an Oval Office bill signing with the president appearing in a photo op at his desk in front of the famous windows with a view of the Washington and Lincoln monuments in the distant background. It is this occasion with which we are concerned.[5]

The bill signing, as one can see from the photograph, was all celebratory of a job well done. It was a little moment of bipartisan, even nonpartisan, triumph for Mr. Nixon. You will recall how the personnel are arranged for such an occasion, as shown in figure 7.3. The president sits at his desk, a White House aide on either side, serving papers from the left and removing them from the right as he signs his name, ceremoniously, on each necessary document. The president uses as many pens as possible, passing these souvenirs of the place and ritual occasion back

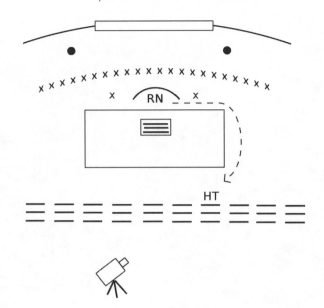

FIGURE 7.3.

to the dignitaries and centrally interested parties who stand in an arc of witnesses behind him. The White House press corps, representing "the people," we trust, comprises the audience who takes all of this in, the cameras recording it all in still and motion pictures behind them.

The president at his desk is the focal point of the ritual event, for in and by his act of signing, he "executes" the bill, rendering it public law. It is a high-ritual performative event, like a marriage, that transforms the social world by the action of a single authorized individual. The president is, after all, the "chief executive" and is ceremonially seated in the very epicenter of presidential authority, which is in the direct line of serial occupancy monumentalized (Washington → ... → Lincoln → ...) outdoors as high points of the entire history of the presidency, of the executive branch. The current president's desk, then, is in a physical sense at the growing tip of leadership as the chief magistrate of the state.

We now know—from many different writers of memoirs, of reflections on his character, as also from the tape-recorded evidence that threatened

Table 7.1.

WASHINGTON [UPI]—President Nixon, a gentleman of the old school, teased a newspaper woman yesterday about wearing slacks to the White House and made it clear that he prefers dresses on women.

After a bill-signing ceremony in the Oval Office, the President stood up from his desk and in a teasing voice said to UPI's Helen Thomas: "Helen, are you still wearing slacks? Do you prefer them actually? Every time I see girls in slacks it reminds me of China."

Miss Thomas, somewhat abashed, told the President that Chinese women were moving toward Western dress.

"This is not said in an uncomplimentary way, but slacks can do something for some people and some it can't." He hastened to add, "but I think you do very well. Turn around."

As Nixon, Attorney General Elliott L. Richardson, FBI Director Clarence Kelley and other high-ranking law enforcement officials smiling [*sic*], Miss Thomas did a pirouette for the President. She was wearing white pants, a navy blue jersey shirt, long white beads and navy blue patent leather shoes with red trim.

Nixon asked Miss Thomas how her husband, Douglas Cornell, liked her wearing pants outfits.

"He doesn't mind," she replied.

"Do they cost less than gowns?"

"No," said Miss Thomas.

"Then change," commanded the President with a wide grin as other reporters and cameramen roared with laughter. [*Philadelphia Evening Bulletin*, 1973]

to impeach him later that very year—that Mr. Nixon was a grotesque, a term we have suggested should be taken in the literary sense, of someone with glaring, larger-than-life character problems and personality dysfunctions, ones that drove, or animated the very plotlines of his biography. Such a grotesque can never leave well enough alone. After the bill had been signed, Mr. Nixon, feeling good, no doubt, and feeling his manly anti-crime oats, as it were—notwithstanding what was happening in the Senate at the other end of Pennsylvania Avenue—got up, came around his desk, and focused his attention on one of the members of the White House press corps.

Here's the report (table 7.1) of that phase of the post-signing transformation of Mr. Nixon, adapted from its presentation at the very outset of the famous paper "Footing" by Erving Goffman (1979).[6]

Recuperating the Prior Text from the Published Text-Artifact

Versions of the report of this incident, which, like the *New York Times* photograph, come from the wire service United Press International, were published in some newspapers on Tuesday the seventh. A very short account appears in the *Times* on page A-31, along with much fuller details of the official occasion, the bill signing; it is appended as part of the personalia tidbits from Washington that supplement the more important or serious news. A more elaborate report, by contrast—the whole UPI filing, in fact—appeared that day in the 7 August *Philadelphia Evening Bulletin*, the late, lamented afternoon paper. It is a narrative account, rich in direct quotation, of what transpired between Mr. Nixon and one of the reporters who was present to witness the bill signing. Read as a narrative report of people's doings and sayings, a bit of what we term 'reportively calibrated metapragmatic discourse', note that it allows us to reconstruct a detailed picture of the interaction turn by turn, social act by social act. In the original event, Mr. Nixon and the reporter and others present are all interacting in particular role incumbencies; in the report, they all become named characters of the story that is being recounted, as it were, to the readers of the *Bulletin*. Ultimately the story has come, originally via the sharp eye of our late colleague Erving Goffman, to us as interested scholars who can retrospectively contemplate what this circulating bit of intelligible cultural Message material says about Mr. Nixon and his time.[7]

In table 7.2 we have reorganized the presentation of the *Bulletin* article to reveal its structure as monologic discourse, thus allowing the examination of its rhetorical force as a descriptive narrative emplotting the interactional sayings and doings of its two central characters, the president and the reporter. Moreover, we have enclosed in boxes the actual direct and indirect quotations of the central characters, so as to reveal the presumptively precise record of the utterances and equivalent denotations of the president and of the reporter whom he targets. With the top-to-bottom serial visual order of "A said ' . . . '" → "B said ' . . . '" → "A said ' . . .,'" the reader of the transcript can understand the original event to be indeed centered on a two-party social interaction unfolding more or less in simple, straightforward adjacency-pair form. Following the Jakobsonian (1960) insights about the role of cotextual cohesion—Jakobson's "poetic function"—in entextualizing a 'text' that is immanent in discourse, the horizontal graphic arrangement of words and expressions in grammatically continuous syntactic construction tries to capture this. Hence, what emerges as a columnar visual arrangement shows the parallelistic repetition of same or semantically clustered words and expressions across chains of two-by-two pairs of linked adjacency-pair parts.

The idea behind the analytic is that interactional segments that are denotationally cohesive (Halliday and Hasan 1976) in this way across multiparty talk serve as the actual diagrammatic means revealing interactional social coherence—an emergent coherence of meaning relative to which participants seem to be playing out their parts over the duration of interaction.[8] Knowledgeable cultural interpreters can reveal how such coherence unfolds, whether in a news report of it, such as in the standard graphic representation of table 7.1, or even more analytically, as in our re-transcription of table 7.2, which attempts explicitly to reveal the dynamic semiotic coherence by using the two-dimensionality of the graphic surface plus various diacritics such as font style.

The first thing to understand about the UPI report is that it is written as a news article, a specific genre of narrative that, in canonical form, starts with a summary of the newsworthiness, the import, of the happenings or doings being described. This article starts: "President Nixon, a gentleman of the old school, teased a reporter." This is news? Well, that he "prefers dresses on women" speaks loudly to those readers of 1973 (and today) who are caught up in one of what would be the wedge political issues for Republicans ever since, second-wave feminism and its battles over what became the sartorial emblems of genderized politico-economic and social stratification: the bra, high-heeled shoes, and here, dresses and trousers.[9] (We have put words designating the potent sartorial emblems at issue in *italics* in the structural transcript so that we can keep track of this recurring focus.) Women wearing pants struck fear into those who would never abide women wearing *the* pants, those fearfully anxious that this would turn men into what were the henpecked husbands of T.V. sitcom-land virtual reality, whether white (Chester A. Riley in *The Life of Riley*) or black (George "Kingfish" Stevens in *Amos 'n' Andy*). Mr. Nixon, it appeared,

Table 7.2.

President Nixon, ["] a gentleman of the old school,["]

teased   a newspaper woman

                    yesterday {**about**

          and   **made (it) clear that**   to the White House}

{he   [her] wearing   *slacks*   on women}.

                                 prefers   *dresses*

The President . . .   UPI's Helen Thomas:

      in a **teasing** voice **said to**

            "Helen, {you x are still   wearing   *slacks*}?:

                  "   you x do   **prefer**   them   actually?:

                              Every time

I   see   {girls   in   *slacks*}

      "   it   }

me x reminds of   China."

            Miss
            Thomas

      somewhat abashed **told**

the President that

            Chinese)   were moving toward   (Western

            Women)   (*dress*

"This [>:] **is** <u>not</u> **said** [to you]

"in an <u>un</u>complimentary   (but) {[wearing] *slacks*}   can do something for

"way,   "some people

"and

"[for]   some [people]   it   can't [ ] —

"but   do very well

you

{[wearing   *slacks*]}.

"I   **think**

"[you]   Turn around!"

As Nixon, Attorney General
  Elliott L. Richardson,
  FBI Director Clarence
     Kelley,
And other high-ranking
Law enforcement officials

  [were]   **smiling** [*sic*],

  Miss
  Thomas   did a pirouette for
the President.

She   {was   wearing white   *pants*},
                              a navy blue   *jersey shirt*,
                              long white   beads
                              and navy blue   patent leather shoes
                                 with red   trim.

Nixon **asked** Miss Thomas

how her husband,
Douglas Cornell, **liked** {her wearing *pants outfits*}.

"He **doesn't mind,**"

replied x she.
[Nixon asked Miss Thomas,]

"...*they*...
x Do ... cost less than *gowns?*"

"No,"

"Then change,"

said Miss Thomas.

commanded ... with a wide grin

. . . the President,

as

other reporters and
cameramen **roared with laughter.**

was firmly on the "old school" side. In fact by 1973, the phrase "[I'm just a] gentleman of the old school" was widely understood as a hackneyed and caricatured attempt at self-excuse uttered by a man for being a "male chauvinist pig," as feminists and their sympathizers saw it. That it is used in description of Mr. Nixon in the news story's lede is, then, quite telling, precisely the kind of polyphonic 'double-voicing' that Bakhtin (1981, 301–308) demonstrates is the hallmark of Dickensian parodic stylization, where the heteroglossic particular phrasings of narrated-world characters break out of their proper world to become the very descriptive terms of the authorial world of narration.

But let us look at the details of what, according to the report, transpired. Let us follow both the framing descriptors in the newspaper report of the actions, **boldfaced** in our diagram, which are labels for ways of doing socially effective things by saying things that then can be quoted, and let us look at the very quoted utterances themselves, rendered in print as what Mr. Nixon and the targeted reporter say.

Breaking ceremonial frame (hence on new 'footing,' as Goffman [1979] termed it), Mr. Nixon addresses the famous woman reporter "in a teasing voice." This reporter is Helen Thomas of United Press International (UPI), a former news agency, whom he calls out by first name, speaking "down" to her in either an assumed superior status or with undue, nonceremonial familiarity. (Note that in American English, the name one uses in direct address works as an indicator of the tenor of social relations between speaker and addressee, equivalent to saying *tu* [as opposed to *vous*] in French. On this equivalence to second-person deictic systems in European languages such as French, German, Russian; cf. Brown and Ford 1961; Ervin-Tripp 1971, 17–29; Murphy 1988). "Helen, are you still wearing slacks?" Mr. Nixon asks with a negative polarity construction, as though asking about any behavior presumed conventionally to be reprehensible ("Are you still beating your husband?" "Are you still smoking dope?").

Since the framing prose of the article states up front that Mr. Nixon "prefers dresses on women," he sets Miss Thomas up as the opposition when he asks her, "Do you prefer them actually?" That is, could it really be the case that she would have this seemingly incomprehensible complementary or opposite preference? Note Mr. Nixon's explanation: that American "girls"—Miss Thomas at the time was a fifty-three-year-old woman—in slacks are like alien others, in particular the Communist Chinese, stereotypically both men and women, Americans thought, dressed in Mao outfits.[10] The great diplomatic triumph of Mr. Nixon's administration, in fact, had been his state visit to mainland China early in 1972,[11] in effect opening up relations with a country of—to Middle America—racialized enemy others that since 1949 had been seen as being across the great divide of the Cold War. Because Miss Thomas is wearing pants rather than a skirt or dress, he associates her with the unisex—that is, gender effacing—customs of the Maoist Chinese, in 1973 still a potent emblem of otherness and enemy opposition, notwithstanding Mr. Nixon's diplomatic entente.

Note, as shown in the diagram of the adjacency pair in table 7.3, that Miss Thomas declines the invitation to inhabit an alien identity by politely reminding the president—she was, as he no doubt knows, one of the press corps members accompanying him on his trip to China—that "Chinese women were moving toward Western dress." In other words, they were, in a sense, realizing their femininity in terms that should be legible even to someone like him. So—but exceedingly politely!—"Buzz off, Bozo!" Notice that Miss Thomas has not answered the main question here about her preference for wearing pants outfits; she simply avoids it, attempting to close down the offending intrusion.

But her nonresponse doesn't succeed. Mr. Nixon starts another round of "teasing," by announcing a "no[n] uncompliment." Uh-oh! Something said not uncomplimentarily is, as any speaker of English (except maybe a logician) knows, not the same thing as something said as a compliment. The double negative does not make a positive; it indexically conveys an almost grudgingly neutral but still somewhat negative evaluation. Here's the interactional move Mr. Nixon has made: it's 'let's-see-if-we-can-make-her-interactionally-uneasy-on-her-feet; self-conscious-and-embarrassed-in-footing' time. He notes, "[wearing] slacks can do something for some people and [for] some [wearing slacks] can't." So which category is Miss Thomas in? "I think you do very well," Mr. Nixon says, rendering judgment with a grudging modicum of graciousness.

Table 7.3.

NIXON:

Helen Thomas

Woman wearing dress : Woman wearing pants [outfit]

::

American woman : Communist Chinese woman

THOMAS:

American women <<< Communist Chinese women

But again he can't seem to stop. "Turn around!" he says, with what we term, grammatically, a bald imperative construction, the most peremptory, or even rude way of formulating a verbal request for someone to do something (Ervin-Tripp 1976; Brown and Levinson 1978, 196). It's quite consistent with calling her "Helen"; it confirms a kind of register consistency that is emergent in the text of this interaction, speaking down the cline of status and power.

What we all have to put up with good-naturedly from organizational status superiors! With all of the male law-enforcement brass "smiling" at her compliant gesture, Miss Thomas metaphorically becomes a fashion model. Just as happens at the end of the fashion-show runway, the model pirouettes so that we can see the colors, the weaves, the lines, and the drapes of the couturier outfit being offered. Here, offered for the president's judgment and approval. Note how the news article now goes into the language of the traditional women's page or style section of the newspaper. At the time, 1973, in fact, one could not read even a serious interview with a woman executive in the business pages of a newspaper that did not go into an elaborate description of her clothing, her office furnishings (feminized interior design), and other gender-marking details. So note that Miss Thomas's outfit, fittingly enough for a government occasion in summertime, was an ensemble in seasonally—and patriotically—appropriate red, white, and blue.

Having secured Miss Thomas's florid and amusing compliance in response to the direct imperative, however, Mr. Nixon now makes explicit to us the stance he has taken as a controlling judge of her worthiness to appear in her ensemble. In our society, it is the domestic partner before whom we try on and thus try out possible outfits, looking to the spouse or equivalent for a thumbs-up or thumbs-down on individual articles of clothing as well as on the total outfit. Would you be seen with me dressed in this? we essentially are asking. Would you be embarrassed or proud of being known as what Erving Goffman termed "my 'with'?"[12]

Characteristically revelatory, Mr. Nixon presses on with his presumptuousness. Does Douglas B. Cornell, then Miss Thomas's husband of two years and thus her culturally legitimated sartorial opinion-giver— presumably also of "the old school"—"like [her] wearing pants outfits?" Whew! What intrusiveness, and what an obvious way that Mr. Nixon is aligning himself as a male empowered to render judgment. "[Mr. Cornell] doesn't mind," the article reports as Miss Thomas's answer. Well, no traction for Mr. Nixon this way, obviously, if Miss Thomas's husband has given his *nihil obstat*, his imprimatur.

At this point, as we can see, Mr. Nixon falls back on one of the most persistent "old school" masculinist stereotypes: that women are somehow irrational in the face of silly things like fashion, while men are all rationality, all the time. "Do [pants] cost less than gowns?" asks Mr. Nixon, according to the article. Gowns? (See table 7.4.) Anyone who speaks American English knows that in our cultural taxonomy of articles of clothing, 'gowns' are a kind of generally expensive, special-occasion-fancy version of the more general taxonomic category 'dresses' (in Great Britain, 'frocks'). That one wears gowns when dressing "up" might, in fact, lie behind Mr. Nixon's peevishness: that, even as chief correspondent of her bureau, Miss Thomas does not think that coming into the Oval Office, into the exalted presence of the chief executive, demands of a woman that she wear a "gown."

Regardless of this, the point presumed here is that if a woman were rational, she would wear the lower-cost article of clothing. So if pants outfits do not cost less than "gowns," why would one wear them? And they do not, Miss Thomas admits, cost less than dresses.

Table 7.4.

CLOTHES IN PUBLIC	
Traditional Men's Clothing	Traditional Women's Clothing
Formal >. . . > Informal	*Formal > . . . > Informal*

			Sportcoat			Skirt
Tails >	Tux >	Suit >	&	Gown > Dress >		&
			Slacks			Blouse

Aha! Nixon's final gotcha! "Then change!" the president "command[s]"—for he is, of course, the 'commander in chief'—"with a wide grin." This final bald imperative to the woman, who has obviously not justified her taste in rational terms, elicits from her male peers and colleagues, as the article notes, roars of laughter. A crescendo of mirth among the boys, first the Justice and FBI brass, who earlier had smiled at Miss Thomas's fashion pirouette, and then the news corps, Miss Thomas's peers, who now roar with laughter at Mr. Nixon's getting the last word of masculine rationality. From the position of power ritually emphasized by the bill-signing ceremony, the "commander in chief" *commands* Miss Thomas to change her style of clothing from the feminist-innovative to the antifeminist-retrograde.

This news story, then, is a report of an event within a ritual event that anthropologists—and psychiatric personnel—immediately recognize. It is an instance of ad hominem—or ad feminam—ritual degradation of the female reporter at the hands of the male president of the United States, a show ritual before an audience of the president's peers and the reporter's peers itself embedded within a larger show ritual for the American people: the signing of a bill to beef up funding and tighten law enforcement at the federal level (increased punishments for certain crimes; sentencing guidelines for judges; fewer rights for those arrested and imprisoned—in short, "law and order" as the right wing of American politics likes to emphasize).

The Circulation of the Newspaper Account

As a newspaper article, the story in and of itself is not particularly interesting. What is interesting is that it reveals—or verbally constructs for the readership as it construes—something of the character of this president: both as a small-minded person willing to attempt this sort of "private," interpersonal degradation at a moment of public triumph for his political persona—and, as the figural head of the United States, as someone who serves as the emblem of antifeminist small-mindedness. Mr. Nixon is revealed to be a brute in his own way. The occasion reported thus associates law-enforcement machismo with taking advantage of the good nature and subordinate position of power of the woman reporter, who through Mr. Nixon's aggression becomes the butt of laughter of the attorney general, the solicitor general, the director of the FBI, other officials, and her peers in the White House press corps.

So why did the reporter file this "objective" report? Key here is the fact that this was filed as a UPI report, as revealed in the *Evening Bulletin*. Of course, the chief UPI reporter at the White House was none other than Helen Thomas herself. This is what we term "payback" time. Mr. Nixon has humiliated Ms. Thomas with his antics. Ms. Thomas uses the institutionalized form of circulation of White House news through her wire service to retell the story, a story that reveals Mr. Nixon naked in his worst characterological ugliness: not merely a cowardly bully, pushing people around from an assumed or inhabited position of presumed power, but one who obviously sees women—even women of Ms. Thomas's age and distinction—as targets for not-so-innocent pranks of devaluing and control as misplaced demonstrations in public of his (male-gendered) power. Note that these are precisely the claims of second-wave feminists about masculinist social formations in general! But here it is right at the top and center of political, and we daresay politico-economic, power at a peak moment when Mr. Nixon's subjective sense of agentivity—as chief executive, executing new law for the country, as it were—was most juiced up, most energized, most grotesque.

Whatever the original event—we are still searching for the original footage in news archives—the communication of that event in subsequent events of communication frames the cultural values emergent in the first event with an overlay of those of the second.[13] Thus, note that the institutional self-placement of journalism as our Fourth Estate rests on the notion that there is an "objective" mode of reportage embodied in the true, fair, and accurate denotational standard of the news article, whether print or broadcast or even on the Internet. However, any careful examination of the texts through which news is reported reveals that it is impossible to avoid the cultural values associated with any form of report by a member of society to and about other members of society. (One need not be a Birmingham School media critic to see this, though, to be sure, "bias" in news has long been a chestnut of such research in media communication.[14])

Here, for example, the emphasis on Richard Nixon's actual utterances summons up particular cultural signs that put him right in the middle—and on the politically "wrong" side—of the second-wave feminist struggle, and in two ways. First is his explicitly articulated view about whether or not women—"girls" of Ms. Thomas's age and distinction—should be wearing pants outfits rather than dresses. Note the potency of these indexicals of political position around restrictive sartorial codes. Second is his naked use of masculine presumption in speaking down to Ms. Thomas, speaking rudely or peremptorily to her, playing with her personal dignity, invading the personal space of her then-recent marital domesticity, shamefully seeking to degrade her in front of colleagues, and so forth. The list is long, but it is everything second-wave feminists had been associating with the male-versus-female gender divide, here revealed in concentrated form. Plus the fact that the guy was so out of it, he didn't even seem to know the difference between men's slacks and women's pants, between the general category of dresses and the idea of formal gowns for evening and similar wear. Yet he had retrograde opinions about these matters that he would impose on Ms. Thomas and, presumably, on the "little lady" upstairs at the White House, in popular presumption ironing his clothes, the late, long-suffering political wife Patricia Nixon.[15]

What is exceedingly interesting to us is that this particular report was not posted on page one of the 7 August *Evening Bulletin*, where other, very damaging news of the Nixon administration was posted in the right two columns (fig. 7.4): Mr. Nixon's louche vice president, Spiro T. Agnew, it was reported, had been notified by the Justice Department that he was under investigation (which, as noted above, would later lead to his resignation); Mr. Nixon's White House counsel, Herbert Kleindienst, revealed that knowledge of the Watergate matter went straight to the Oval Office staff. To be sure, there was more bad news from that very day, paralleling that of Monday's news reported in the *Times* that morning.

But this particular story about Mr. Nixon and Ms. Thomas occurs inside the second, or B, section of the paper on page 7 (fig. 7.5), "Women Today," directed—by an editor who herself may have felt somewhat outraged—at evening-newspaper-reading women, perhaps professional women who, like their male counterparts, in those days read an evening paper on the commuter train home from work. Even the headline of the actual article (fig. 7.6) is somewhat mocking, "Nixon Turns Fashion Critic," then quoting his presumptuous command as though Ms. Thomas had just sashayed down the runway, "'Turn around.'" As if to highlight the outrage, it has a nice UPI colleague's telephoto shot of Ms. Thomas, in her rather fetching outfit, sashaying along the North Portico of the White House after the bill-signing ceremony. "Take that, Tricky Dick!" as if to say on behalf of its women readers. For surely all this is not by chance: mass-communication news is targeted to those who are imagined to be interested in particular ways.

But this is true more generally as well. We know that "circulation" of cultural knowledge and values is accomplished by interdiscursivity of communicative events—events of communication linked to and in various ways incorporating other events of communication that are in turn linked to and incorporating other events of communication, dot dot dot.[16] Such processes of interdiscursivity (Agha and Wortham 2005) move those cultural values through the social space-time of our experience (what the literary critic Mikhail Bakhtin [1981, 84] called a *chronotope*) in sometimes characteristic, sometimes innovative ways.

These paths of interdiscursivity become in effect trajectories of propulsion of cultural knowledge and value, even when they seem most innocently to be mere reports of happenings or doings of certain sorts involving people positioned in certain ways one to another. In the example

íng Bulletin

WITH SUNDAY MORNING EDITION

4 ★★★★ SPORTS
CLOSING STOCKS
SEE PAGE 38

UGUST 7, 1973   DAILY HOME DELIVERY 70¢ PER WEEK; WITH SUNDAY $1.05 PER WEEK   TEN CEN

l in Kickback Scheme

children gather in their Jenkintown home.

od $150 Weekly

U.S. Probes Payments By Maryland Builders

By JERRY LANDAUER
Wall Street Journal

Washington — Vice President Spiro T. Agnew was formally notified by the Justice Department last week that he is a target of a far-ranging criminal investigation by the U. S. Attorney's office in Baltimore.

Possible allegations of bribery, extortion and tax fraud are involved in the case.

The investigation is being carried on in strictest secrecy. On receiving the Justice Department notice, the vice president sought a White House audience, presumably to inform President Nixon.

Agnew Statement

[At about the time today's Journal story appeared on the streets late last night, Agnew issued a statement through his press secretary that said in full:

["I have been informed that I am under investigation for possible violations of the criminal statutes. I will make no further comment until the investigation has been completed, other than to say that I am innocent of any wrongdoing, that I have confidence in the criminal justice system of the United States and that I am equally confident my innocence will be affirmed."]

Not Related

The Justice Department notification, sent by U. S. Attorney George Beall, was hand-delivered to Agnew. Essentially, the investigation stems from the award of state contracts during Agnew's tenure as governor of Maryland in 1967 and 1968—and of federal contracts in Maryland let by the General Services Administration since Agnew be-

Spiro T. Agnew
". . . I am innocent."

came the vice president in January 1969.

The GSA is the agency in charge of constructing federal buildings.

The investigation by the U. S. Attorney's office started last January, initially probing reports of kickbacks and payoffs by contractors, consulting engineers and architects to current office-holders in Baltimore County. Baltimore County, a mushrooming bedroom community bordering the city of Baltimore, is where Agnew launched his political career just a dozen or so years ago, beginning as a zoning official and moving up to county executive, a post he left to become governor in 1967.

In recent months, that investigation has been broadened to embrace state contracts awarded during Agnew's two

Please turn to Page 13, Col. 1

"Big families pay off sometimes."

While this might seem a bit of a contradiction to the average shopper in this day when a smile in the supermarket has become nearly as extinct as the supply as beef, to the Martin family it makes perfect sense.

For along with the logistical problem of feeding his hungry horde, Joseph Martin has the advantage of having four chil-

dren who work, and contribute financially to help surmount the family's staggering food tab.

"The rise in food prices has affected us in terms of the amount of money we spend, but not in what we eat," said Martin, 46, a territory salesman with Pepsi-Cola Metropolitan Bottling Co. Inc. in Philadelphia.

Roasts Go Farthest

"I still shop on the basis of supply and demand," said his 45-year-old wife, Marie. "I buy what I know we will eat. I still buy the same amount and quality of food. I buy a lot of roasts because they go farthest."

Having just finished a roast beef dinner, Mrs. Martin described the family's standard fare as "roast beef one night, chicken the next and maybe hamburger the next. So far we haven't been affected by the beef shortage."

"We eat a lot of meat," said

Kleindienst Tells Of Nixon Shock

Washington — (AP) — Former Attorney General Richard G. Kleindienst said today President Nixon seemed "dumbfounded" when told last April 15 that his top aides had been accused in the Watergate case.

But Kleindienst said the in-

being made to prosecutors by John W. Dean 3d, former White House counsel and Jeb Stuart Magruder, former Nixon campaign deputy director.

Kleindienst said Justice Department officials told him—and he told the President — that Dean and Magruder had

FIGURE 7.4.

THE GREAT INDOORS—Bi-level Oxford Valley Mall receives finishing touches after two years in the making. First level looks in...

Now It's Instant Downtown in Su...

IT TOOK Billy Penn and friends decades to execute plans for downtown Philadelphia, but the Oxford Valley folks did it in two years.

The opening of the new Oxford Valley Mall in Langhorne, Lower Bucks County, on Thursday will introduce a new American concept—an instant downtown in suburbia.

Although the bi-level 1.2 million square foot indoor shopping center was still at a stage of disarray last Friday, Ted Fox, vice president for management of M. A. Kravitz Co., mall manager, was confident that it would be ready for its debut.

Woolworth's and J. C. Penney's won't open until the fall. But Gimbels, Wanamaker's and Bamberger's will be in business, along with most of the mall's about 130 specialty shops.

Conceived as suburbia's answer to a downtown area, Oxford Valley's got all the trappings. It produces its own electricity, pipes in its own water, and has a couple of traffic signals on the road surrounding the site. It even has its own trash compactors.

It boasts a large community room, a small police force, 25-foot trees, a bevy of fountains and even an old-fashioned town square with an outdoor colonnade of shops. Unlike most cities, however, it has 7,000 free parking spaces.

Most of the center is under one roof, a design described as a space frame which looks like an airplane hangar with a see-through roof. And while the top level looks like your run-of-the-mill mall, the first floor has the atmosphere of a bustling city street.

On its grounds is yet another shopping center with a supermarket and a host of discount stores including a Woolco, Lincoln Plaza, as the stepchild of the big mall is called, is on a 8-acre plot.

The Great Indoors, as Oxford Valley dubs itself was a private airport and a couple of farm houses two years ago.

Now it's a shopping mecca. And in the near future, a five-acre lake built for flood control will be used for recreation.

The best way to get to the mall is right up Route 1, since 313 or exit 24 of I-95. It's six miles from exit 28 of the turnpike to Oxford Valley—suburbia's instant center city.

Wearing white pants, a navy blue jersey shirt and long white beads, UPI's Helen Thomas leaves the White House through the North Portico. President Nixon asked Miss Thomas yesterday if pants outfits were less expensive than dresses. When Mr. Nixon was informed they were not, the Chief Executive commanded: "Then change."

Nixon Turns Fashion Critic 'Turn Around...'

WASHINGTON—UPI—President Nixon, a practitioner of the old school, teased a newspaper woman yesterday about wearing slacks to the White House and made it clear that he prefers dresses to slacks.

When a happening ceremony in the Oval Office, the President asked up from his desk and walked over toward the... to UPI's Helen Thomas. "Helen," he said, "are..."

Miss Thomas ...

JOHN WANAMAKER'S famous eagle goes modern in front of its new store in Langhorne.

Joseph X. Dever ... At Marine Corps Reunion

Lugging Volcanic Ash to Rea...

JUST BEFORE we joined the Bulletin half a dozen years or so back, Sen. Henry L. Bellmon, then governor of Oklahoma, invited us to accompany him as an aide on a return to the Pacific battlegrounds where we had fought together during World War II — Saipan, Tinian, and Iwo Jima.

Due to a comedy of errors we never made the trip, but for those who joined us as a comedian not prize, a 25-minute short sound made one an anthem and fall of the black vagabond and of fog, as remote through all these years as most moves.

GUADALCANAL ...

GEORGE H. Rodrue with a lot...

AS IT TURNED out, we were sad we were. You...

UPI Telephoto

Wearing white pants, a navy blue jersey shirt and long white beads, UPI's Helen Thomas leaves the White House through the North Portico. President Nixon asked Miss Thomas yesterday if pants outfits were less expensive than dresses. When Mr. Nixon was informed they were not, the Chief Executive commanded: "Then change."

Nixon Turns Fashion Critic 'Turn Around...'

WASHINGTON—(UPI)—President Nixon, a gentleman of the old school, teased a newspaper woman yesterday about wearing slacks to the White House and made it clear that he prefers dresses on women.

After a bill-signing ceremony in the Oval Office, the President stood up from his desk and in a teasing voice said to UPI's Helen Thomas: "Helen, are you still wearing slacks? Do you prefer them actually? Every time I see girls in slacks it reminds me of China."

Miss Thomas, somewhat abashed, told the President that Chinese women were moving toward Western dress.

"This is not said in an uncomplimentary way, but slacks can do something for some people and some it can't." He hastened to add, "but I think you do very well. Turn around."

As Nixon, Attorney General Elliott L. Richardson, FBI Director Clarence Kelley and other high-ranking law enforcement officials smiling, Miss Thomas did a pirouette for the President. She was wearing white pants, a navy blue jersey shirt, long white beads and navy blue patent leather shoes with a red trim.

Nixon asked Miss Thomas how her husband, Douglas Cornell, liked her wearing pants outfits.

"He doesn't mind," she replied.

"Do they cost less than gowns?"

"No," said Miss Thomas.

"Then change," commanded the President with a wide grin as other reporters and cameramen roared with laughter.

above, even those who may not have had already highly articulated feminist views can see the ugliness of the bundle of associated traits that someone like Mr. Nixon manifested, among them being on the "wrong" side—and floridly inhabiting the negatively portrayed and unenlightened masculine image—of second-wave feminism. Everything he did interactionally, doubling everything he overtly claimed in his quoted denotational-text utterances, pointed to his negative positionality from beginning to end of the story.

This structure of analogic associations of such potently indexical material all built around the centrally emblematic (men-in-) PANTS versus (women-in-) DRESSES dichotomy moves along the paths of its circulation and grows and matures as a revelatory configuration through the telling and retelling of the story, here, in particular, by the reading and rereading of the print text artifact. In our mass societies such telling and retelling always occur through such highly fashioned (no pun intended) instruments of mass broadcast or equivalent print journalism or, now, of robust presence on accessible websites. Such a structure of analogic associations as those in which Mr. Nixon has wrapped—or dressed—himself by denotation and role-inhabitance comes to define the named characters in these exemplary stories of incidents involving them. Conversely, the public comes to understand such incidents by invoking such structures of analogic associations as are already in circulation about the figurated characters, automatically bringing them to bear on what must have been going on in the reported event. This is, of course, what is called in the political world, one's Message.

Message for political figures, like brand for products and services more generally, makes particular incidents involving them intelligible, just as the accumulated lamination of such incidents aligning them to people's interests and to the issues about which people care allows a communicational public to bring political figures into focus. As an imaginable character about whom stories are narrated, a political figure is thus endowed with a biographical aura. In the history of the American presidency, Message, as we have several times noted, has been absolutely central, no matter the era one considers.

So let us consider what is at risk in the way of Mr. Nixon's Message on 7 August 1973 in the media universe of his presidency.

The Media as Messengers of Message

As noted, in American political life Message is the characterological aura of a persona, much like a character in realist literature, who not only has said and done things but also has the potential, as in the fictive universe of plot, to be imaginable as acting in certain ways in situations that are still unrealized in a plot's chronotope—the plot's "future." Everything visible to various political publics, whether directly in televisually mediated spectacle or indirectly in reporters' narrative accounts, revolves around this characterological, this biographical illusion: positions taken on so-called issues; ways of becoming visible against backdrops, with significant others, even caught quote-unquote unawares in candid Goffmanian "backstage" moments. All of this is part of rolling out a candidate's—or, increasingly, maintaining an incumbent's—Message.[17] You can see, we hope, why modern politics—since General Eisenhower's campaign of 1952, to be precise—has merged both conceptually and organizationally with modern advertising, and why political campaigns have long been managed by people who come out of brand-centered advertising or marketing backgrounds, including that special kind of marketing to and through sponsored—that is, purchased or at least rented—legislators called "lobbying." In a sense the communicative aspects of electoral politics have become just one more province of the advertising industry and its person-focused sub-branch, public relations.

A politician's life in U.S. politics, we have noted, involves a lengthy sequence of communicative extravaganzas made up of events in long, long interdiscursive chains punctuated by elections. Especially before election time, this life has long revolved around an *agōn*—Greek for competitive engagement—of positive and negative Message-focused events. In campaign mode, each such event has to develop one's own positive Message and/or to develop one's opponent's negative Message. In incumbency mode, strengthening one's own positive Message in the face of constantly shifting events is central.

These particular semiotic flotsam, the very design elements of communicated Message, become what we term *emblems of political identity* that can be deployed to remind the folks of who—that is, of course, sociologically speaking, what—the political figure is. What are his or her defining qualitative dimensionalities? It is strategically essential to inhabit the semiotic space defined by these emblems of one's own making, and to constantly use them as the building blocks of one's spectacular availability—that is, availability through spectacle—all the while evading the constructions prepared and put forth for you by opponents. Most importantly, one must not seem to be hapless in Message-worthiness, passively defined by events and circumstances that develop and swirl about one. Controlling one's own Message, or being "on message," it is called in the trade: this state of being is seen by insiders to the business of politics as a metaphor for being in control of government, as when thinking about a candidate's possible future of incumbency; controlling Message always remains a desideratum for an incumbent administration.

Such quality-revealing emblems position political figures, allowing a public to identify them in a structural space of relative possible social identities, like protagonists and villains in the emplotments of most of the narratives to which we are otherwise exposed (saliently, a soap opera of grotesques, as we have termed the dominant genre). Such a contrast space provides relative places for political figures to stand in our—the electorate's and the general public's—imaginations, defined thus publicly as personalities by processes that either they have controlled or that circumstances, or their opponents, have managed to shape (as one can see, easily understood as a figuration of being a "winner" or "loser").

The chief way we come to "know" our political figures is through the art of their words and their surroundings, which creates and maintains a biographical world in which they can seem to exist—in which, so seeming, they do, in fact, exist. Political figures, then, depend on the mediation of mediatization to maintain that illusory existence, just as the media are intermediaries who relay the semiotics of the political figure to us in the public sphere by descriptive accounts of these on-stage and off-stage events in which the political figure inhabits Message. The press in America was central to this process in this moment of Mr. Nixon's political career.

In this way the professionals in the press corps, to be sure, play a critical role in broadcasting Message, serving as mediating nodes for relayed accounts of events and thus continuing circulation of them in the public sphere. Press corps personnel certainly understand the nature of the contributory partials of Message, as we have termed them, and become sometimes doubly conscious connoisseurs of them, allowing themselves to be, as it were, used by the political establishment and at the same time making judgment calls as to how much of the artifice of Message-focused communication to expose, to render critically on the public's behalf. As we've noted earlier, the press corps has its own Faustian bargain to make, since goodwill of the political establishment, giving privileged access to inner circles and their inner workings, is the "opportunity cost" of being able to get desirable scoops and exclusives for one's sponsoring print or broadcast or webcast organization. This is the curious institutional position of political reporting, especially of presidential-level reportage, operating completely within a mutually negotiated institutional form—"politics as usual," let's call it—as their continued insider status compels them to. The press learns to live within the parameters that the currently evolved system of Message-ing offers to them. When they stray, they are frequently punished, as several reporters and commentators—Maureen Dowd of the *Times* (New York, not Washington) and Joe Klein of *Newsweek*, for example—were during the 2008 presidential campaign season by being thrown off the McCain and Palin campaign jets and made to arrange their own travel to cover political events of these candidates.

Damage: Controlled?

Now let us return to the Nixon White House of 6 August 1973. It was being defined that summer by the inexorable and unending parade of witnesses before the Ervin Committee, broadcast live on television. Their shocking—or perhaps, in retrospect, not so shocking—testimony about the workings of the Committee to Re-Elect the President (amusingly, with the acronym CREEP) and of the administration itself in the last campaign was daily summarized and elaborated on the front pages of newspapers all across the country. Leaks that filled out the picture were emerging through investigative reporting, the most notable case of which was the *Washington Post* team of Carl Bernstein and Bob Woodward (whose 1974 book, *All the President's Men,* gives overall narrative order to their earlier piecemeal revelations), whose information was in turn relayed in other print and broadcast commentaries.

In a somewhat desperate attempt to counter the leaking and listing of Nixon's torpedoed ship of state, this front-page exposure of the bill-signing ceremony was a kind of journalistic life preserver tossed by the established press. It gave the president a commanding centrality in an event of making public law precisely within the Message he had commandeered in 1968, against the hapless Hubert Humphrey, who, after the bruising winter of the Tet Offensive and the bloody spring of assassinations of Martin Luther King Jr. and Robert F. Kennedy, was followed around by noisy, unruly, unkempt protesters who were angry because however Left Hubert was, he was not Left enough. During that campaign, Mr. Nixon and his campaign crew had merely to point to this noisy and messy stuff as what was in store if people voted Democratic. Mr. Nixon had sustained this Message as president and especially in the triumphal 1972 reelection campaign, another one in which the Democrats managed to scare the electorate by revealing the noisy, messy thing that is participatory democracy. Consistent with his Message, the occasion of the bill signing bespoke Nixonian "law and order" in the controlled confines of the Oval Office that Monday afternoon. Looking at the page-one UPI photograph, we see governmental bipartisanship and unity of the executive and legislative branches around this theme. So no matter how bad all the news on the whole rest of the first page was, this picture, and the story to which it sent the reader on page A-31, was a countervailing tonic resulting from editorial decisions from within that delicate contract between the establishment press and the White House: "Let's give the poor bastard a break."

Ms. Thomas of UPI, by contrast, was always a somewhat unreliable press corps figure in this respect, not much of a player—and, quite unusually in the Washington, D.C., of the era, a woman who worked her way by longevity and seniority to the front row at White House press events.[18] As we see from this incident, in which she attempts to get even

FIGURE 7.7. Bonding over cupcakes: Her due or just dessert?

with—rather than getting mad at—President Nixon, she personifies the risks of Message politics in the institutional communicative economy of the somewhat stodgy, male-dominated establishment that itself represents organizational conventions unenlightened by the second wave. She could write truthfully of the differently "footed" individual behind the official Message that the establishment vehicles colluded with the Nixon administration to present. Their establishment bonhomie shows a Nixon at the helm of an efficiently functioning three-branched government apparatus, countervailing all the bad news they were otherwise spewing forth as the administration expired from self-administered poisons. In a curious way, Ms. Thomas's little story reveals the poisonous fraud being pictured on page one for what it was, and along a line of Message-ing not of the administration's choosing, the "social issue" of gender equity and gender equality. The *Times* buries a short summary account inside, as noted above; the *Post* has no mention of it, as also the other major newspapers. How delicious, then, that an editor of the women's page at Philadelphia's second paper sees fit not only to publish the whole UPI wire story but also to include a photograph of Ms. Thomas—perhaps published with a visual ironic "voice"—illustrating the very pants outfit at issue on 6 August.

As a postscript to this matter of Ms. Thomas's place in the White House press corps, we should point out that when UPI folded definitively in 1999, and with it, her position as head of its White House bureau, she moved over to write commentary for Hearst News Service. Up to recently, she has endured in various relationships to presidential Message-ing. Here is a recent example to consider, which was photographed in the James Brady White House press corps briefing room on the fourth of August 2009: Ms. Thomas's eighty-ninth birthday, and, as it turns out, the forty-eighth birthday of the current president, Professor Obama—whose Message is, of course, "no 'message'" (fig. 7.7).[19]

Mr. Nixon's singling her out missed Ms. Thomas's fifty-third birthday by two days. One wonders if he would have served her birthday cupcakes.

NOTES

1. Celebrity as corporate industry, moreover, depends on a complicated set of relationships that mediate a celebrity's persona, performance, and "privacy" for the masses, which draw together public relations experts working on behalf of celebrity interests, the press in various institutionalized roles (critics, gossip columnists, "lifestyle" reporters, and commentators in all print, broadcast, and web venues), working all as representatives of sometimes global corporate entities with financial interests therein.

2. For details, see Silverstein 2010.

3. As suggested earlier, we use the term "mediatized" broadly to denote processes of mediation by media. While there is no space to develop the argument here, "mediatization," as Agha (2011) has suggested, is best understood by clarifying its relation to semiotic mediation generally. "Semiotic mediation," writes Agha (2011, 174), "is the generic process whereby signs connect persons to each other through various forms of cognition, communication and interaction. It is a process that bridges or links moments of thought/action/conduct involving persons to each other through the use of perceivable signs, making such moments jointly relevant to persons and to their subsequent activities." Mediatization, then, is semiotic mediation via the circulatory processes of mass media.

2. GETTING IT "JU . . . ST RIGHT!"

1. Invoking political philosopher Karl Schmidt and economist Joseph Schumpeter, U.S. federal appellate court judge Richard A. Posner (2003) takes what he terms a self-styled "pragmatic" view of government that sees this as an optimum state-of-affairs of state. The low level of actual citizenly participation and the high level of citizenly tolerance of governance as (others') insider elite business on behalf of the aggregate polity is to be appreciated in this view as what "works." It does strike us as a view of national politics that rationalizes complacency in the face of generally falling voter turnouts in all of the advanced (post-)industrial democracies (that of 2004 in the United States being only a slight upward

blip, perhaps as a function of incredibly costly mobilization of Message on both sides of the contest; that of 2008 only slightly better overall).

2. As we noted in our introductory chapter, the dominant American mass narrative genre, soap opera, is to the point here in structuring the interdiscursive field within which Message operates. American media audiences are well socialized at this time to consume a very great fraction of their mass narrative communication, whatever the medium, under this broad schematization of plot and character development (even in Spanish-language media in which *telenovela* rules). As political communication itself is drawn into the space of such interdiscursive semiosis, the reaction to political figures will itself take on the character of a popular criticism informed by concepts such as "favorite characters" and their chronotopes (Bakhtin 1981), their movements through the space-time of emplotment in the audience's media experience. In this connection, recall too that characters in classic soap opera are grotesques, as literary critics were once wont to term the larger-than-life character, whether they are morally loaded as good or bad. Being understood by an electoral public to be just such a grotesque may increasingly be a communicational opportunity cost of being elect-ably political at the higher realms of our current Message politics: forget trying to run as a decent enough person with some policy ideas (Wendell Willkie? Michael Dukakis? Tim Pawlenty?). In point of fact, we might have seen this forcefully demonstrated on the politi-cal horizon exemplified in the special California gubernatorial recall election of 2003, in which the very gray Gray Davis was blown away by the basically issue-less, though celebrity grotesque, insurgency of Arnold "The Terminator" Schwarzenegger.

3. See, for example, the history of communication in and around electoral politics in Great Britain and the United States revealed in Robertson (1995). For an accessible history of nineteenth-century American English as it was mobilized to communication in the pub-lic sphere, see Cmiel (1990). For a profound analysis of the role of Enlightenment language ideology as a leitmotif of American political history and letters up to the Civil War, see Gus-tafson (1992) on *Representative Words*. Silverstein (2010) treats the problematic implications of such ideology as it focuses on identifying the language community with the political one.

4. As noted in our discussion of Mr. Nixon, pop semioticians of Message like the reporter Joe McGinniss were able to shock the public in 1969 with the explicit comparison of Mr. Nixon to a branded political product made available by advertising professionals for full-press marketing techniques. It was like the first instance of reporting what was just a public secret in the realm of presidential pornography. "Hey! That's my electoral democracy you're talking about! I know what the Constitution says!" the offended Whiggish intellectu-als sniffed in reviewing Mr. McGinniss. (It is amusing to think that he positioned his own book, *The Selling of the President, 1968*, in relation to a brand that was already established, the series of best-selling pop-poli-sci or pop-history books by Theodore H. White titled *The Making of the President 1960, . . . 1964, . . . 1968*. Preach what you practice, we guess!) But of course the involvement of national, even international, advertising in U.S. presidential campaigns hardly began with Mr. Nixon. The heads of the most clout-heavy advertising agencies pleadingly called upon General Eisenhower in 1950 or thereabouts to offer their full array of packaging, marketing, and distributing services gratis if only he would run as a Republican in 1952, not as a Democrat. Recall also that the very popular movie star Robert Montgomery had an office in the West Wing, advising Ike and shaping his media appearances.

5. Given how the American public of 2012 overwhelmingly views the two Bush-Cheney military invasions of 2003, this retrospective revisionism is extraordinarily poignant. It reveals how Message is bound to a fragile and labile sociopolitical here-and-now.

3. ADDRESSING "THE ISSUES"

1. "Debate Analysis: ABC Asked Most Scandal Questions, Obama Was Clear Target," 20 April 2008, http://www.huffingtonpost.com/2008/04/20/debate-analysis-abc-asked _n_97599.html. Accessed 22 October 2008.

2. Will Bunch, "An Open Letter to Charlie Gibson and George Stephanopoulos," 17 April 2008, http://www.philly.com/philly/blogs/attytood/An_open_letter_to_Charlie _Gibson_and_George_Stephanopoulos.html. Accessed 6 November 2008.

3. "Taking Liberties in Philadelphia," 17 April 2008, http://www.factcheck.org /elections-2008/taking_liberties_in_philadelphia.html. Accessed 22 October 2008.

4. FactCheck.org is now joined by a number of comparable services, like PolitiFact.com and fact-checking services linked to national news media (e.g., WashingtonPost.com's Fact-Checker). Issue-monitoring sites include OnTheIssues.org, Project Vote Smart, and news media that offer tracking services, like CNN.com's Issue Tracker. Tellingly, some of the dedicated Issue-watching sites explicitly position themselves as 'compensatory' in the field of public-sphere deliberation about candidates. OnTheIssues.org's site says its "mission is to provide non-partisan information to voters in the Presidential election, so that votes can be based on issues rather than on personalities and popularity" (http://www.ontheissues.org /join.htm, accessed 30 October 2008).

5. Nearly all sites list candidate positions on Issues. Exceptions from the 2007–2008 primaries include Hillary Clinton's site, which only added an [ISSUES] link to her front page sometime between 19 April and 17 May 2007. For quite some time, G. W. Bush's website didn't have "issues," it had an "agenda," though this does not appear to be a widely used descriptor on campaign websites. Having Issues on campaign websites extends to senate and congressional pages, with occasional exceptions (e.g., Elizabeth Dole's site, accessed in October 2008).

6. Unlike McCain's list, Obama's is alphabetized, just like a number of past Democratic campaign websites (e.g., John Edwards and John Kerry in 2004, Gore and Lieberman in 2000). Obama's site appears to have alphabetized its Issues only in late December 2007. Besides the fact that this rubricization of Issues admits of a kind of membership analysis, the alphabetization itself suggests that no one issue (and hence constituency) is more important than another. In addition, the Issue captions in the new web format differ. Instead of predominantly gerundive captions like "Strengthening America Overseas," "Cleansing Washington," and "Fighting Poverty," the new web format features Issues that do not signal Obama's agentive positioning and involvement: "Civil Rights," "Defense," "Disabilities," "Economy," and so on. (Taken together, these two mutually reinforcing patterns may even be seen to resonate with the campaign's post-partisan 'unity' message.) Expectedly, care has been taken to rename Issues during this web edit to preserve a second order of messaging, laminated upon the first. In his non-alphabetized 7 September 2007 site, for instance, the number one Issue (out of fourteen) was "Strengthening America Overseas," but in his newer, alphabetized format, this Issue appears to be renamed "Defense" so that it can remain near the top of the list (second out of twenty-four), just below the new top Issue, "Civil Rights."

7. No individualized "agency" of the stance-taking subject is presumed here. It is the felt presence of the topicalized Issue that interpellates the stance-taker, that summons him or her to assume that role. More precisely, it is a kind of schooled spectatorship of politician-before-the-Issue (by members of the news media, commentariat, and consultants from competing campaigns) that ultimately assigns positions to candidates, even when the latter hem and haw, and even when they produce a null stance, as it were (more on such Issue infelicities below; on stance ascription, see especially Irvine 2009). In interaction-centered literature on stance, the "stance-taker" is sometimes imagined as hardwired followers of a liberal-democratic credo, as if naturally endowed with the capacity and hence the right to evaluate discourse and (dis)align with others. It would be misleading to speak of Issue avoidance from such an actor-centric perspective here, because it is less a stratagem of Message-maximizing rational actors and more an artifact of mediatized ways of interpreting stance-taking for the benefit of a public who needs to be informed.

8. The candidates in this MSNBC-sponsored debate were Joe Biden (senator, Delaware), Hillary Clinton (senator, New York), Chris Dodd (senator, Connecticut), John Edwards (formerly a senator for North Carolina and vice presidential candidate in 2004), Dennis Kucinich (member of the House of Representatives, Ohio), Barack Obama (senator, Illinois), and Bill Richardson (governor, New Mexico).

9. Audio transcript available at http://media.nashuatelegraph.com/projects/edits /primary/clinton/spitzer. Accessed 3 August 2009.

10. CNNPolitics.com, "Transcript of Thursday's Democratic Presidential Debate," 31 January 2008, http://www.cnn.com/2008/POLITICS/01/31/dem.debate.transcript. Accessed 5 August 2009.

11. Transcript of MSNBC "Live with Dan Abrams," 31 January 2008. Accessed through Lexis-Nexis, 21 September 2009.

12. Bill Adair, "Introducing the Flip-O-Meter," PolitiFact.Com from *St. Petersburg Times*. Published on 5 August 2008, http://www.politifact.com/truth-o-meter/article/2008/aug /05/introducing-flip-o-meter. Accessed 24 October 2008.

13. Though not investigated here, it is possible that campaigns drew on this figure so frequently in 2007–2008 because of the senator-heavy nature of the field. Senators are vulnerable to the charge of being "beltway insiders" in ways that governors are not.

14. Katharine Q. Seelye, "On the Road: Clinton's Very Bad Day," 24 May 2008, http://thecaucus.blogs.nytimes.com/2008/05/24/on-the-road-clintons-very-bad-day /?scp=1&sq=clinton%27s%20very%20bad%20day&st=Search. Accessed 9 August 2009.

4. ETHNO-BLOOPEROLOGY

1. It should be noted, in retrospect, that this line of associative stigmatization continued with increasing frequency and shrillness for the entire presidential political season, and it was ratcheted up especially as the presidential campaign moved into the post-convention phase leading up to the election of 4 November 2008. Nor, in fact, has it ceased for any period while Mr. Obama has been in office as president. A whole professionally created and media-stirred Potemkin "movement"—"AstroTurf™," in the parlance, rather than "grassroots"—has come into existence that will not be dissuaded from various assertions to the effect that notwithstanding other evidence Mr. Obama is a Muslim born in Kenya, educated in religious madrassas in Indonesia, and a secret agent of radical Islam.

2. See Silverstein (1976, 47–48) for an outline of four metadiscursive strategies—two of them speaker or sender focused, the other two focused on the addressee or recipient—by which one tries, in effect, to "take back" what has been a consequential move or act[ion] in discursive interaction. One of these strategies, *residual semanticity*, involves sticking to the concept that utterances, it can be officially claimed, have only "literal" meanings, each formulable in a standard and unproblematic way. When one shouts to a noisy theatergoer sitting nearby, "Shut the fuck up!" and is then challenged, one can say, relying on the intuition of semantically equivalent (if interactionally non-equivalent) alternatives, "But all I said was, 'Please be quiet [during the movie]'!" Here, too, in the political blooper one relies on the always available fallback of residual equivalence underlying what seems to be one's mere formal dysfluency or semantic inappropriateness, or referential lapse, or misfire of verbal register, or whatever.

3. There is, to be sure, a vast literature about brand and branding, much of it in a professional "how-to" genre or in the business school "case study" mode. Much of this, non-disciplinary in nature, seems to confuse the socio-semiotic fact of brand with the text-artifactual entity, the brand logo or trademark (which, of course, is the focus of high-stakes legal and economic anxieties and activities). The semiotic study of brand, while vigorous on its own terms, and the anthropological study of branding as a contributory aspect of com-modification, have yet to be developed together with the duplex sophistication required by the phenomenon, though there are "decodings" of advertisements as "cultural texts" (see, e.g., Van Leeuwen 2005) and studies of branding as the focus of marketing organiza-tions (see, e.g., Mazzarella 2003). See the overview by Manning (2010), informed both by politico-economic and semiotic theory.

4. See the retrospective by Rick Perlstein (2008) on this watershed moment in modern American history and its effects. See also the much earlier account of the "Southern Strat-egy" in wresting the Old South and former Confederacy from Democratic control, Kevin Phillips's *The Emerging Republican Majority* (1969).

5. Michael Silverstein's blooperological assistant Brenden Raymond-Yakoubian, re-searching media coverage, found, for example, that the *New York Times* continued to hold on to the unfortunate turn of phrase in stories and commentaries for thirty-one days after it broke as a reportable news item. Imagine the *Washington Times* or *National Review*!

6. All of this is very ironic in light of what finally moved from rumor to newsworthy scandal during the 2008 presidential cycle: not only that Senator Edwards had been car-rying on an affair with a campaign photographer, but also that he was the biological father (genitor) of a child born of this sexual relationship.

7. It took four more years of the Bush-43 administration before the country was ready to accept the syntactic complexity and semantic nuance of a great speaker, Barack Obama, whose return to an older—Kennedyesque, vintage 1961—rhetoric of public political com-munication turned out to be refreshingly new to, meaning heretofore not experienced by, the large number of relatively young voters and, to be reassuring to older ones who recalled the original.

8. Richard Bauman has been collecting and investigating the recorded genres of politi-cal parody, which apparently date back virtually to the beginning of Ediphone cylinder recording. It was this tradition that W. C. Fields, in his various comedies, was building upon, a kind of sesquipedalian bombast that said nothing much about thematic issues but appealed to a cynical consciousness of politics as humbuggery and the mountebank's craft.

For an analysis of Senator Kerry's attempts at countering at least one aspect of this negative Message about him, wantonly "flip-flopping" on issues, see chapter 5.

9. Observe that in the 2008 presidential primaries, then Senator Clinton's campaign made much of the celebrity grotesque surrounding then Senator Obama, and that in the general election Senator McCain's campaign did the same. Following McCain's surprise choice of a vice presidential running mate, the celebrity grotesquery of then Gov. Sarah Palin of Alaska and her truly soap-opera-worthy persona, biography, and family situation riveted the entire political apparatus—campaigns, press, public—and captivated the particular demographic of the Republican Party base who seemed to identify with her and still do. She, not the candidate at the top of the ticket, became the main protagonist of a 2012 made-for-TV film, *Game Change,* set in autumn 2008, thus a fictively real double played by an actress in a plot about the fictive "reality" Governor Palin was asked to inhabit at that time. And all during the lead-up to the film's broadcast Governor Palin was tweeting to her Twitter base her own first-person critique of this or that detail that wide pre-press coverage had been reporting!

10. That is why we pay attention to such things as the time-sensitive trajectory of adjectives that political reporters and analysts use—or even the themes of their cartoons—to help track a sometimes continuously morphing Message in both its positive and negative aspects.

5. UNFLIPPING THE FLOP

1. The transcription by no means exhausts the poetic structure in Kerry's turn. In fact, if one were to re-transcribe lines 1–7 with an eye toward prosodic prominences in intonation units, one would observe, first, that 'message'-related points are foregrounded. (' = high pitch accent;: = lengthening): (line 1) I ' ca:n; (line 2) I be' lie:ve; (line 3) con' victions; (line 5) ' strongest. Though other prominences occur between these four lines, these major beats appear rhythmically integrated, in the sense that they occur at (relatively) regular intervals (5.6 sec., 6.03 sec., and 5.59 sec., respectively) and form (to our ear) a 'perceptual gestalt' (Auer, Couper-Kuhlen, and Müller 1999). What is more, no attempt has been made here to parse Kerry's turn into rhetorically relevant units by attending to metricalized denotational text, as we've done at length in chapter 7.

2. Another objection: might some of Kerry's epistemic phrases, notably I think, express weak 'certainty' or 'commitment' and thus not contribute to this branded image of 'conviction'? In her research on British political discourse, Anne-Marie Simon-Vandenbergen (1996, 2000) observed that I think wasn't typically used to express 'non-commitment' (Jucker 1986). 'Tentative' meanings were overshadowed by authoritative, 'deliberative' ones (Aijmer 1997). Simon-Vandenbergen found that I think tended to occur clause-initially (see also Aijmer 1997; Kärkkäinen 2003); that the complement clauses tended to lack adverbs like perhaps or modal auxiliaries like epistemic might; and that these clauses often had, in contrast, 'grading terms of the maximising type or inherently graded words,' like 'I think it's been a brilliant piece of negotiation'; this, even when the politician was addressing a controversial issue (Simon-Vandenbergen 2000, 53). For Simon-Vandenbergen, this suggested that her politicians use I think to index a certain authoritativeness in the face of contestation. In the 2004 debate, Kerry produced no clause-final tokens of I think, and a mere two clause-medial tokens; of these two, only the first clearly admits of a 'tentative' reading. (About

Bush's shifting positions on North Korea, Kerry says: "Now, that, I think, is one of the most serious, sort of, reversals or mixed messages that you could possibly send.").

3. In terms of density of epistemic phrases, only one other speaking turn by Kerry is comparable to his final turn—namely, the thirteenth turn (6 out of 393). In his final turn, Kerry uses four personalized epistemic phrases based on the predicate believe, which reso-nate, as they did in turn one, with a parallel series of first-person-singular subject-predicate constructions. Before his declaration of conviction and this repetition of I believe, he also uttered two other epistemic phrases: (I think, I know).

4. As counterevidence one might cite Bush's own litany of epistemic phrases midway through his closing statement, featuring four successive tokens of I believe. That these aren't doing the same characterological work as Kerry's is evident especially from the opening of Bush's turn. After thanking Lehrer, he says: "If America shows uncertainty or weakness in this decade, the world will drift toward tragedy." Here, as elsewhere in the debate and in the attack ads on Kerry, Bush links certainty/conviction with strong leadership, and if one substitutes "Kerry" for "America" we get the Message: that Kerry is uncertain, vacillating, weak; that Bush is certain, steadfast, strong.

5. We train our attention on one critical moment in the campaign and do not address how candidates were branded and rebranded over time. Nor do we suggest that the same linguistic and semiotic resources were mobilized across time. In this respect, consider Kerry's ascription of conviction to himself in this debate. In a sample of forty public ad-dresses by Kerry, from 6 July to his concession speech on 3 November, not once does he predicate conviction of himself. (Dates of addresses examined in 2004: for the month of July: 6, 15, 16, 22, 23, 29; August: 5, 7, 12, 18, 19, 24; September: 1, 2, 6, 8, 9, 11, 14, 15 (x 2), 16, 20, 24; October: 2, 3, 11, 14, 15, 16, 18, 19, 20, 21, 22, 24, 26, 27, 29; November: 3). As for the three presidential debates, the second contains one token of conviction in his final turn: ("Obvi-ously the president and I both have very strong convictions. I respect him for that.") The third debate also contains one token, which again occurs in Kerry's final turn.

6. Flip-flopper (and related terms) is not a caption for some monolithic figure. In some inflections it was Kerry's patrician pretentions that were foregrounded, where his lack of decisiveness was a function of his extensive retinue (a charge bolstered by attention to his wife, Teresa Heinz-Kerry, heiress of the Heinz ketchup fortune). In other readings flip-flopping was symptomatic of Kerry's failure to commit to country, a lack of patriotism. This charge was aided by citing his turn against the Vietnam War, by suspicion of his war medals, and by recalling his vote against an $87 billion resolution to supply emergency funds for the troops in Iraq and to support reconstruction there and in Afghanistan. (Again, it is surely no accident that Kerry used his first turn of the first presidential debate to say, "President Bush and I both love our country equally.") Still, common to these indictments is the charge of displaced principal-ship, where the candidate is said to have ceded commitment to The Issues over to some alter(s). It is this displacement that interests us.

6. THE MESSAGE IN HAND

1. Transcription conventions are as follows: line breaks mark intonation unit [IU] boundaries; "(. . .)" = parentheses are used for unfilled pause durations (generally 5 sec-onds or more for inter-IU pauses, with a lower pause-length threshold for intra-IU pauses); "(.)" = unfilled micro-pause, noticeable but generally less than 0.4 seconds; ":" = lengthen-ing; "[_____]" = left and right brackets with underlined text mark stretches of discourse

with precision grip; specifically, the left bracket marks precision-grip "onset"—that is, the first stroke in a series of similar strokes (see note 5 below); the right bracket marks the end of precision-grip hand shape; "[＿＿＿＿]" = left and right brackets with wave-underlined text marks discourse with listing gesture; "P" = precision-grip strokes; "p" = lower-amplitude precision-grip strokes; "L" = list strokes; "l" = lower-amplitude list strokes. Note that only the focal gestures (precision grip, listing gestures) are marked in the transcript; others are left untranscribed.

2. Obama's longest stretch of precision grip in the debate was 18 seconds; the second longest in this debate was slightly under 13 seconds; the average was 6.5. And it's not that Obama was inspired by Edwards's or Clinton's gestural accompaniments, either. Clinton's answer to the earlier question, which promised swift retaliation, featured no precision-grip gestures. Edwards's answer, which also led with the promise to act "swiftly" and "strongly" in response to the hypothetical terrorist attack, featured just a brief stretch of precision-grip gesture, despite his 75-second-long speaking turn.

3. A more detailed discussion and theorization of Obama's IFT precision-grip gestures can be found in Lempert (2011b). This essay discusses how precision grip's distinct values can be understood in terms of a theory of indexical order (Silverstein 2003b).

4. Barack Obama's IFT precision-grip gestures were analyzed in a corpus of twenty-eight televised debates, which include twenty-one 2007–2008 primary debates, the three 2008 presidential debates against Republican candidate John McCain, and four debates from Obama's 2004 senate race against Republican Alan Keyes. A number of non-debate events (especially public oratory at "stump" speeches, delivered before supporters) were considered as well, and Obama's precision-grip gestures were also compared with precision-grip gestures by the seven other 2008 Democratic candidates, using eight consecutive debates stretching from 26 April to 26 September 2007. The other candidates were Joe Biden (senator, Delaware), Hillary Clinton (senator, New York), Chris Dodd (senator, Connecticut), John Edwards (formerly senator for North Carolina and vice presidential candidate in 2004), Mike Gavel (former senator for Alaska), Dennis Kucinich (member of the House of Representatives, Ohio), and Bill Richardson (governor, New Mexico).

5. This thumb position permits precision grip to shade into a pointing gesture, specifically when the hand is rotated so that the palm faces outward and away from speaker, as illustrated in fig. 6.1(b). This hand shape is indeed sometimes used by Obama for gestural deixis and for repeated, downward-directed lectern tapping. Precision grip should not be conceived as a discrete, circumscribed category of gesture but as a caption for a range of features that share a family resemblance and that overlap partially with features of other families. That said, it may well be the case that the precision-grip gestures documented here—and presumably in the repertoires of most American-English speakers—are comparatively fuzzier or "sloppier" in gestural articulation relative to the Neapolitan precision-grip gestures studied by Adam Kendon. For the latter population, distinct types of precision grip exist, and intermediate types do not often occur (Kendon, personal communication).

6. Obama's precision-grip gestures differ along certain dimensions and in varying degrees from the seven other Democratic candidates with whom he competed in 2007 and early 2008. In a sample of eight debates from 26 April to 26 September 2007, variation was most pronounced in terms of hand shape and less pronounced with respect to motion, stroke amplitude, and gesture space. For all eight candidates, amplitude overwhelmingly tended to be low, and gesture space tended to be center, right-center, or left-center

(following Pedelty's 1987 division of gesture space; see also McNeill 1992). In these five debates, all of Obama's onset strokes (the initial IFT stroke rather than successive tokens of the gesture) were precision grips that involved either thumb to tip of forefinger's distal phalange or to the distal interphalangeal joint ([a] and [b] in fig. 1). With the exception of Gov. Bill Richardson, all the candidates tended to resort to a precision-grip shape of thumb to tip of forefinger, though several used finger bunches (thumb touches tips of two or more fingers) in varying proportions (e.g., 71 percent [122/172] of John Edwards's precision grips were thumb to forefinger while 29 percent [49/172] were finger bunches). Richardson was the only candidate for whom a finger bunch was the default precision-grip gesture (95 percent [119/125]). While we have not investigated this systematically on a larger corpus, from this sample the argument made about precision grip for Obama seems to apply to the other candidates, despite the variation in shape noted above.

7. There is no place here to reflect on what terms like "exactness" and "delicacy" and "fineness" could or should mean with respect to precision grip. Is it, on analogy with language, some epistemic 'modal' or quasi-modalizing function that precision grip contributes? Or perhaps precision grip's contribution should be studied even more broadly in terms of "stance" (e.g., Matoesian 2005; Englebretson 2007; Du Bois 2007; Jaffe 2009; Lempert 2008). While contextualized tokens of precision grip can help motivate a wide range of semantic and pragmatic effects, some of which may be glossable as 'exactness,' as argued below, it is the last on Kendon's (2004, 240) list of what precision grip generally does (namely, "making prominent some specific fact or idea") that most closely approximates what is found in the data analyzed here.

8. Germane here is Kendon's (1995, 2004) research on southern Italian gesture, where he describes two precision-grip subfamilies: the "finger bunch" or "*grappolo*" (or G-family) and the "ring" (R-family). In the former the fingers are fully extended and the thumb touches their tips, forming a "bunch"; in the latter the thumb touches only the tip of the index finger, forming a circular "ring" shape while the rest of the fingers remain spread (see Kendon 2004; compare with [d] in fig. 1). While both groupings may be considered to belong to the more general family of "precision grip," based on the common act of grasping something small, Kendon showed that, at least in the Italian material he studied, the contexts of use of the G-forms differed from the R-forms. In both groupings, Kendon found that distinct form and movement types correlated with distinct information-based construals, ranging from topic marking, to comment marking, to what he has sometimes captioned broadly as "making precise." For the R-forms, in contrast to the G-forms, "the semantic theme that seems to unite all of these usages is the theme of 'making precise.' That is to say, these gestures are used in conjunction with spoken expressions that either quote some exact fact or figure, or clarify an idea, a description, an observation or opinion" (241). For a more detailed comparison with Kendon's research, see Lempert (2011b).

9. Effort to secure recipiency is evidenced by the tendency for gaze shifts (not just those of Obama but also those of the other candidates) to occur immediately before the onset stroke (i.e., during the gesture's preparation phase) or during the onset stroke's execution.

10. In a sample of seven consecutive debates (26 April to 7 August 2007) and ten non-debate campaign events (21 April to 3 August; almost all of which were campaign stump speeches to Obama's supporters, held both indoors and outdoors) from the same period, precision grip had almost three times the average density in debate relative to non-debate settings (14.4 percent and 4.9 percent respectively).

11. The other Democratic candidates tended to use precision grip in a manner similar to Obama, despite variation in precision-grip hand shape (see note 6).

12. Using ELAN (a multimedia annotator developed by the Max Planck Institute for Linguistics), precision-grip "density" was assessed by coding as single annotations stretches of precision grip, defined on the left boundary by onset stroke (excluding any preparation). Any successive precision-grip strokes and lower-amplitude repetitions were included as part of the annotation, and the right boundary was delimited using the moment the precision-grip hand shape ends. All stretches of Obama's speech in which his gestures were visible (not obstructed by camera position or cuts to the crowd) were then separately annotated, and then the ratio of the total duration (measured in milliseconds) of precision-grip highlighting to the total time in which gestures could have been displayed was assessed. As discussed later, the first two debates (26 April and 3 June) were low in precision-grip density and comparable to that of non-debate events from the same period, though this changes dramatically in late June. For now, the basic observation is that no corresponding spike in precision-grip density occurs during the same period and that, on average, precision-grip density in debates greatly exceeds that of non-debates.

13. Clinton's response in full:

> Well again having been a Senator uh during nine eleven, I understand very well the extraordinary horror of that kind of an attack and the impact that it has far beyond those who are directly affected. I think a president must move as swiftly as is prudent to retaliate. If we are attacked and we can determine who was behind that attack, and if there were nations that supported or gave material aid to those who attacked us, I believe we should quickly respond. Now that doesn't mean we go looking for other fights. You know, I supported President Bush when he went after Al Qaida and the Taliban in Afghanistan. And then when he decided to divert attention to Iraq, it was not a decision that I would have made had I been President, because we still haven't found Bin Laden. So let's focus on those who have attacked us and do everything we can to destroy them.

14. It is unclear whether this reported strategy was operative in the first couple of debates. There is some discursive evidence of this strategy in July. It may be that the plan either took on more urgency in the wake of Obama's initial, weak performance or perhaps was even developed as a response to his subpar performance.

15. While there is little evidence of a change in debate strategy in the second debate, held on 3 June 2007, one does at least sense a small shift on the 'decisiveness' front. The debate's first question, directed to Obama, raised the very issue that had sunk him in April: terrorism.

> SCOTT SPRADLING, WMUR: Senator Obama, you get the first question of the night. It has been nearly six years since 9/11. Since that time, we have not suffered any terrorist attacks on U.S. soil. Just yesterday, the FBI arrested three men for a terror plot at JFK Airport. Could it be that the Bush administration's effort to thwart terror at home has been a success?
>
> SEN. BARACK OBAMA (D) ILLINOIS: No. Look, all of us are glad that we haven't had a terrorist attack since 9/11, and I think there's some things that the Bush

administration has done well. But the fact of the matter is that we live in a more dangerous world, not a less dangerous world, partly as a consequence of this president's actions. (CNN 2007)

Obama replies with a punchy, decisive, turn-initial <u>no</u>—not a discourse-marker <u>well</u> followed by an answer that reads like a laundry list. Obama, the *Game Change* authors report, "had a lot to say and wasn't good at spitting it out quickly or concisely, tending to back into his responses. Rather than sell one idea well, he tried to squeeze in as many points as possible" (Heilemann and Halperin 2010, 110). At this moment at least, he sounded sharper, and post-debate coverage did register some improvement from the first debate.

16. Obama's 2004 debate appearances featured little in the way of precision grip, but that was not true of his celebrated speech later that year at the Democratic National Convention. Not only was the density of precision grip high relative to his 2004 debates (11.8 percent), but there was an unprecedented diversity of precision-grip forms, most of which never appeared again in the 2007–2008 video corpus of debates. In his 2004 speech, more than a third of his precision-grip gestures were finger bunches in which thumb touches the tips of index and middle fingers, and there was an instance of a finger bunch where thumb touches the tips of three fingers. Slightly more than a fifth of his precision-grip gestures were thumb to tip of middle finger, not index finger. This event was clearly an exception.

7. WHAT GOES AROUND . . .

1. Among recent studies of such relationships by political scientists and communication theorists, mostly centered on Western democracies and their mass media, note Bennett and Entman 2001; Brader 2006; Hajer 2009; Meyer 2001; Negrine 2008; Norris 2000; Rawnsley 2005; Rozell 2003; Sanders 2009; Stanyer 2007; Trent and Friedenberg 2004. For a "how to" manual by a noted practitioner, see Luntz 2007. A recent linguistically centered collection is Fetzer and Lauerbach 2007.

2. See Moore 2003 and Manning 2010 for recent discussions from within linguistic anthropology. The recent crop of books by marketing professionals is interesting for the way their subtitles, rather than their titles, seem to offer "brands" of brand consciousness and marketing strategy. Among the more colorful: "the alchemy of brand-led growth" (Sherrington 2003); "creating unique brands that stick in your customers' minds" (Post 2005; the book is titled *Brain Tattoos*); "insights on the art of creating a distinctive brand voice" (Duffy 2005); "translating virtual world branding into real world success" (De Mesa 2009); "humanizing brands through emotional design" (Gobé 2007); "unleashing the power of storytelling to create a winning marketing strategy" (Vincent 2002); "how to build brands, redefine markets, and defy conventions" (Grant 2006); "building extraordinary brands through the power of archetypes" (Mark and Pearson 2001; the book is titled *The Hero and the Outlaw*); "rediscovering the lost art of the big idea" (Schley and Nichols 2005). Because of the pecuniary value of branded entities projected out into market futurity, the semiotic paraphernalia of brand, including the brand name—think of McDonald's—become trademarks that can be legally registered and defended against infringement by competitors. Celebrities in entertainment and related cultural industries have had a certain success in defending their public personae as brands, given the direct pecuniary interest they have in sustained uniqueness over their performance careers, while politicians, whose interests in "public service" are presumptively independent of such interest (violations are

in some cases actionable as offenses against integrity, i.e., "corruption"), have brands—that is, "messages"—that are inherently in the public domain and subject to multiple potentially transformative effects on them. (Many thanks to the anonymous reviewer who ruminated on the difference between the two to our benefit.)

3. According to testimony by several of those eventually convicted, there had also been an earlier, undetected break-in on 28 May 1972. This did not figure centrally in the brewing public scandal leading everyone's attention to the Oval Office itself.

4. Mr. Agnew would soon resign the vice presidency on 10 October 1973 as part of a plea agreement reached with federal prosecutors. The looming alternative, conviction on all counts after a trial, would have brought a long jail sentence.

5. In the official record, *Public Papers of the Presidents of the United States; Richard Nixon . . . 1973,* Appendix B, p. 1079, we find for 6 August: "In a ceremony in the Oval Office, the President signed into law the Crime Control Act of 1973 (HR 8152 approved August 6, 1973, as Public Law 93–83, 87 Stat 197)." The original vote in the House of Representatives, on 18 June, was 391–0 with 42 abstentions; the Senate appears to have passed their version originally on 28 June without even the necessity of a roll call.

6. In the paper, it served Goffman as an illustrative starting point in his discussion of how interactants manage to change 'footing'—that is, social role-relational incumbencies with respect to segments of an ongoing denotational text the unfolding of which mediates interaction. Managing a change of 'footing' frequently involves, among other changes, a rearrangement of physical placement of the body and of face-to-face exclusivities in participant frameworks, as Goffman pointed out and as illustrated here.

7. Goffman himself, interested in the 1979 paper in 'footing' in the micro-sociological contexts of actual face-to-face interaction, passes over matters of gender in silence. As will be seen below, matters of the cultural politics of gender in the macro-sociological context of 1973 America seem to be central in this material, both as a metapragmatic narrative text and as an institutionally circulating potential news article available on, but not widely adopted from, a wire service feed. That Goffman was collecting visual print material in the early 1970s for his 1976 "Gender Advertisements" may indeed have facilitated his coming across the print article and thus may have rendered this example of change of 'footing' particularly noteworthy to him, even if it was for use in another study.

8. This is the thesis that 'what-we-say'—that is, the denotational text properly seen in both its grammatical and cotextual ("poetic") structurations—is projectable as a Peircean indexical icon that dynamically figurates, or plays out in real space-time, 'what-we-do' in-and-by utterance—in other words, what social acts our communication "counts as." See Silverstein 1985, 1997, 2004, 2005a, 2007; and now the further developments of Lempert 2005, 2008, 2009 that redefine old chestnuts such as 'force', 'stance', etc. in these terms.

9. Radical New York Feminists organized guerilla theatrical demonstrations on the Atlantic City, New Jersey, boardwalk outside the venue of the 1968 Miss America Pageant on 7 September, throwing sartorial emblems of women's felt sense of oppression—high-heeled shoes, girdles, bras, curlers, tweezers—as well as mops, pots and pans, and copies of *Playboy* magazine into a "Freedom Trash Can." Although a proposal to burn the contents was made by the crowd, and a small fire may have in fact been briefly started, police soon prevailed on grounds of potential damage to the boardwalk. But, via inaccurate press reports, ever after this event feminists have been labeled as "bra-burning" radicals by political opponents. See

Bonnie J. Dow's (2003) wry account of the rhetorical back-and-forth with the Miss America Pageant producers in the wake of the 1968 action and its media aftermath.

10. The word "girls" was one of the most salient indexical shibboleths of "male chauvinist pig" register at the time. See R. Lakoff 1973, 61n9, a passage transferred to the main text in the latest reprinting (2004, 56).

11. From 21 to 28 February 1972, the president traveled to Beijing, Hangzhou, and Shanghai, meeting with Chairman Mao Zedong and with Premier Zhou Enlai. The "Shanghai Communiqué" jointly issued at the conclusion of the trip, pledged a full normalization of relations on the basis of the recognition by the United States that there is only one China, both on the mainland in the People's Republic and on Taiwan. On his return, Mr. Nixon proclaimed: "This was the week that changed the world, as what we have said in that Communiqué is not nearly as important as what we will do in the years ahead to build a bridge across 16,000 miles and 22 years of hostilities which have divided us in the past. And what we have said today is that we shall build that bridge." Mr. Nixon's perceived bold move in traveling to the People's Republic of China was milked for Message-worthiness even as part of his semiotic self-redemption after being forced from office in disgrace. In a way, old "Tricky Dick" never stopped running.

12. That is, the one with whom I am associated by others as being part of a social dyad, such as a domestic-group couple, either member of which can elevate or lower the dyad's status. Hence, intimacy's licensing to one of the right of critique of the other on behalf of the dyad.

13. The network news archives seem not to have such footage at this late date, and the collection in the Nixon Presidential Library has not yet been calendared sufficiently for searching, given how much of the material has been subject to litigation and other impediments to public use.

14. For a Bakhtinian reading of the contribution in particular of metapragmatic discourse devices to such inevitable "biasing" by indexing evaluative stance on the moral loading of narrated events, see Locher and Wortham 1994 and Wortham and Locher 1996, 1999. Metapragmatic descriptors of segmentable speech-event segments constitute the basic vocabulary of Conversation Analysis descriptions as well, to be sure; cf. Levinson 1983, 336, for terminology applied to first- and second-adjacency-pair parts in interactionally coherent sequences. As if braced for such critique, Silverstein's wife's graduate journalism school instruction circa 1980 strictly forbade any metapragmatic framing verb other than say-, for fear of introducing non-"objectivity" into news reportage.

15. See the interesting portrait of Patricia Nixon by her daughter, Julie Nixon Eisenhower (1986), subtitled "The Untold Story." The one possible excuse for Mr. Nixon's taking such liberties with Ms. Thomas is that Mrs. Nixon was friendly to her through her husband, Douglas Cornell, who had long worked for Associated Press (see Thomas 1999, 232–33). But certainly as the interaction developed into an interactional text of ritual degradation, it went beyond friendly "teasing," the adult equivalent of a boy's pulling on the ponytail of the girl sitting in the seat in front of him. Male-male ritual insults, too, cannot be invoked here except as a misplaced analogue.

16. See Urban's (1996, 2001, 2010) interesting formulations of the roles of 'metaculture' and of presupposable social structure, including institutionalization, in the "circulation" of cultural texts.

17. Of course, the precise methods for building and maintaining this kind of image, and for keeping it in circulation, have changed over time as technologies of communication have changed in the broadcast mode—from a source to a self-selecting "market" of addressees, sometimes in stages or phases of circulation. Today, for example, it is rare for us to feel that we live in an era of the unforgettable and quotation-worthy speech on a carefully, thematically constructed occasion, as in Mr. Lincoln's day (see Silverstein 2003a), which relied on verbatim quotation in newspaper circulation and then many further echoes in popular phraseology for a certain image-building half-life. Today, as in contemporary product branding, a multimodal or cross-modal media strategy is necessary to reinforce all the components of a message in which the political persona—not necessarily the actual individual politician concerned—is to exist in the communicational interface with the public. That this became blatant for the first time in Mr. Nixon's 1968 presidential campaign led some people to be "shocked, shocked" that *The Selling of the* [Republican] *President, 1968* (McGinniss 1969) would follow upon *The Making of the* [Democratic] *President* in 1960 and 1964 (White 1961, 1965).

18. See Ms. Thomas's 1999 autobiography, *Front Row at the White House: My Life and Times,* in which she notes the struggle to be recognized as in the first line of presidential reporters.

19. Ms. Thomas had a spectacular and precipitous fall from her stance of populist objectivity when, after a rabbi's unexpected question to her on 27 May 2010 about her views on Israel, she blurted out, "Tell them to get the hell out of Palestine!" AIPAC—Anti-Defamation League—World Zionist Congress Red Alert! Ms. Thomas resigned and retired from Hearst on 7 June, the day after the Obama White House commented on the clip of this that went viral on YouTube and for which her apologies were to no avail.

REFERENCES

ABC. 2008. "The Candidates Debate: And the Winner Is?" *Nightline*. Transcript. 26 September.

Adair, Bill. 2008. "Introducing the Flip-O-Meter." *St. Petersburg Times*. 5 August. Available at http://www.politifact.com/truth-o-meter/article/2008/aug/05/introducing-flip-o-meter. Accessed 24 October 2008.

Agha, Asif. 2005. "Voice, Footing, Enregisterment." *Journal of Linguistic Anthropology* 15 (1): 38–59.

———. 2007. *Language and Social Relations*. Cambridge, UK: Cambridge University Press.

———. 2011. "Large and Small Scale Forms of Personhood." *Language and Communication* 31 (3): 171–80.

Agha, Asif, and Stanton E. F. Wortham, eds. 2005. Special issue. "Discourse across Speech Events: Intertextuality and Interdiscursivity in Social Life." *Journal of Linguistic Anthropology* 15 (1).

Aijmer, Karin. 1997. "I Think: An English Modal Particle." In *Modality in Germanic Languages: Historical and Comparative Perspectives,* edited by T. Swan and O. J. Westvik. 1–47. Berlin: Mouton de Gruyter.

Auer, Peter, Elizabeth Couper-Kuhlen, and Frank Müller, eds. 1999. *Language in Time: The Rhythm and Tempo of Spoken Interaction.* New York: Oxford University Press.

Bakhtin, Mikhail M. 1981. *The Dialogic Imagination.* Translated by C. Emerson and M. Holquist. Edited by M. Holquist. Austin: University of Texas Press.

———. 1986. *Speech Genres and Other Late Essays.* Austin: University of Texas Press.

Bauman, Richard. 1983. *Let Your Words Be Few: Symbolism of Speaking and Silence among Seventeenth-Century Quakers.* Edited by P. Burke and R. Finnegan. Cambridge Series in Oral and Literate Culture. New York: Cambridge University Press.

Bauman, Richard, and Charles L. Briggs. 2003. *Voices of Modernity: Language Ideologies and the Politics of Inequality.* Cambridge, UK: Cambridge University Press.

Benen, Steve. 2008. "Political Animal." 8 October. *Washington Monthly*. http://www
.washingtonmonthly.com/archives/individual/2008_10/015092.php. Accessed 11 July
2011.

Bennett, W. Lance, and Robert M. Entman, eds. 2001. *Mediated Politics: Communication in
the Future of Democracy*. Cambridge, UK: Cambridge University Press.

Bernstein, Carl, and Bob Woodward. 1974. *All the President's Men*. New York: Simon and
Schuster.

Biber, Douglas, and Edward Finegan. 1989. "Styles of Stance in English: Lexical and
Grammatical Marking of Evidentiality and Affect." *Text* 9 (1): 93–124.

Blow, Charles M. 2012. "Mitt, Grits and Grit." *New York Times*. Op-Ed. 9 March. http://
www.nytimes.com/2012/03/10/opinion/blow-mitt-grits-and-grit.html?_r=1&ref=
charlesmblow. Accessed 11 March 2012.

Blumenthal, Sidney. 1980. *The Permanent Campaign: Inside the World of Elite Political
Operatives*. Boston: Beacon Press.

Bourdieu, Pierre. 1984. *Distinction: A Social Critique of the Judgement of Taste*. Translated by
R. Nice. Cambridge, MA: Harvard University Press.

Brader, Ted. 2006. *Campaigning for Hearts and Minds: How Emotional Appeals in Political
Ads Work*. Chicago: University of Chicago Press.

Brown, Penelope, and Stephen C. Levinson. 1978. "Universals of Human Politeness."
In *Questions and Politeness: Strategies in Social Interaction,* edited by Esther N. Goody.
56–289, 295–310. Cambridge, UK: Cambridge University Press.

Brown, Roger, and Marguerite Ford. 1961. "Address in American English." *Journal of
Abnormal and Social Psychology* 62 (2): 375–85.

Bunch, Will. 2008. "An Open Letter to Charlie Gibson and George Stephanopoulos," 17
April. http://www.philly.com/philly/blogs/attytood/An_open_letter_to_Charlie
_Gibson_and_George_Stephanopoulos.html. Accessed 6 November 2008.

Campbell, Karlyn Kohrs, and Kathleen Hall Jamieson. 1990. *Deeds Done in Words:
Presidential Rhetoric and the Genres of Governance*. Chicago: University of Chicago Press.

———. 2008. *Presidents Creating the Presidency: Deeds Done in Words*. Chicago: University
of Chicago Press.

CBS News. 2008. "Face the Nation." 29 June. http://www.cbsnews.com/video/watch
/?id=4217703n.

Chicago Sun-Times. 2007. "What's Romney Bin Thinking? Get Those Names Right."
Editorial. 25 October 25. 33.

Clarke, Thurston. 2004. *Ask Not: The Inauguration of John F. Kennedy and the Speech That
Changed America*. New York: Henry Holt.

Cmiel, Kenneth. 1990. *Democratic Eloquence: The Fight over Popular Speech in Nineteenth-
Century America*. Berkeley: University of California Press.

CNN. 2004. "Cheney, Edwards Spar over Iraq Policies." Transcript part I. 7 October. http://
www.cnn.com/2004/ALLPOLITICS/10/05/debate.transcript/index.html. Accessed 24
April 2007.

———. 2007. "New Hampshire Democratic Presidential Candidates Debate." 3 June.
http://transcripts.cnn.com/TRANSCRIPTS/0706/03/se.01.html. Accessed 18 February
2012.

————. 2008a. "Analyzing the First Presidential Debate." *Anderson Cooper 360 Degrees.* Transcript. 26 September. http://transcripts.cnn.com/TRANSCRIPTS/0809/26/acd .02.html. Accessed 20 March 2012.

————. 2008b. "The Week's Political Events in Review." *This Week in Politics.* Transcript. 28 September.

————. 2008c. "Transcript of GOP Debate at Reagan Library." CNN Politics. http:// articles.cnn.com/2008-01-30/politics/GOPdebate.transcript_1_governor-romney-budget-gap-mitt-romney?_s=PM:POLITICS. Accessed 14 March 2012.

————. 2008d. "Transcript of Thursday's Democratic Presidential Debate." 31 January. http://www.cnn.com/2008/POLITICS/01/31/dem.debate.transcript. Accessed 5 August 2009.

De Mesa, Alicia. 2009. *Brand Avatar: Translating Virtual World Branding into Real World Success.* Basingstoke: Palgrave Macmillan.

Dow, Bonnie J. 2003. "Feminism, Miss America, and Media Mythology." *Rhetoric and Public Affairs* 6 (1): 127–49.

Du Bois, John W. 2007. "The Stance Triangle." In *Stancetaking in Discourse: Subjectivity, Evaluation, Interaction,* edited by R. Englebretson. 139–82. Amsterdam: John Benjamins.

Duffy, Joe. 2005. *Brand Apart: Insights on the Art of Creating a Distinctive Brand Voice.* New York: One Club Publishing.

Dulio, David A. 2004. *For Better or Worse? How Political Consultants Are Changing Elections in the United States.* Albany: State University of New York Press.

Dunham, S. Ann. 2009. *Surviving against the Odds: Village Industry in Indonesia.* Durham, NC: Duke University Press.

Efron, David. 1972. *Gesture, Race and Culture: A Tentative Study of the Spatio-Temporal and "Linguistic" Aspects of the Gestural Behavior of Eastern Jews and Southern Italians in New York City, Living under Similar as Well as Different Environmental Conditions, Approaches to Semiotics.* The Hague: Mouton.

Eisenhower, Julie Nixon. 1986. *Pat Nixon: The Untold Story.* New York: Simon and Schuster.

Ekman, Paul, and W. Friesen. 1969. "The Repertoire of Non-verbal Behavior: Categories, Origins, Usage and Coding." *Semiotica* 1: 49–98.

Englebretson, Robert, ed. 2007. *Stancetaking in Discourse: Subjectivity, Evaluation, Interaction.* Pragmatics and Beyond New Series 164. Amsterdam: John Benjamins.

Ervin-Tripp, Susan. 1971. "Sociolinguistics." In *Advances in the Sociology of Language.* Vol. 1. *Basic Concepts, Theories, and Problems: Alternative Approaches,* edited by Joshua A. Fishman. 15–91. The Hague: Mouton.

————. 1976. "Is Sybil There? The Structure of American English Directives." *Language in Society* 5 (1): 25–66.

FactCheck.org. 2008. "Taking Liberties in Philadelphia." 17 April. http://www.factcheck .org/elections-2008/taking_liberties_in_philadelphia.html. Accessed 22 October 2008.

Feldman, Jeffrey. 2007. *Framing the Debate: Famous Presidential Speeches and How Progressives Can Use Them to Change the Conversation (and Win Elections).* Brooklyn, NY: Ig Publishing.

Ferrara, Kathleen. 1994. "Repetition as Rejoinder in Therapeutic Discourse: Echoing and Mirroring." In *Repetition in Discourse: Interdisciplinary Perspectives,* edited by B. Johnstone. 66–83. Norwood, NJ: Ablex.

Fetzer, Anita, and Gerda Eva Lauerbach, eds. 2007. *Political Discourse in the Media: Cross-cultural Perspectives*. Amsterdam: John Benjamins.

Filmer, Paul. 2003. "Structures of Feeling and Socio-cultural Formations: The Significance of Literature and Experience to Raymond Williams's Sociology of Culture." *British Journal of Sociology* 54 (2): 199–219.

Fox News Network. 2008a. "'Body Language': Joe Biden, Sarah Palin, Barney Frank." *The O'Reilly Factor*. Transcript. 6 October.

———. 2008b. "'Body Language': Sarah Palin, O'Reilly's 'View' Appearance." *The O'Reilly Factor*. Transcript. 24 October.

Fraser, Nancy. 1993. "Rethinking the Public Sphere: A Contribution to the Critique of Actually Existing Democracy." In *The Phantom Public Sphere*, edited by B. Robbins. 1–32. Minneapolis: University of Minnesota Press.

Gabler, Neal. 2008. "The Maverick and the Media." *New York Times*. Op-Ed. 26 March. http://www.nytimes.com/2008/03/26/opinion/26gabler.html?pagewanted=all. Accessed 9 March 2012.

Gobé, Marc 2007. *Brandjam: Humanizing Brands through Emotional Design*. New York: Allworth Press.

Goffman, Erving. 1959. *The Presentation of Self in Everyday Life*. Garden City, NY: Doubleday.

———. 1967. *Interaction Ritual: Essays on Face-to-Face Behavior*. New York: Anchor Books.

———. 1974. *Frame Analysis: An Essay on the Organization of Experience*. New York: Harper Colophon Books.

———. 1976. "Gender Advertisements." *Studies in the Anthropology of Visual Communication* 3 (2). Washington, DC: Society for the Anthropology of Visual Communication. [Reissued in book form, New York: Harper and Row, 1979.]

———. 1978. "Response Cries." *Language* 54: 787–815.

———. 1979. "Footing." *Semiotica* 25 (1–2): 1–29.

———. 1981. "Footing." In *Forms of Talk*, edited by E. Goffman. 124–59. Philadelphia: University of Pennsylvania Press.

Goodwin, Marjorie Harness. 1990. *He-Said-She-Said: Talk as Social Organization among Black Children*. Bloomington: Indiana University Press.

Gouldner, Alvin Ward. 1971. *The Coming Crisis of Western Sociology*. New York: Avon.

Graham, Michael. 2007. "Anyone behind Wheel, Hillary?" *Boston Herald*. Op-ed. 1 November. Available at http://www.bostonherald.com/news/opinion/op_ed/view.bg?articleid=1041769&srvc=next_article. Accessed 15 February 2012.

Grant, John. 2006. *The Brand Innovation Manifesto: How to Build Brands, Redefine Markets, and Defy Conventions*. Chichester, Eng.: John Wiley and Sons.

Gustafson, Thomas. 1992. *Representative Words: Politics, Literature, and the American Language, 1776–1865*. Cambridge, UK: Cambridge University Press.

Habermas, Jürgen. 1984. *The Theory of Communicative Action*. Boston: Beacon Press.

———. 1989. *The Structural Transformation of the Public Sphere: An Inquiry into a Category of Bourgeois Society*. Translated by T. Burger. Cambridge: MIT Press. [Original 1962]

Hajer, Maarten A. 2009. *Authoritative Governance: Policy Making in the Age of Mediatization*. Oxford: Oxford University Press.

Halliday, M.A.K., and Ruqaiya Hasan. 1976. *Cohesion in English*. London: Longman.

Haviland, John B. 2006. "Gesture: Sociocultural Analysis." In *Encyclopedia of Language and Linguistics,* edited by A. Anderson and E. K. Brown. 66–71. Boston: Elsevier.

Heilemann, John, and Mark Halperin. 2010. *Game Change: Obama and the Clintons, McCain and Palin, and the Race of a Lifetime.* New York: Harper.

Hobson, Dorothy. 2003. *Soap Opera.* Cambridge, UK: Polity Press.

Holland, Steve. 2007. "It's the Year of the Flip-Flop in U.S. Politics." Reuters.com. 10 June. Available at http://www.reuters.com/article/2007/06/10/us-usa-politics-flipflops-id USN0836055720070610. Accessed 115 February 2012.

Horowitz, Jason. 2007. "Biden Unbound: Lays into Clinton, Obama, Edwards." *New York Observer.* 5 February. http://www.observer.com/2007/politics/biden-unbound-lays-clinton-obama-edwards. Accessed 15 February 2012.

Irvine, Judith T. 2009. "How Mr. Taylor Lost His Footing: Stance in a Colonial Encounter." In *Stance: Sociolinguistic Perspectives,* edited by A. M. Jaffe. 53–71. Oxford: Oxford University Press.

Irving, Washington, William Irving, and James Paulding. 1871 [1807]. *Salmagundi.* Philadelphia: J. B. Lippincott.

Iser, Wolfgang. 1974. *The Implied Reader: Patterns of Communication in Prose Fiction from Bunyan to Beckett.* Baltimore: Johns Hopkins University Press.

Jaffe, Alexandra M. 2009. *Stance: Sociolinguistic Perspectives.* Oxford: Oxford University Press.

Jakobson, Roman. 1960. "Closing Statement: Linguistics and Poetics." In *Style in Language,* edited by Thomas A. Sebeok. 350–77. Cambridge: MIT Press.

Jameson, Fredric. 1991. *Postmodernism; or, The Cultural Logic of Late Capitalism, Post-Contemporary Interventions.* Durham, NC: Duke University Press.

Jamieson, Kathleen Hall. 1988. *Eloquence in an Electronic Age: The Transformation of Political Speechmaking.* New York: Oxford University Press.

———. 2006. *Electing the President, 2004: The Insider's View.* Philadelphia: University of Pennsylvania Press.

Johnson, Dennis W. 2007. *No Place for Amateurs: How Political Consultants Are Reshaping American Democracy.* 2nd ed. New York: Routledge.

Jucker, Andreas H. 1986. *News Interviews: A Pragmalinguistic Analysis.* Amsterdam: John Benjamins.

Kärkkäinen, Elise. 2003. *Epistemic Stance in English Conversation: A Description of Its Interactional Functions, with a Focus on* I Think. Amsterdam: John Benjamins.

Kavanagh, Dennis. 1995. *Election Campaigning: The New Marketing of Politics.* Oxford: B. Blackwell.

Keane, Webb. 2001. "Voice." In *Key Terms in Language and Culture,* edited by A. Duranti. Malden, MA: Blackwell.

———. 2002. "Sincerity, 'Modernity,' and the Protestants." *Cultural Anthropology* 17 (1): 65–92.

———. Forthcoming. "On Spirit Writing: The Materiality of Language and the Religious Work of Transduction." *Journal of the Royal Anthropological Institute.*

Kendon, Adam. 1990. "Gesticulation, Quotable Gestures, and Signs." In *Culture Embodied,* edited by M. Moerman and M. Nomura. 53–78. Osaka: National Museum of Ethnology.

———. 1992. "Some Recent Work from Italy on 'Quotable Gestures' ('Emblems')." *Journal of Linguistic Anthropology* 2: 92–108.

———. 1995. "Gestures as Illocutionary and Discourse Structure Markers in Southern Italian Conversation." *Journal of Pragmatics* 23: 247–79.

———. 2004. *Gesture: Visible Action as Utterance.* Cambridge, UK: Cambridge University Press.

Kiesling, Scott F. 2005. "Norms of Sociocultural Meaning in Language: Indexicality, Stance, and Cultural Models." In *Intercultural Discourse and Communication: The Essential Readings,* edited by S. F. Kiesling and C. B. Paulston. Malden, MA: Blackwell.

Lakoff, George. 2004. *Don't Think of an Elephant! Know Your Values and Frame the Debate: The Essential Guide for Progressives.* White River Junction, VT: Chelsea Green.

Lakoff, Robin Tolmach. 1973. "Language and Woman's Place." *Language in Society* 2 (1): 45–80.

———. 2004. *Language and Woman's Place: Text and Commentaries.* Rev. and exp. ed. Edited by Mary Bucholtz. Oxford: Oxford University Press.

Latimer, Matt. 2011. "Is Romney the Next Kerry?" Daily Beast. 9 October. http://www.thedailybeast.com/articles/2011/10/09/romney-a-flip-flop-used-to-be-more-liberal-than-ted-kennedy.html. Accessed 15 February 2012.

Lefort, Claude, and John B. Thompson. 1986. *The Political Forms of Modern Society: Bureaucracy, Democracy, Totalitarianism.* Cambridge: MIT Press.

Lempert, Michael P. 2005. "Denotational Textuality and Demeanor Indexicality in Tibetan Buddhist Debate." *Journal of Linguistic Anthropology* 15 (2): 171–93.

———. 2008. "Poetics of Stance: Text-metricality, Epistemicity, Interaction." *Language in Society* 37 (4): 569–92.

———. 2009. "On 'Flip-Flopping': Branded Stance-Taking in U.S. Electoral Politics." *Journal of Sociolinguistics* 13 (2): 223–48.

———. 2011a. "Avoiding 'The Issues' as Addressivity in U.S. Electoral Politics." *Anthropological Quarterly* 84 (1): 187–208.

———. 2011b. "Barack Obama, Being Sharp: Indexical Order in the Pragmatics of Precision-Grip Gesture." *Gesture* 11 (3): 241–70.

Levinson, Stephen C. 1983. *Pragmatics.* Cambridge, UK: Cambridge University Press.

Lim, Elvin T. 2008. *The Anti-Intellectual Presidency: The Decline of Presidential Rhetoric from George Washington to George W. Bush.* Oxford: Oxford University Press.

Locher, Michael A., and Stanton E. F. Wortham. 1994. "The Cast of the News." *Pragmatics* 4 (4): 517–33.

Lopez, Kathryn Jean. 2008. "Running for President of Europe?" National Review Online. 7 October. http://www.nationalreview.com/corner/171547/running-president-europe/kathryn-jean-lopez. Accessed 9 July 2011.

Luntz, Frank I. 2007. *Words That Work: It's Not What You Say, It's What People Hear.* 1st ed. New York: Hyperion.

Luo, Michael. 2007. "Romney Makes Obama-Osama Gaffe." *New York Times.* 23 October. "The Caucus" [political blog]. Available at http://thecaucus.blogs.nytimes.com/2007/10/23/romney-makes-obama-osama-gaffe. Accessed 15 February 2012.

Malcolm, Andrew. 2008. "Barack Obama Makes a One-Fingered Gesture While Speaking of Hillary Clinton." *Los Angeles Times.* 17 April. http://latimesblogs.latimes.com/washington/2008/04/obamaflipsoffcl.html. Accessed 18 February 2012.

Manning, Paul. 2010. "The Semiotics of Brand." *Annual Review of Anthropology* 39: 33–49.

Mark, Margaret, and Carol S. Pearson. 2001. *The Hero and the Outlaw: Building Extraordinary Brands through the Power of Archetypes*. New York: McGraw-Hill.

Mason, Jeff. 2008. "Clinton Upstages Republicans with Stimulus Plan." Reuters.com. 11 January. http://mobile.reuters.com/article/politicsNews/idUSN0264367920080111?i=5. Accessed 15 March 2012.

Matoesian, Gregory. 2005. "Struck by Speech Revisited: Embodied Stance in Jurisdictional Discourse." *Journal of Sociolinguistics* 9 (2): 167–93.

Mauser, Gary A. 1983. *Political Marketing: An Approach to Campaign Strategy*. New York: Praeger.

Mazzarella, William. 2003. *Shoveling Smoke: Advertising and Globalization in Contemporary India*. Durham, NC: Duke University Press.

McGinniss, Joe. 1969. *The Selling of the President, 1968*. New York: Trident Press.

McLaughlin Group. 2007. Transcript. McLaughlin.com. 27 April. http://www.mclaughlin.com/transcript.htm?id=595. Accessed 18 February 2012.

McNeill, David. 1992. *Hand and Mind: What Gestures Reveal about Thought*. Chicago: University of Chicago Press.

———. 2005. *Gesture and Thought*. Chicago: University of Chicago Press.

Mendelsohn, Matt. 2008. "McCain Injures Fingers Making Quotation Marks Sign, Suspends Campaign." *Huffington Post*. 29 October. http://www.huffingtonpost.com/matt-mendelsohn/mccain-injures-fingers-ma_b_138754.html. Accessed 18 February 2012.

Meyer, Thomas. 2001. *Mediokratie: die Kolonisierung der Politik durch das Mediensystem*. Frankfurt/M: Suhrkamp.

Moore, Robert E. 2003. "From Genericide to Viral Marketing: On 'Brand.'" *Language and Communication* 23 (3–4): 331–57.

Morris, Desmond. 1977. *Manwatching: A Field Guide to Human Behaviour*. London: Jonathan Cape.

MSNBC. 2007a. *Hardball*. "Post-Democratic Presidential Candidates Debate Coverage for October 30." Transcript. 30 October. http://www.msnbc.msn.com/id/21562767/ns/msnbc_tv-hardball_with_chris_matthews/t/post-democratic-presidential-candidates-debate-coverage-oct.

———. 2007b. "South Carolina Democratic Debate Transcript." 26 April. http://www.msnbc.msn.com/id/18352397/print/1/displaymode/1098. Accessed 18 February 2012.

———. 2008a. *Hardball*. Transcript. 26 September. http://www.msnbc.msn.com/id/26947279/ns/msnbc_tv-hardball_with_chris_matthews/t/hardball-chris-matthews-friday-september/#.T1FldnnrsZc. Accessed 28 February 2012.

———. 2008b. *Live with Dan Abrams*. Transcript. 31 January. http://www.lexisnexis.com.proxy.lib.umich.edu/lnacui2api/api/version1/getDocCui?lni=4RR7-BXT0-TWD3-10VK&csi=257765&hl=t&hv=t&hnsd=f&hns=t&hgn=t&oc=00240&perma=true Accessed 28 February 2012.

Muller, Judy. 2008. "McCain's Debate Air Quotes Badly 'Misfired.'" *Huffington Post*. 16 October. http://www.huffingtonpost.com/judy-muller/mccains-debate-air-quotes_b_135296.html. Accessed 18 February 2012.

Murphy, Gerald. 1988. "Personal Reference in English." *Language in Society* 17 (3): 317–49.

Needham, Catherine. 2006. "Brands and Political Loyalty." *Journal of Brand Management* 13 (3): 178–87.

Negrine, Ralph M. 2008. *Transformation of Political Communication: Continuities and Changes in Media and Politics.* Basingstoke : Palgrave Macmillan.

New York Times. 2003. "Dr. Dean and the Pickup Truck." Editorial. 6 November. A-30.

———. 2007. "The Democratic Debate on MSNBC." Transcript. 30 October. http://www.nytimes.com/2007/10/30/us/politics/30debate-transcript.html?pagewanted=all.

———. 2008. "First Presidential Debate." Transcript. 26 September. http://elections.nytimes.com/2008/president/debates/transcripts/first-presidential-debate.html.

Newman, Bruce I. 1994. *The Marketing of the President: Political Marketing as Campaign Strategy.* Thousand Oaks, CA: Sage Publications.

Newman, Bruce I., and Jagdish N. Sheth. 1985. *Political Marketing: Readings and Annotated Bibliography.* Chicago: American Marketing Association.

Norris, Pippa. 2000. *A Virtuous Circle: Political Communication in Postindustrial Societies.* Cambridge, UK: Cambridge University Press.

Obama, Barack. 1995. *Dreams from My Father: A Story of Race and Inheritance.* New York: Times Books/Random House.

Pedelty, L. L. 1987. "Gesture in Aphasia." PhD dissertation. Department of Behavioral Sciences, University of Chicago, Chicago.

Penn, Mark J., and E. Kinney Zalesne. 2007. *Microtrends: The Small Forces behind Tomorrow's Big Changes.* 1st ed. New York: Twelve.

Perlstein, Rick. 2008. *Nixonland: The Rise of a President and the Fracturing of America.* New York: Scribner.

Phillips, Kevin P. 1969. *The Emerging Republican Majority.* New Rochelle, NY: Arlington House.

Pitney, Nico. 2008. "Debate Analysis: ABC Asked Most Scandal Questions, Obama Was Clear Target." 20 April. http://www.huffingtonpost.com/2008/04/20/debate-analysis-abc-asked_n_97599.html. Accessed 22 October 2008.

Posner, Richard A. 2003. *Law, Pragmatism, and Democracy.* Cambridge, MA: Harvard University Press.

Post, Karen. 2005. *Brain Tattoos: Creating Unique Brands That Stick in Your Customers' Minds.* New York: AMACOM.

Prince, Ellen F. 1981. "Toward a Taxonomy of Given-New Information." In *Radical Pragmatics,* edited by P. Cole. 223–55. New York: Academic Press.

Public Papers of the Presidents of the United States; Richard Nixon . . . 1973. Washington, DC: USGPO.

Quintilian. 1902. *Quintilian's Institutes of Oratory; or, Education of an Orator.* In twelve books. Translated by R. J. S. Watson. London: George Bell and Sons.

Rawnsley, Gary D. 2005. *Political Communication and Democracy.* Basingstoke: Palgrave Macmillan.

Robertson, Andrew W. 1995. *The Language of Democracy: Political Rhetoric in the United States and Britain, 1790-1900.* Ithaca, NY: Cornell University Press.

Rozell, Mark J., ed. 2003. *Media Power, Media Politics.* Lanham, MD: Rowman and Littlefield.

Rubin, Trudy. 2008. "After Debate, Still No Clarity on Exit Strategies." Philly.com. 20 April. http://articles.philly.com/2008-04-20/news/25251379_1_clinton-adviser-hillary-clinton-democratic-debate. Accessed 15 March 2012.

Rutenberg, Jim. 2007. "One Candidate's 'Personal Evolution' Is Another's 'Flip-Flop.'" New York Times. 4 November. http://www.nytimes.com/2007/11/04/world/americas /04iht-camp.4.8180760.html. Accessed 13 February 2012.

Sanders, Karen. 2009. *Communicating Politics in the Twenty-first Century.* Houndmills, Basingstoke: Palgrave Macmillan.

Schley, Bill, and Carl Nichols Jr. 2005. *Why Johnny Can't Brand: Rediscovering the Lost Art of the Big Idea.* New York: Portfolio.

Schulman, Bruce. 2007. "Beware the Politician Who Won't Flip-flop." *Los Angeles Times.* 1 April. Available at http://www.latimes.com/news/opinion/commentary/la-op-schul man1apr01,0,894880.story.

Schwartz, John. 2008. "Who You Callin' a Maverick?" *New York Times.* 4 October. Available at http://www.nytimes.com/2008/10/05/weekinreview/05schwartz.html.

Sherrington, Mark. 2003. *Added Value: The Alchemy of Brand-Led Growth.* Basingstoke: Palgrave Macmillan.

Silverstein, Michael. 1976. "Shifters, Linguistic Categories, and Cultural Description." In *Meaning in Anthropology,* edited by K. H. Basso and H. A. Selby. 11–55. Albuquerque: University of New Mexico Press.

———. 1985. "On the Pragmatic 'Poetry' of Prose: Parallelism, Repetition, and Cohesive Structure in the Time Course of Dyadic Conversation." In *Meaning, Form, and Use in Context: Linguistic Applications (GURT 1984),* edited by Deborah Schiffrin. 181–99. Washington, DC: Georgetown University Press.

———. 1997. "The Improvisational Performance of Culture in Realtime Discursive Practice." In *Creativity in Performance,* edited by R. Keith Sawyer. 265–312. Greenwich, CT: Ablex.

———. 2003a. *Talking Politics: The Substance of Style from Abe to "W."* Chicago: Prickly Paradigm.

———. 2003b. "Indexical Order and the Dialectics of Sociolinguistic Life." *Language and Communication* 23 (3–4): 193–229.

———. 2004. "Cultural Concepts and the Language-Culture Nexus." *Current Anthropology* 45(5): 621–52.

———. 2005a. "Cultural Knowledge, Discourse Poetics, and the Performance of Social Relations." In *LACUS Forum XXXI: Interconnections,* edited by Adam Makkai, William J. Sullivan, and A. R. Lommel. 33–52. Houston: LACUS.

———. 2005b. "The Poetics of Politics: 'Theirs' and 'Ours.'" *Journal of Anthropological Research* 61 (1): 1–24.

———. 2007. "How Knowledge Begets Communication Begets Knowledge: Textuality and Contextuality in Knowing and Learning." *Intercultural Communication Review* (Tokyo) 5: 31–60.

———. 2010. "Society, Polity, and Language Community: An Enlightenment Trinity in Anthropological Perspective." *Journal of Language and Politics* 9 (3): 339–63.

———. 2011a. "Presidential Ethno-Blooperology: Performance Misfires in the Business of 'Message'-ing." *Anthropological Quarterly* 84 (1): 165–86.

———. 2011b. "The 'Message' in the (Political) Battle." *Language and Communication* 31 (3): 203–16.

———. 2011c. "What Goes Around . . . : Some Shtick from 'Tricky Dick' and the Circulation of U.S. Presidential Image." *Journal of Linguistic Anthropology* 21 (1): 54–77.

Simonini, R. C. Jr. 1956. "Phonemic and Analogic Lapses in Radio and Television Speech." *American Speech* 31: 252–63.

Simon-Vandenbergen, Anne-Marie. 1996. "Image-Building through Modality: The Case of Political Interviews." *Discourse and Society* 7 (3): 389–415.

———. 2000. "The Functions of *I Think* in Political Discourse." *International Journal of American Linguistics* 10 (1): 41–63.

Sperber, Dan, and Deirdre Wilson. 1995. *Relevance: Communication and Cognition.* Oxford: Blackwell.

Spetalnick, Matt. 2007. "Goof Reveals Phonetic Guide for Bush." Reuters. Posted 26 September on AOL News.

Stanyer, James 2007. *Modern Political Communication: Mediated Politics in Uncertain Times.* Cambridge, UK: Polity Press.

Streeck, Jürgen. 2008. "Gesture in Political Communication: A Case Study of the Democratic Presidential Candidates during the 2004 Primary Campaign." *Research on Language and Social Interaction* 41 (2): 154–86.

Taylor, Charles. 1994. "The Politics of Recognition." In *Multiculturalism: Examining the Politics of Recognition,* edited by C. Taylor, A. Gutmann, and C. Taylor. Princeton, NJ: Princeton University Press.

Thomas, Helen. 1999. *Front Row at the White House: My Life and Times.* New York: Scribner.

Trent, Judith S., and Robert V. Friedenberg. 2004. *Political Campaign Communication: Principles and Practices.* Lanham, MD: Rowman and Littlefield.

Trilling, Lionel. 1972. *Sincerity and Authenticity.* Cambridge, MA: Harvard University Press.

Tulis, Jeffrey. 1987. *The Rhetorical Presidency.* Princeton, NJ: Princeton University Press.

Urban, Greg 1996. "Entextualization, Replication, and Power." In *Natural Histories of Discourse,* edited by Michael Silverstein and Greg Urban. 21–44. Chicago: University of Chicago Press.

———. 2001. *Metaculture: How Culture Moves through the World.* Minneapolis: University of Minnesota Press.

———. 2010. "A Method for Measuring the Motion of Culture." *American Anthropologist* 112 (1): 122–39.

Van Leeuwen, Theo. 2005. *Introducing Social Semiotics.* London: Routledge.

Vincent, Laurence. 2002. *Legendary Brands: Unleashing the Power of Storytelling to Create a Winning Marketing Strategy.* Chicago: Dearborn Trade Publications.

Wall Street Journal. 2003. "Dean's Rebel Yell." Editorial. 7 November. A-10.

Warner, Michael. 1990. *The Letters of the Republic: Publication and the Public Sphere in Eighteenth-Century America.* Cambridge, MA: Harvard University Press.

———.1993. "The Mass Public and the Mass Subject." In *The Phantom Public Sphere,* edited by B. Robbins. 234–56. Minneapolis: University of Minnesota Press.

White, Theodore H. 1961. *The Making of the President, 1960.* New York: Atheneum.

———. 1965. *The Making of the President, 1964.* New York: Atheneum.

———. 1969. *The Making of the President, 1968.* New York: Atheneum.

Williams, Raymond. 1977. *Marxism and Literature.* Oxford: Oxford University Press.

Williams, Raymond, and Michael Orrom. 1954. *A Preface to Film.* London: Film Drama.

Wills, Garry. 1992. *Lincoln at Gettysburg: The Words That Remade America.* New York: Simon and Schuster.

Wortham, Stanton, and Michael Locher. 1996. "Voicing on the News: An Analytic Technique for Studying Media Bias." *Text* 16 (4): 557–85.
———. 1999. "Embedded Metapragmatics and Lying Politicians." *Language and Communication* 19 (2): 109–25.

INDEX

MICHAEL LEMPERT is Assistant Professor of Anthropology at the University of Michigan and author of *Discipline and Debate: The Language of Violence in a Tibetan Buddhist Monastery*.

MICHAEL SILVERSTEIN is Charles F. Grey Distinguished Service Professor of Anthropology, of Linguistics, and of Psychology and in the Committee on Interdisciplinary Studies in the Humanities at the University of Chicago. His published works include *Talking Politics: The Substance of Style from Abe to "W."*